SLEEPING

WITH

A

PSYCHOPATH

SLEEPING WITH A PSYCHOPATH

CAROLYN WOODS

Leabharlanna Poiblí Chathair Baile Átha Cliath
Dublin City Public Libraries

HARPER
element

HarperElement
An imprint of HarperCollins*Publishers*
1 London Bridge Street
London SE1 9GF

www.harpercollins.co.uk

HarperCollins*Publishers*
1st Floor, Watermarque Building, Ringsend Road
Dublin 4, Ireland

First published by HarperElement, 2021

3 5 7 9 10 8 6 4

© Carolyn Woods 2021

Carolyn Woods asserts the moral right to
be identified as the author of this work

A catalogue record of this book is
available from the British Library

ISBN 978-0-00-839866-8

Printed and bound in Great Britain by
CPI Group (UK) Ltd, Croydon

MIX
Paper from
responsible sources
FSC™ C007454

This book is produced from independently certified FSC™ paper
to ensure responsible forest management.

For more information visit: www.harpercollins.co.uk/green

For Lara and Emma

He will choose you, disarm you with his words, and control you with his presence. He will delight you with his wit and his plans. He will show you a good time, but you will always get the bill. He will smile and deceive you, and he will scare you with his eyes. And when he is through with you, and he will be through with you, he will desert you and take with him your innocence and your pride. You will be left much sadder but not a lot wiser, and for a long time you will wonder what happened and what you did wrong. And if another of his kind comes knocking at your door, will you open it?

From an essay signed 'A Psychopath in Prison',
Robert Hare, *Without Conscience*

CONTENTS

PROLOGUE

15 June 2013

I am in shock. I lie here unable to move a muscle. Every nerve in my body is under attack. I am so tired, but if I close my eyes, I'm assaulted by sickening flashes of psychedelic light. So I lie here, motionless, eyes wide open, hardly daring to breathe.

I want to die. I feel myself being sucked into the vortex of a black hole as white noise crackles in my head and three words spool around my mind, over and over, screaming to get out, louder and louder, until I think I'm going to pass out.

YOU FUCKING BASTARD!

It's Thursday, 13 June 2013. Eighteen months ago, I was a sophisticated, educated woman of a certain age – sociable, gregarious, full of confidence and enjoying my independence. I had put my divorce, the death of my parents and redundancy behind me, and was looking forward to a fresh start. My two daughters had flown the nest and I had sold up and moved to a friendly Cotswold town where I was looking for a new home to buy. I was renting a lovely cottage and I'd found myself a job, helping to run a stylish clothing and lifestyle shop locally, which gave me an excuse to dress smartly every day to serve our well-heeled customers. Once I even wore a top hat and tails; it was that type of place – so refreshing after the rather stuffy atmosphere of the pharmaceutical company where I had worked for nearly ten years previously.

I was socialising and integrating into the life of the town and trying to make new friends. Old friends admired my courage and remarked that I was 'living the dream'. I could hardly have been happier. And I certainly wasn't looking for romance.

Then, one evening, a man walked into the shop and into my life and changed everything. He was unlike anybody I had ever met, and I was instantly attracted to him, as he was to me. He was handsome and dashing and paid me lots of attention. As we quickly got to know each other he told me he was a wealthy tax exile, a Swiss banker; then later, he swore me to secrecy, confiding that his job was a cover for his work as a spy.

I know it sounds extraordinary, but I believed every word he said. He certainly looked the part, and lots of things happened to convince me that he was a real-life James Bond. I fell in love with him and looked forward to our marriage. An expensive wedding dress hung in my wardrobe.

All that seems a long time ago now, as I agonise about our relationship. I have got used to Mark's erratic lifestyle, but now I haven't seen him in several months, and although he phones and texts me every day I am worried about his health.

Mark has gradually taken over control of my life, persuading me to give up the job I loved and move out of the cottage I was renting and into a mansion he bought for us, while another – even grander – house was being renovated as our eventual home. He has isolated me and I have become frightened, depressed and introverted. I am very confused. It feels as though someone has opened the top of my head and put a blender into my brain. I have lost all my confidence and am spending much of my time as a recluse, sitting alone and miserable, waiting for Mark's phone calls and texts with news of when we might see each other again.

When I look in the mirror I hardly recognise the woman staring back at me. People have always said I look younger than I am, but now I look terrible. I am suffering an identity crisis. I don't even know who I am. It's as though each month of our relationship has added a year to my age. I used to take great pride in my appearance – always smartly dressed, made up every day, going to the hairdresser every couple of months – but that has had to stop. The grey is showing and there are dark circles under my eyes. I am living from one day to the next, never sure where I will be staying.

It is six months since I fled the loneliness of the £3 million Georgian townhouse Mark had bought in Bath, and I am staying with an old friend. With no money and mounting debts, I am leading a nomadic existence, relying on the goodwill of others to give me a room for short periods.

Part of me still clings to the hope that I am overreacting and that my new life with Mark will be all that he keeps promising. At the outset, he told me that it would take him eighteen months to sort out his life. I'd said I would wait for him. But that time is almost up, and I am at my wits' end, barely coping. I have been let down by Mark so many times, but I still try to convince myself that he is honourable. Hope is all I have left.

It's 4.22 in the morning with the first hint of daylight filtering through the curtains. I haven't slept all night.

I can't take any more.

My fingers fumble in the dark on the bedside table. I pick up my mobile phone and tap out three words:

Please help me.

Another two hours pass before James Miller responds to my text and says I can call him if I like. I don't know James well at all. He did some business with Mark, who once told me that if ever he and I were unable to talk and I was worried about anything at all, I should contact James for information and reassurance, because he would know everything.

I ring James, apologising for calling him so early. Our brief conversation offers none of the reassurance I am looking for. I tell him, 'For the past couple of weeks Mark has been telling me that you're going to collect me, bringing air tickets and money, and that we'll be flying out to see him wherever he is, because you have some work to do for him. Do you know anything about this?'

'No, no, I'm sorry,' says James, 'I don't know anything at all about that.'

I am stunned by what comes next:

'Carolyn, I'm really sorry, but I've been having a difficult time with him myself. My business has virtually gone down the pan and my reputation is in tatters. I don't know how I'm going to survive. I've found out quite a bit about him that I think you should know.'

I ask James if we can meet up, and he agrees to come up to London from Gloucestershire on Saturday to see me and answer more of my questions. I have plenty.

Two days later I have moved on and am staying with an old schoolfriend in Twickenham. It's 9.00 a.m. James parks his motorbike at the house and we walk the short distance to Twickenham Green, exchanging rather awkward pleasantries, both of us apprehensive about what is going to happen next.

Arthur's Bistro on the edge of the green is empty. It's still early. We choose a table in an alcove, as private as is possible, and order coffee. James orders scrambled eggs too; I have no appetite. It is a sunny June morning but I feel icy cold and I know I must look terrible, but it strikes me, as the café begins to fill up, that no one looking at the two of us would guess that anything is wrong, let alone that my world is collapsing around me. We are just another couple chatting over coffee. It is a relaxed, informal place where, at first glance, we probably blend in well, me in my brown leather jacket and jeans and James with his motorbike jacket and helmet. But I feel as though I'm wearing a placard declaring 'Heartbroken', or 'Suicidal'.

It's difficult to know where to begin, but I sit engrossed in conversation with James as the hours fly by. The revelations come thick and fast, and I am finding it hard to take it all in.

His name isn't Mark Conway.

How on earth has this happened to me? How have I let this man ruin my life to a point where I want to kill myself?

And if he isn't Mark Conway, who the hell is he?

1

ONE MEMORABLE DAY

That was a memorable day to me, for it made great changes in me and in my fortunes. But it is the same with any life. Imagine one selected day struck out of it, and think how different its course would have been. Pause, you who read this, and think for a moment of the long chain of iron or gold, of thorns or flowers, that would never have bound you, but for the formation of the first link on one memorable day.

Charles Dickens, *Great Expectations*

As I drew back the curtains on the morning of 19 January 2012, there was nothing to indicate that the events of the next twenty-four hours would dramatically alter the course of my life. The grey skies that had stared blankly back at me remained obstinately metallic all day, turning leaden by the time evening wrapped its cloak around the small Cotswold town of Tetbury, and darkness fell.

Customers had been few and far between in the post-Christmas lull, but there was still half an hour to go before I could lock up and go home. Nina Simone sang softly in the background, as I sat at the counter, writing up my end-of-day report. Then I heard the familiar sound of the bell as the door opened and I looked up to greet a late customer.

'Hello,' I smiled. 'Can I help you?'

Lone male customers were few and far between, and those men who did come in were usually dressed casually in jeans or crumpled cords, often paired with an equally crumpled tweed jacket. The dress code around here was definitely country casual. Smart casual hardly got a look-in. And smart was rarely seen.

But this man was immaculate. He was of medium height and build, with thick dark brown hair, brown eyes, a very closely trimmed beard and moustache and an olive complexion. He wore a crisp white shirt (no tie), and what looked like a designer suit and designer glasses. He had a continental air about him and exuded confidence. The atmosphere was electric. He looked straight at me, held my gaze, and smiled.

'I noticed the jacket in the window. I wondered if you had it in my size?'

'I'll have a look. The menswear's in the back. Let me show you.'

I showed him into the back room.

'What size do you normally take? A forty-two?'

I picked through the jackets hanging on the rail, but to no avail.

'Well, it looks as though that's the last one – in the window. I'll get it for you.'

'No, really, don't bother. I was just looking.'

'It's no bother. Why don't you have a look through here while you're waiting? There are a couple of other really nice designs.'

I picked out some alternative jackets, pointing out the colourful linings and the mismatched buttons and buttonholes that were a trademark of the brand, and left him to try them on while I went to get the jacket out of the window. He carried on chatting.

'I've been driving up and down Long Street every day for a few weeks now. That jacket caught my eye. Actually, I wouldn't normally have stopped, but today I was desperate to get my hair cut. But the hairdresser closes at five. Five o'clock – it's insane! Probably just as well. I'd never normally get it cut in a place like that. But this shop has style. How long have you been here?'

'About eighteen months. We've only recently started selling menswear. What do you think of it?'

I helped him into the jacket I had brought in for him.

'Well it's not really what I'm used to, but I do like this particular jacket. It doesn't really fit properly though, does it? What do you think? I think perhaps a size bigger.'

'I think it looks good, but I can see if we can order you the next size up, if you like.'

'I'll think about it. I might get something similar made to measure. It's the only way to get things to fit properly. What's your name, by the way?' He was looking straight at me, still smiling.

'I'm Carolyn.'

'I'm Mark. It's good to meet you.'

We moved back through to the front of the shop and chatted on easily, but were suddenly interrupted when my friend Uma burst in with her dog, Lulu. Uma was windswept and dishevelled, dressed in a long, brown waxed coat and sheepskin hat. We used to joke and say that we would make a good double act, privately referring to ourselves as 'Shabby Chic'. We were a good example of opposites attracting. I liked Uma and her partner, Antony, who had both been exceptionally hospitable and generous to me since Uma and I had become friends – a friendship that started with a first encounter in the shop.

'Hi, Carolyn. Listen, I've just been out for a walk past that house at Doughton you were looking at. I know you discounted it, but I really think you should take a second look. There's real potential there; you could really add some value. I just wanted to come and tell you.' Uma had previously worked as an estate agent and was keen to help.

'Thanks, Uma, but you know I really don't want a project.'

Uma glanced at Mark and shot me a questioning look, but I didn't introduce them. In fact, I was rather keen for her to leave so that I could continue my conversation with my intriguing new customer.

'OK, well I'm off home now. Pop in after work for a drink if you feel like it and I'll try to change your mind.'

'Thanks, Uma. I will. But my mind's made up on that one.'

Uma left, and Mark and I resumed our conversation. I explained that I had only recently moved to Tetbury and was looking for a place to buy, but it was proving more difficult than I had anticipated. Mark was so easy to talk to, I felt as though I'd known him all my life. He asked me about my family and I told him about my grown-up daughters, Lara and Emma. I picked up a copy of *Cotswold Life*, which lay open on the table, to show him photographs of my younger daughter, Emma, who had modelled for a feature on the shop.

'Isn't she lovely?'

'She certainly is.'

'And her sister is equally beautiful, and I don't mean just physically. They are lovely girls. I am very lucky.'

'Are you married?'

He had already mentioned that he had been married three times.

'No.'

'Is there anyone special in your life?'

He was very forward, and I paused momentarily before answering him.

'Maybe …'

It was none of his business, but ever since childhood I have always felt compelled to answer when questioned about anything, and I can't lie to save my life.

'I've met a couple of men since I've been here,' I continued, 'but only one who turned my head. Sadly, his manners let him down. No, I'm happy being single.'

I looked at him as I said it and he held my gaze as a wry smile crossed his lips.

'I see.'

'Anyway, you'll have to excuse me, I need to shut up shop now.'

Although I am a naturally open person, I felt that perhaps I had given away too much, but he invited it and was so easy to talk to.

'Do you work here every day?'

'No. Usually four days a week, but never the same four.'

I didn't like routine and enjoyed working irregular hours. I felt it added to my freedom somehow, and it also made it difficult for people to pin me down.

'So how will I know which days you'll be working?'

'You won't.'

'So how can I find you?'

I looked straight at him.

'I really don't know.'

The tension was palpable.

'Will you give me your number?'

He was holding his mobile phone, thumbs poised.

And I gave it. Just like that. He keyed it into his phone, then looked directly at me.

'So why did you just give me your number?'

'I really don't know. It's not something I usually do.'

I felt slightly flustered. Why *had* I given him my number? It was so out of character.

Suddenly, I heard my phone ringing from inside the cabinet behind me.

'Just to make sure,' he smiled. 'Good.'

Then he reached out, took my hand and leaned forward to kiss it. I apologised because it was cold.

'Cold hands, warm heart,' he ventured, and he held my gaze again. Then he turned on his heels and left, glancing back through the glass of the door, still smiling, before disappearing into the darkness.

The ping of my mobile phone alerted me to a new message.

17.25 Did I turn your head?

I didn't even have to think before responding.

A few degrees perhaps …

I shut up shop and went to buy a bottle of wine and some cigarettes. I didn't normally smoke, but I must have detected a faint trace of tobacco on him, and already I was falling under his spell, mirroring him. I set off to see Uma. I was looking forward to a glass of wine and a cigarette. I wanted to reflect on what had happened. A man walked into the shop: it was the most ordinary thing, but it felt completely extraordinary – and significant. It was not like any other encounter I had ever had.

'So, who was that guy with you in the shop?'

Uma was pouring out three large glasses of chilled white wine. She and Antony always enjoyed an evening drink or two.

'I don't know. His name's Mark. He's doing some work up at the airport. He just came in to look at a jacket and we got talking.'

'Bloody hell! I couldn't work out what was going on. I wondered why you didn't introduce me. I thought he was a friend of yours – I mean I got the impression you knew each other pretty well. I definitely felt as though I was interrupting something.'

'Well, you were! Look at this.'

I showed them the message on my phone.

'Nice reply,' said Antony with a wry smile.

As he spoke, another message came in and I felt my pulse quicken as I read it. Mark was asking me if I wanted him to be honest with me, about what he was looking for:

17.55   Actually, wasn't looking, just found.

God! He certainly wasn't backward in coming forward.

'Take a look at this.'

I showed Antony and Uma, who exchanged knowing glances.

'Looks like you've scored there,' Uma remarked as she raised her glass to mine. 'Cheers, darling!'

I felt excited, but wary. I had been caught off guard. I wouldn't respond immediately. I needed to compose myself. But he was persistent.

19.24   Did you get my message.

This time I couldn't resist.

Yes, I did. What exactly do you think you just found?

I am very honest.

He went on to explain that he had no way of being in a full-time relationship for at least eighteen months, but that he liked me a lot, saying he found me 'very, very attractive', and that 'everything happens for a reason'.

> **19.45**   Thanks for the compliment. I also think things
>   happen for a reason but before we talk about
>   marriage number 4 how about a drink? Aren't you
>   being a little premature?
>
>   Lol! Where are you?

I let it rest. Let him stew for a bit.

> **20.20**   You are perfect for me.

Bloody hell! Nobody had ever come on to me this strongly before. I liked it – I was attracted to him, and I was flattered – but I didn't respond. Uma and Antony exchanged another glance, eyebrows raised. Suddenly, my phone rang – it was him. I excused myself and went out of the room to take the call.

'It's Mark. I've been texting you. Why don't you respond to my messages?'

'I'm busy. I'm with friends.'

'Well, I'm not used to being kept waiting. Look, I really like you and want to see you again – soon. Are you free tomorrow evening? We could meet for that drink. I could come and pick you up.'

'I can't talk now, but I'd like to see you again too. Call me tomorrow and perhaps we can arrange something.'

'Great. I just can't wait to see you again.'

'We'll talk tomorrow then. Bye.'

I hung up. Every nerve in my body was on red alert.

'So, what did he say?' Uma asked, as I returned to the kitchen.

'He wants to see me again. We'll probably meet up tomorrow evening for a drink. He's going to call tomorrow.'

'Well, this is all very sudden. You be careful. You know nothing about him.'

'Of course I'll be careful. We're only meeting for a drink.'

But it wasn't long before another message pinged in and my heart sank. 'Perhaps we won't be meeting after all,' I said.

I passed my phone to Uma.

22.16   What are you wearing now?

'Well, he's blotted his copybook there, hasn't he? Bloody men – always following their dicks!'

I didn't like the question either, and a frisson of doubt crossed my mind. I felt as if my heart had brushed a cobweb. I shook it off, but had the sense I should tread carefully. I didn't respond, but almost an hour later, after I had got home, another message came in.

23.09   I take it … you haven't read my message?

That was enough for one evening. Let him wait. I really didn't like the question about what I was wearing, which lodged uncomfortably at the back of my mind. But I couldn't stop thinking about him. Well-meaning friends had previously tried to set me up on dates, and a few men had come on to me of their own accord. Now, in my mind's eye, I went along the identity parade of rejects. And then I thought of Mark again. He was completely different. It had been a veritable *coup de foudre* when I had looked up to greet him.

I hardly slept a wink that night, thinking about him, and the next day, at work, I couldn't resist responding to his text of the night before.

10.14   Hello. I did read your message, eventually, but I
             didn't like the question.

Let's see how he responds to that, I thought.

10.55 The question was because I like your style.

He went on to say that he wondered if I had changed for dinner, and he couldn't wait to see me later. I didn't believe for one minute that was what the question was about, but I liked his explanation all the same. Here was someone who, like me, favoured a more formal style, and understood things like changing for dinner. It struck a chord with me.

> Bring a business card. I'll bring my car – I would
> hate to be at your mercy, although I do like good
> manners so appreciate the offer of a lift. Send me
> some info, like your full name, so I can Google you.
> You can't be too careful and I was caught totally on
> the back foot yesterday. Where and when this eve?
> Nice and local would be good.

> I don't know your name nor does it bother me.

He said that he would know in time, told me that he just liked me, which he thought was 'nice', and invited me to pick a place for a drink, while suggesting the Hare and Hounds in Westonbirt himself.

> Re the rest I find your lack of trust insulting.

His bluntness was softened by the reassurance that although I may well have been hurt in the past, that didn't mean he would hurt me too. He went on to say that he had a LinkedIn account and one on Twitter, but that he hated social media, so had no Facebook or anything like that.

I liked that. He was like me. He valued his privacy and didn't go in for opening up his life to the rest of the world on social media.

12.33   Hmm. I am sorry you feel insulted. No insult was intended. That's one of the reasons I generally don't spend a lot of time texting or emailing in this sort of situation. It's difficult to gauge the tone of what is being said and easy to have a misunderstanding – as I did re your question about what I was wearing. Let's wipe the slate clean and talk this eve. Hare & Hounds is fine. What time?

PS I also have no time for Facebook, or Twitter, or internet dating, or a whole host of other popular activity. I prefer the real world.

7?

See you then.

All day I was excited and later that afternoon I texted my best friend, Anne, to tell her that I was going out on a date. She replied immediately.

16.31   Well, who is he? Is he the one you told me about?

No, this is someone else. Very confident and straight talking but could be a total bull-shitter. We shall see. He's been married three times, perhaps a bit of a player. I don't know. He came into the shop yesterday and I ended up giving him my phone number, God knows why. I am very out of practice with all this. Wish me luck.

That afternoon, as the working day drew to a close, I thanked God I had no last-minute customers. Today I wanted to leave promptly and get home in time to spend a leisurely hour relaxing and getting ready to go out. When I got back home, I had a bath, touched up my make-up and put on a simple, short black tweed shift dress with a slight sparkle woven into it and gold fringing on the pockets. I loved this dress. It was very 'Chanel' and I felt good in it. I'd got it in the shop and received countless compliments on it. I could have sold it ten times over. With it I wore opaque black tights, simple black suede court shoes and a short black cardigan. My favourite black bag and a faux fur coat completed my outfit. It was time to go. As I was getting ready to leave another message pinged in on my phone.

18.43   I am here! Early for the first time ever. xx

He added that there was little coverage there, but I would find him in the library on the right-hand side of the main entrance.

He was keen! And I noted the kisses.

I arrived at the hotel twenty minutes later, parked in the car park a short walk away and strode briskly towards the hotel. I could see Mark in the yellow glare of the floodlights, standing outside the main entrance, smoking. I was aware of him watching me, but felt relaxed and confident as I approached him, smiling.

'Hello.'

'Hi.' He was smiling too. 'You look great. Come in.'

He stubbed out his cigarette and held the door open for me.

'I'm through here. What can I get you to drink?'

I looked into the library where I could see a glass on a table next to the fireplace, a wood fire blazing in the hearth. The setting was warm and inviting and utterly romantic.

'Are you drinking champagne?'

'Yes, I am.'

'I'll have the same.'

Mark disappeared to the bar and I went through to the library and sat down in a large armchair by the fire, directly opposite where he had obviously been sitting. We had the room to ourselves. He returned with my champagne and once more we slipped into easy conversation. I asked him about his day and he told me he had flown back in from Geneva that evening specially to see me. I was flattered and impressed. He said he was a Swiss banker and a tax exile but that he was spending some time in the UK working on some projects of his own. The conversation flowed and we sat chatting for over an hour. He was such easy company, and I found him absolutely riveting. It seemed he worked at least twenty hours a day. He flew his own plane, spoke seven languages and had a photographic memory. Somehow, the more open he was, the more mysterious he became.

Then there was a brief lull in the conversation. He was looking intently at me.

'Do you smoke?'

'Occasionally.'

'I knew it! Like I said, you are perfect for me. Shall we?'

He gave a slight tilt of his head towards the door. I put on my coat and we went outside for a cigarette. Marlboro Reds. Spanish. Mark lit two and offered me one. I put my bag on the ground as I took the cigarette from him, but he immediately picked it up and hung it on the door handle.

'You must never put your bag down like that,' he scolded. 'It's bad luck. If you do that all your money will run away.'

'Luckily, I'm not superstitious,' I laughed, as I took a drag on my cigarette and felt the effects of the nicotine. I was feeling slightly light-headed but was enjoying smoking with him. It felt companionable and rather conspiratorial – slightly wicked, even.

I had always been such a 'good girl'. I was pleased that I had brought my thick, warm coat with me as it was very cold outside and I could feel myself beginning to tense up.

'God, it's cold out here!'

'Precisely! That's why I don't live in this country. The climate's terrible. I have houses all over the world, but for me the Mediterranean is the place to live. This is crap. How anyone can live in this country I just don't understand.'

He held the door open for me and we went back inside. Mark started to tell me about his family, his childhood, his education, his marriages, his money – everything. It was all quite extraordinary. He told me that he hated his mother who, he explained, was Spanish, and preferred the company of her dogs to her children.

'Every time she gave birth she got herself another poodle, and lavished all her attention on the dog. I can't stand her,' he said, shaking his head.

Despite being born into a very wealthy family (and a house of over one hundred rooms!) he had never been given pocket money and had always worked for everything. He had even paid for part of his education, in some sort of a two-fingered gesture at his father. He had gone to Eton and then on to Oxford.

'Which college?' I enquired eagerly. My father and one of my daughters had gone to Oxford. Wouldn't it be funny if he had attended one of the same colleges?

'New College,' he responded, 'but I didn't finish my degree there. I found the course dull, so I left and went to LSE. I was their top student.'

'I see,' I said, seeing no reason to disbelieve him. His CV sounded impressive, and although, as I write this, I can see how on the page he may come across as obnoxiously boastful, in real life, as we sat in front of the fire in a lovely hotel, I didn't find him so. On the contrary, I enjoyed his confidence and found him refreshingly open, and the way he told me about himself and the way he looked at me were thoroughly captivating.

He went on to tell me more about his family. He hardly ever saw his brother or his sisters, one of whom he said was a brain surgeon, and the only person he seemed to have any contact with was an uncle. His relationships with women seemed equally strange. He told me that he had married very young and that his first wife was a beautiful Finnish model.

'Beautiful but stupid,' he said, claiming her lack of intelligence had driven him mad.

His second marriage – one of convenience, made for the mutual benefit of the two families – was to a woman who was intelligent but no beauty. She was from a good background with good connections, but she was a member of Opus Dei. He told me that the marriage was a disaster as it was never consummated, and eventually his wife had sought a divorce on the grounds that he was addicted to pornography.

'Well, what was I supposed to do? And anyway, how much better to be watching porn than to be sleeping around with other women,' he explained. 'I have no time for that sort of thing.'

He told me that he had discovered that the judge in his divorce case was having an affair, so he soon put him in his place.

'Knowledge is power,' he told me with a wicked smile, looking deep into my eyes.

More recently he had been married to another woman who had a son, Pedro, now fourteen years old. That relationship had ended a couple of years ago, but they had remained on good terms and he had undertaken to educate Pedro, as the boy's father, despite being ferociously wealthy, just didn't give a shit about him.

'Poor kid. I couldn't just abandon him because his mother and I didn't want to be together any more. That just wouldn't be right.'

'Do you have any children of your own?' I asked him.

'No. I thought I did. I thought I had two by my first wife, but when one of them became ill a DNA test revealed they weren't mine. I've had no contact with them since.'

What a bizarre life he had lived. I admired the fact that he'd made his own way and not relied on his family's fortune to get on in life, but I didn't envy him his background and thought how lucky I was to have such a close-knit family – that was everything to me.

Mark went on to tell me about his lifestyle: luxury homes all over the world, tables available at a moment's notice in the best restaurants, expensive everything. He liked only 'the best' and he had the money to pay for it. He began name-dropping and show-ing off, and, although I suppose he had been doing that all evening, he overstepped the mark and I remember pulling him up short.

'I'm not interested in your money,' I interjected.

'No, I know you're not.'

'But you have had an extraordinary life.'

'You're right. It is totally extraordinary. My life is like a film; you couldn't make it up … But there's something I have to tell you,' he confided, as he leaned across the table towards me. 'I'm not normal.'

I couldn't deny it – but I liked 'not normal'. Indeed, my old university motto was 'Do Different'. I had always liked that and felt that it suited my character. Being and doing different was refreshing. It meant that you thought for yourself and didn't follow the crowd. Mark had style and charisma. I found him very attractive, physically, and he was obviously highly intelligent. I had always found intellect attractive. He also appeared to have boundless energy and I found that exciting. He was so unlike any of the other men who had shown an interest in me since I had found myself footloose and fancy-free, one of whom had spent an entire lunchtime telling me all about his many ailments, a dicky heart among them – hardly the sort of information to set my pulse racing! Mark was something else entirely.

I was at that stage in my life where I was enjoying my independence, but at times I could feel quite isolated. Single women are not readily accepted socially. I had made some big changes in my life and everything was working out better than I could have imagined. Soon I would have my own home again and would have enough money left over to provide me with a financially secure future. The only thing missing was a partner – a lover. I didn't want to marry again; I didn't want to live with anyone, but I did think my life would be richer and more fun with a man in it. I liked what Mark represented. Even his arrogance had a certain appeal. He was so sure of himself. I certainly wasn't looking for another conventional relationship, and he seemed to offer something completely different – something that was missing from my life: excitement.

Suddenly, the conversation changed. Mark had been looking intently at me the whole evening.

'You know, I can sum people up within a few minutes of meeting them. I can read people like books. I often know them better than they know themselves. People are so transparent. Now you I like. I find you very attractive, and you're intelligent. You're a good person too. And you're classy. I like that. You're a real lady, but I think there's another side to you. You have a very high libido. Am I right?'

He was out of order, but I didn't object. In fact, I liked his full-on approach, and found him very entertaining. I laughed and shook my head.

'And *you* are very direct.'

'Well, you don't deny it. As I said, I can read people. How old are you, by the way?'

'Fifty-four.'

People had always said I could be taken for ten years younger, but I had never lied about my age.

'And you?'

'Guess.'

'Hmmm …' I was hopeless at judging people's age. I was sure he was younger than me, but how much?

'Forty-seven?'

'Forty-six.'

'Hmmm.' I was looking directly at him. 'You know I've never been able to see myself with a younger man.'

'Why ever not?' He was smiling wickedly at me.

'I always thought it would make me feel old.'

'Nonsense, it will make you feel young. I love older women. All the women I have had relationships with have been older than me. Young women are just so dull. They have no conversation, no real confidence – no life experience.'

As he finished speaking, he stuck his tongue out at me.

'I do that when I'm nervous,' he said, at the same time pulling at his right eyebrow. And then he did it again.

It was time to go. The evening had gone by in a flash. Mark had to get back to the airport to fly back to Switzerland, although he told me he had a house in Bath and would be back the following day. He was unlike anybody I had ever met before and my mind was in a spin.

'I'll walk you to your car.'

'Just wait till you see what I drive!'

After all his talk of mansions, private planes and fast cars I wondered what he would make of mine.

'I already know. I saw you drive in.'

We stopped by my car, a ten-year-old Ford KA, and suddenly (and to this day I don't know how he did it), he had one hand up my dress and the other one down it.

'Stop it!'

'But I want you so much. You know you want me too.'

'Not now.'

'Yes, you do. You know you do.'

'Stop it!'

I meant it, although I was laughing. Someone later told me that it sounded like an assault, but it didn't feel like that and he stopped almost immediately. I extricated myself and got into the car; he sat down on the door sill.

'Don't sit there, it's filthy, you'll wreck your suit.'

'Never mind about that. I have to see you again. I have to see you again, very soon.'

'I'd like that too.'

He was very close and staring intently into my eyes.

'You know what I really do, don't you?' he enquired.

'I think you're a secret agent,' I whispered back to him.

'I'll call you.'

He stood up, shut the car door and watched as I started the car and drove away. When I got home, I texted Uma.

> **OMG!!!!! I really like him. This is the beginning of a big adventure.**

2

A MAN IN A HURRY

It is vain to say human beings ought to be satisfied with tranquillity: they must have action; and they will make it if they cannot find it.

Charlotte Brontë, *Jane Eyre*

The next morning, I was up early. I had hardly slept a wink, but when I got up, I didn't feel tired. On the contrary – I felt alive. There were messages on my phone from Anne and the owner of the shop, Kerry. I couldn't wait to tell them how it had gone.

All my senses felt heightened, but I couldn't settle to anything. I wasn't working that day, so to take my mind off things I threw myself into cleaning the house. I often resorted to cleaning when I felt the need to regain control. I was bursting with energy and I swept through my cottage like a whirlwind, changing the sheets on my bed, gathering up laundry, scrubbing, hoovering, dusting and polishing, plumping up cushions and making sure everything was in its place. When the place was gleaming I sat down with a cup of coffee and tried to read my book, but I couldn't concentrate and found myself reading the same paragraph over and over again, still not registering anything. It was hopeless. In the end, I gave in and picked up my phone. I knew I should play it cool, but I also knew that something extraordinary was happening.

12.00   Did you sleep well? I hardly slept a wink but I found
myself laughing out loud when I thought of some of
the things you said. You are so full on and very
funny. I really like that and altogether I like you a lot.
A bientôt. Hasta la vista. Mi piace quando parli
italiano

I pressed 'send' and waited for a response. It seemed like for ever
before I heard a message come in.

Ti amo.

I want to make love to you so much.

Slept at 5am and just got up!

**I am so distracted I can hardly do a thing. When are
we going to see each other?**

Me too. Will call you around 5

I couldn't bear it. How could I wait all that time to speak to him?
It would seem like years. I had to do something to take my mind
off things, so I phoned Uma and suggested a walk. The fresh air
and exercise would do me good, and I needed company. We
walked for a couple of hours, but although I usually turned my
phone off when out walking, or even left it at home, now I kept
an ear open, waiting for it to ring. Five o'clock came and went,
then five-thirty, then six o'clock. Perhaps he wouldn't call me,
after all, but I felt sure he would. At around six-forty, I got a
message:

I can escape for an hour! Where do you want me?

What? Where was he?

> **I'm completely thrown! If you're in Bath and I'm here, an hour gives you barely enough time for the round trip.**

> Yes but I am now already near M4 going over it

> **I can't make love in a hurry – well I can but that's not what I want now. Do you understand?**

> Yes, but you can kiss me. Would you like to kiss me?

> **Yes**

> Where am I driving?

I couldn't resist. I gave him my address.

> OK 20 mins

I was thrown into turmoil. I had spent the afternoon out walking and was wearing old jeans, old everything. My hair was unwashed, as was the rest of me. I wished I was looking less scruffy, but I hadn't expected to be seeing him and there was no time to do much. I wanted to look good for him but, on the other hand, the fact that I was unwashed and wearing my least attractive but most comfortable walking underwear would ensure I kept my clothes on. He had been right the night before. I really wanted him.

It wasn't long before I heard the crunch of a car on the gravel outside and went to the door to meet him. It was so good to see him. He came in and immediately started kissing me. We moved over to the sofa. I was deeply attracted to him and every nerve in my body felt like a tightly coiled spring.

'Do you like that?' he murmured.

'Mmm. I do,' I whispered back.

Suddenly, he jumped up, and in a flash, he had removed all his clothes. I noted that he went 'commando'. He stood there in front of me, stark naked, fully aroused, muscles like steel, show-ing off to me. I liked what I saw, but there was no way this was going any further just now.

'What are you doing? Stop it! Put your clothes back on. Right now!' I protested, but he took no notice and sat down next to me and started kissing me again.

'Baby, you know you want me just as much as I want you. Come on.'

'I am not going to sleep with you. Forget it!'

I was laughing. He was just so funny, and I had to admit I was enjoying his full-on, no-holds-barred approach.

'Baby, I have to make love to you. Why waste time? It's what we both want. How many people have what we have? I knew the minute I saw you that you were the one for me. Come on, baby, you know you want it too.'

He had undone the button on my jeans and was already pulling at the zip. My jeans were tight and not easy to remove, but I offered up little resistance. I was living in the moment and in a trice, all my clothes were off too. He turned me over and took me vigorously from behind, slapping me as he drove himself deep inside.

'Don't hit me. I don't like that,' I told him.

He said nothing, turned me over and drove himself deep inside me again.

I couldn't relax. 'Let's go upstairs,' I said, softly, looking deep into his eyes. I have always been very private and was worried that we might be seen through the small window that looked out on to the driveway from the stairs. 'Come on.'

I took his hand and led him quickly upstairs where we fell on to the bed and Mark wasted no time claiming me again. Now I was relaxed and uninhibited. He felt so good and I felt so happy my heart was singing. But all of a sudden, he stopped and pulled himself away. He was staring into my eyes.

'This is a nightmare! A fucking nightmare!'

'What's wrong?'

I didn't have a clue what was going on.

'I'm falling in love with you. It's a fucking nightmare!'

Then he was all over me again. He was passionate, but loving and tender with it, kissing me, holding my face and staring deep into my eyes.

'I don't know what to do,' he murmured, 'this is insane. You know I have never truly loved or been loved by anyone before.'

I was playing with his hair, and oh, so happy.

'I don't really know how to make love,' he continued.

I disagreed. 'Yes, you do,' I said, smiling and stroking his hair – and I meant it.

Afterwards, we lay there, exhausted, chatting easily to each other. Then he suddenly sat up.

'When did you last have sex?' he asked.

'That's for me to know and you to wonder,' I told him evasively before turning the question back on him. 'And you?'

'Nothing for two years.'

'What? You must be joking.'

I was truly surprised, for Mark struck me as a very highly charged, red-blooded man.

'That's the truth. I am very fussy. But I need to come three times a day or I can't function properly.'

'What?'

'I mean it. Three times a day. I've mastered the art of masturbation.'

'You're crazy! Mark, if we become lovers, will I be the only one?'

'God, yes!' A look of disgust crossed his face and he spoke as though the thought of others repulsed him. I liked that. He took my hand.

'Who gave you that ring you're wearing?' He was looking intently at the diamond solitaire on the ring finger of my right hand.

'It was my mother's engagement ring. I always wear it.'

'I just wouldn't want you wearing another man's ring, that's all.'

'And what about yours?' He too wore a ring on the ring finger of his right hand.

'My grandmother gave it to me. I loved my grandmother.'

The mood lightened and Mark picked up my camera, which was on the chest of drawers. Photography was a big passion of mine and I loved to go out walking and taking photographs. He started taking pictures.

'Put it down!' I protested, but he wouldn't stop.

He clicked away as we fooled around, both of us in fits of laughter.

All too soon it was time for him to go. I wanted him to stay. I wanted to lie there with him – to talk, cuddle, spend the night together – but he had to go.

'I'm sorry baby, Pedro's staying with me. I told you about Pedro, remember? My ex's son? I have to be with him in the morning.'

'Who's he with now?'

'A nanny. I just dropped him off with the nanny and ran. I had to see you. We'll see each other again soon.' He got up from the bed and we went downstairs where he retrieved his clothes, dressed almost as quickly as he had undressed, kissed me and was gone.

No sooner had he left than I heard a message ping in.

> I miss you already

And I responded immediately:

> **I am lonely!**

That was a big thing for me to confess, for in all the time I had been single I had never really felt lonely. As I lay in bed, I mulled it over in my mind and thought that I had probably never felt lonely because there hadn't been anyone I really wanted to be with. Mark was different. I really wanted to be with him, and now he had gone I did feel lonely. It was a strange feeling, and not one I wanted to have to get used to.

Thinking back on those first heady encounters, with the knowledge I have now, I can see exactly how Mark was operating. I believe him to be a psychopath.

Psychopaths are social predators who have no conscience and are unable to feel love, compassion, guilt or remorse (Mark told me that he had never loved or been truly loved before). They are completely lacking in empathy, and their only motivation is self-gratification, which they achieve using charm, manipulation and the ruthless exploitation of others. They are often smooth talkers with a lot to say. They are supremely confident and relaxed and experience no social anxiety, making it easy for them to put their targets at ease. Mark exhibited all these characteristics. One of the things that I remember very clearly from those early encounters is the intense eye contact he made with me. I took this as a sign that he was telling the truth, but I didn't know then about the 'psychopathic stare', a look of such intensity that many people find totally disarming. Looking back over his early text messages I can see how he flattered me, and how he stressed his 'honesty' (for the duration of our relationship he frequently stressed how honourable he was). I can also see that, initially, I sensed danger. I told him, 'I would hate to be at your mercy', and told my friends that he may be a 'bull-shitter … a bit of a player', but I didn't even flinch on our first date when he admitted to watching porn, something that would normally have been a big turn-off. I found his openness refreshing, and I liked the aura of mischief that surrounded him. After all, bad boys are often especially attractive to good girls.

We don't realise how much we give away in small talk, especially if we are unknowingly being closely watched, and mined for information and reactions. In those first three encounters, Mark was working out exactly what made me tick, and adapting himself to meet my hopes and desires. He was also, from the word go, toying with me, even telling me, 'I don't know how to make love'. Psychopaths are exceptionally good at working out what makes people tick. He openly told me he could read people like books, that he often knew them better than they knew themselves. 'Knowledge is power,' he announced before brazenly confiding, 'I'm not normal'. How he must have been congratulating himself when I drove off after that first date!

As for me, I did everything I could to ensure my safety – I didn't accept Mark's offer of a lift and I told him to bring a business card so that I could Google him. Then he threw the ball back at me, telling me that he felt insulted by my lack of trust. That put me on the back foot again and made me feel bad (a distracting and undermining tactic often used by psychopaths), and it wasn't until days later that I realised I still didn't even know what his surname was. With a skilled manipulator like him though, I stood no chance, and I am sure that had I insisted on some form of ID, he would have supplied one. I can also see how he deliberately sowed the seeds to make me think he was a spy, when he told me that he flew his own plane, spoke seven languages and had a photographic memory.

When I look back on my relationship with Mark, I realise just how much people take on trust, and how little is needed in the form of suggestion before we start joining the dots and construct-ing the picture we want to see – or that someone else wants us to see. I was brought up to be honest and see the best in people, a strategy that served me well for over fifty years; and if you have been brought up to trust people, it is impossible to deal with someone whose whole life is a lie. Just stop for a moment and think how much you take on trust every time you have a conver-sation, even with people you have never met before. I had never indulged in internet dating, for fear of not knowing who I would be dealing with, but it never occurred to me that in 'real-life' encounters you can be deceived just as easily.

Although I never thought of myself as being vulnerable, with the benefit of hindsight I can see that I was. Having recently moved to a new place to start a new life I was experiencing a rather heady freedom. I was suddenly unimpeded by everyday family responsibility and I think I was also lulled into a false sense of security by my idyllic surroundings and a feeling of great confidence and pride in having made such a big change in my life. Living on my own, somewhere other than what had been the family home, was liberating, and when Mark walked into my life, I was ready to throw caution to the wind and experiment a little. This was my time to be just a little bit irresponsible.

3

FALLING IN LOVE

But trouble can come to nice places, too; trouble travels, trouble visits. Trouble even takes holidays from the places where it thrives … it began, as trouble often does, with falling in love.

John Irving, *The Cider House Rules*

I remember thinking, on my first visit to Tetbury, that nothing bad could happen in a place like that, deciding on the spot that this was where I was going to live. I felt completely safe there – but when you feel safe, as I now know, you let your guard down and you are, by definition, at your most vulnerable.

The weeks that followed my first date with Mark were turbulent, and I hardly had time to draw breath. Just days after we met, he took me to the Cotswold Airport, to see his collection of aeroplanes. I couldn't believe my eyes. The hangar he showed me into was vast, containing at least twenty aircraft. I know nothing about planes, but Mark's collection was certainly impressive, and as he walked me around, my attention was drawn to a beautiful, romantic-looking, vintage silver aircraft with two open cockpits. I also recognised a DC3 and a Spitfire.

'I'm setting up a business restoring Spitfires,' Mark explained. 'The Spitfire is the iconic British aeroplane. Just look at this one. Isn't she beautiful? Everyone loves the Spitfire, and they will just go up and up in value. It would be a fantastic investment for you, if you're interested. Much better than buying property.'

'Property is the only investment I understand,' I replied. 'At least you always have a roof over your head, and I need a home. Anyway, I know nothing about Spitfires – but I'd love you to teach me to fly one day.' Only four days into the relationship I was deliriously happy, and, like all new couples, Mark and I texted sweet nothings to each other.

23 Jan 2012

10.24   I can't wait to see you. I feel sick with excitement. You have turned my world upside down.

Me too, sexy!

My heart is singing. I can't wait to see you this evening. I can't bear the suspense. I feel sick!

That evening, Mark came to my cottage. I loved his company and felt completely at ease with him. We made love, chatted and chatted and just couldn't believe our luck in having found each other.

Suddenly, he jumped up, gathered up my clothes and tossed them towards me.

'Get dressed, baby, we're going for a drive. Come on.'

We got dressed, messing about and laughing, and made our way downstairs and outside, into the dark, sharp January air.

'You're driving,' he said, lobbing his car keys over to me.

He directed me to Culkerton, about four miles away, where we stopped outside an empty farmhouse with high wooden electric gates. Illuminated in the beam of the headlights I read the name of the property – West End Farm.

'Paul's been looking for somewhere suitable for us to live – you'll meet Paul, he works for me – but there's hardly anything available.'

My jaw dropped.

'Anyway, I thought you might like to take a look at this. We can't go into the house, but I can get us through the gates into the courtyard, and we can look through the windows. I can get the security code to any house in the country!'

'What?' I couldn't believe what I was hearing.

'Why are you looking at me like that? We're going to live together. Don't argue; you know it's what you want. It's what we both want. There's no point wasting time.'

My mind was swimming. Mark was so commanding and decisive. And what had he said – that he could get any security code he wanted? I felt as if I had walked through the back of the wardrobe into another world.

'Wait here,' Mark ordered as he jumped out of the car and went over to the security keypad. I heard him talking on his mobile phone, checking the code with someone. Then he keyed in some numbers and the gates opened.

'Drive, baby!'

I drove into the courtyard and parked the car. Mark opened the door for me and I climbed out.

'So, what do you think? Like I said, we can't go in right now but let's take a walk around. You'll get a feel for it. Personally, I'd like something grander, but I thought you might like it. You seem to like living in the middle of nowhere. It will do for a while, and it's really close to the airfield – I have to be there quite a bit at the moment … Honestly, baby – I can't stand to see you in that tiny cottage. I can't cope with it. If we're to see anything of each other, we need a place together.'

'Well, I like my cottage. It's home to me. But I like the look of this too. Isn't all this a bit sudden though?'

'Darling, we have to be together. Some things are just meant to be. You know it as much as I do. Don't try to resist it.'

'I'll take a look at the inside on Rightmove when I get back and let you know what I think.'

'I love you so much.' Mark was kissing me.

'I love you too.'

'Come on, baby, time to go home. I've got to get back.'

This time Mark took the driver's seat. He drove fast back to my cottage where he dropped me off and I watched the lights of his car fade away as he made his way back down the long drive. When I got inside, I immediately got out my laptop and took a look at the interior of West End Farm. I liked it, and I liked the idea of living with Mark – of starting a new adventure. I laughed to myself, realising I knew both the letting agents, and texted Mark:

> **21.23** Seen the pics of the house. Looks lovely to me. Know both the agents. Hilarious to think of living there. Agents told me I was not earning enough to rent my place. Would love to stroll in to pick up the keys to that and see their faces! I love you but you are mighty dangerous.

The next morning, Mark texted me to say that his assistant, Paul, had been at the Audi dealership first thing getting me an A5. He had already told me that he was worried about me driving about in my KA. He couldn't bear to think what might happen if I was in an accident.

> What?! Wow, this is insane. Thank you. It won't make me love you any more but it is fun! This is like fiction, I love you. Ha! I can't stop laughing. I'll need driving lessons.

Lol

When I arrived home that evening an Audi sales brochure had been posted through my letter box.

The following day, Mark texted to tell me that he'd call round at around eight. I couldn't wait, as there was something I badly wanted to discuss with him.

> 8pm fine. Look forward to it. I was thinking where my tongue was the other day and imagining where yours might be one day soon. Tonight though I need to talk, and you need to listen. A challenge! I love you.

When Mark arrived though, he was highly agitated. He sat down on the sofa running his fingers through his hair, his forehead set in a deep frown.

'God, I've had a hell of a day, Bubba. Get me a coffee, will you? And I've got to have a cigarette.'

I had told him that he couldn't smoke in the cottage, but now I found myself relenting.

'What's wrong, darling?'

'I'm feeling really stressed, Bubba. It's work. They're being such cunts!'

'Why, what's happened?'

He had confirmed my suspicion that he worked for MI6, and explained that his job at UBS in Switzerland was real but was used as a cover. Now his life was being made very difficult by his relationship with me.

'I'm not supposed to be in a serious relationship. They know everything, these people. They gave me a file this thick on you and told me to read it. I can't stand it, baby. I didn't read it. I wouldn't do that. Fuck, I'm sick and tired of this way of life.

I loved it to begin with, but I've been doing it too long. They're such cunts! They won't let me out of my contract and they'll do everything they can to destroy us – and they mean business. Fucking bastards!'

He reiterated what he told me the day we met – that it would be eighteen months before he could be in anything like a normal relationship.

'You know when we first met – not even a week ago! – I thought we might just have some fun together. Well, we both thought that, didn't we? But darling, I've fallen in love with you. Time's so short. They are just such fucking cunts! You'll stick by me, baby, won't you? It's not going to be easy and I need to know you're going to stand by me and be strong. It will be really hard going, but you've got to think of the bigger picture. It will all work out, I promise you. I'll do anything for you, baby – but you mustn't talk to anyone about any of this, do you understand? They're going to do everything they can to fuck us up and the last thing we need is other people interfering.'

'I'll wait the eighteen months, I've already told you that, and I always keep my word.'

'I know, sweetie. That's one of the things I love about you. You're strong and I know I can rely on you. Thank God for that! And another thing, baby – I want you to meet Pedro, but it has to be done sensitively. So many kids get fucked up because they have no stability in their lives and their fathers introduce them to girlfriend after girlfriend. It's just not fair on the kids. I know Pedro's not mine, but even so, having you in my life is going to affect him too. I'll work out the best way to do it.'

I loved the way Mark cared about Pedro, and what he said was perfectly in tune with the way I felt about such things. It was really crucial to be sensitive to the needs of children and I loved that we seemed to share the same moral values and the same outlook about the important things in life.

Mark's phone rang. It was Paul who was outside in the car waiting to drive him to the airport. His visits were so fleeting and I longed for him to stay.

'I know it's hard, sweetheart, but it will all work out in the end. The big picture, remember? Just think of that.'

Later that night, as I lay there trying to get to sleep, I realised that despite all my best intentions I still hadn't managed to get hold of one of Mark's business cards. I wasn't even sure what his surname was. I thought he'd said Conway, but I couldn't be sure. It was time to get things straight.

27 Jan 2012

00.24   Darling, what is your surname? Did you say
        Conway? Sooner or later one of my family will ask
        and it will seem very odd if I don't know. I miss you
        and love you.

He didn't respond.

I only saw Mark very briefly the following day, when he showed up in the shop to tell me that he had to go to Davos to attend the World Economic Forum.

'They need me there. Sorry, baby. It's going to be like this for a while, but I'll make it up to you.'

Seconds after he left, I heard a text message ping in.

You are so beautiful

I felt overwhelmed with love for him as I texted him back.

I can't get over our good fortune. Of all the shops in
all the towns in all the world you walked into mine –
and on a day I was there! I still can't believe it.

His response came back immediately:

> Lol

28 Jan 2012

00.10   Darling, one of my daughters has just asked me
           what your surname is, thankfully in an email. It's a
           reasonable question and if you can't tell me perhaps
           you can explain why?

10.39   Sorry I didn't reply last time as asleep. Conway.

He then asked me what mine was, pointing out that he didn't
really care.

> I picked up on Conway. I don't care either but I don't
> want my family getting over-interested in us or
> feeling suspicious of you. Of course they are
> interested because you are the first man I have
> expressed any interest in in years. My family is very
> important to me, particularly my daughters. I am
> supposed to be seeing my brother and sister-in-law
> this eve. Just back from skiing. When am I going to
> see you?

I didn't hear from Mark again until just before closing time at the
shop later that day. He was back from Davos, asking if I had any
jackets in his size, and whether I could bring one home with me
for him to try. He told me he would call round but wouldn't be
able to stay long.

   When I opened the door to him later that evening he was
not alone. He was accompanied by a little girl of about two

years old. She had blonde curls and was dressed in what were very obviously expensive clothes. Mark kissed me and gave me a squeeze. Then he looked over towards the child, who had made a beeline for my old cat who lay sleeping on the sofa.

'This is Bianca. She goes everywhere with me.'

'Who is she? Is she yours?'

'No, she's my niece, but I want to adopt her.'

'Why do you want to adopt her?'

'It's a long story. Her mother rejected her. She's the product of an abusive relationship. I have no children of my own and I love her to pieces. Anyway, I like to think that if her mother ever changes her mind, she could have her back.'

'How old is she?'

'Two and a half.'

He kneeled down beside Bianca and spoke gently to her in Spanish. It was so touching seeing him with this small child, so loving and gentle. What a doting uncle! It would have melted any woman's heart.

'Do you want to try the jacket?' I asked him.

'Sure.'

I held it out for him and he tried it on.

'Perfect! Well, not quite what I'm used to, but it will do. I'll take it.'

He took a bundle of cash out of his pocket and counted it out. He had three hundred pounds – thirty-five pounds short.

'Sorry, baby, it's all I've got.'

'Don't worry, I'll make it up and you can pay me back.'

'Thanks, baby. I love you.'

'Love you too.'

And it was time for him to go. Off to Weybridge, he said, to play happy families with Bianca, Pedro and his uncle. I was on my way out too, but all evening I was distracted, thinking about

Mark, and my heart leaped when I heard another message come in as I was saying goodbye to my brother and sister-in-law.

22.15 I miss you

Come over. I'm on my way home.

Lol. I just got to Weybridge. I will have dinner and sleep.

Please yourself.

Lol. See you tomorrow sweetie. She loves the cat.

I thought again about the little girl, and how gentle Mark had been with her, and couldn't help thinking that a man like that was bound to want children of his own – something that I could never give him.

The following evening, I was at home waiting for Mark to turn up. He was pretty unreliable about timing and had warned me that he was usually late for everything – something I regarded as the height of bad manners, but which, as I realised very early on, I would have to learn to accommodate. Still, as the evening wore on, I started to fret. The minutes ticked by and I found myself pacing around my cottage, getting more and more agitated. Eventually I gave in and texted him.

20.44 **When can I expect you?**

A heavy twenty minutes ticked by before he responded.

21.03 You will be let down by me a million times

Baby please don't get annoyed at me.

He went on to explain he'd had a nightmare of a day. He'd got up so late that Pedro was two hours late for school. He had been hoping to drop him off at seven and be with me by eight. He said he would call soon.

It seemed an age before he called and I was very upset, fed up with having been kept waiting, annoyed with him for wasting my time.

'But why didn't you call to say you weren't coming? You've really pissed me off. There's nothing that annoys me more than having my time wasted.'

I was also feeling very edgy because he owed me thirty-five pounds. I thought of myself as a generous person, but a previous boyfriend never seemed to have any money on him and it used to irritate me no end. Now I was getting really angry with Mark for not repaying the money he owed me.

'And you owe me some money,' I added.

He seemed shocked that I was making such a fuss about thirty-five pounds.

'Of course I'm going to repay you: what is wrong with you? Don't you trust me? I cannot believe anyone would make such a fuss about a few quid! Look, baby, I'm sorry but I've got to go.'

He hung up and I growled at my phone and slammed it down. I was so exasperated with him. I wouldn't allow him to treat me like this. He had to understand that my time was as precious as his. If he couldn't get to see me at whatever time we'd arranged, all he had to do was call. That was common courtesy. If I hadn't texted him, I doubted he would have contacted me at all. Well, if you're going to behave like that you can piss off, I thought to myself.

Later that evening I heard the crunch of a car on the gravel outside. I went to the door and Mark was standing there.

'I shouldn't be here, baby. I'm already late, but I couldn't bear hearing you so upset.' It was so lovely to see him. His mere presence poured a balm over my hard-edged resolve and irritation, and it dissolved in an instant as he held me and kissed me.

'Here, I've got something for you.' He felt in his pocket, drew out thirty-five pounds and handed it to me, still teasing me about my 'hysterical behaviour'.

'All that fuss over thirty-five pounds! Honestly, baby, I can't get over it. You are going to be a very wealthy woman. You'd better get used to it. This is just chicken feed.'

He was kind, loving, and oh so reassuring (indeed, whenever I saw him I had no doubt that everything would be just fine), and I ended up feeling faintly ridiculous for having made a fuss over such a paltry sum of money.

'I love you so much, baby,' he said, kissing me. 'I'm doing everything I can to get to see you. I'm so sick and tired of it all. I just want to be with you.'

Then he had to leave, worried he'd miss his flight slot.

22.01   Love you.

I love you too. I'm sorry. Have got my head around things and look forward to talking to you soon. Love you.

Mark told me he was falling in love with me only two days after we met, and he followed up by sending me a text message that read 'Ti amo', but although it was less than seventy-two hours since we had first met, I didn't find this odd or off-putting. I am an incurable romantic and believe in love at first sight, and because I found him very attractive I just found this exciting, especially as he declared it in Italian, my favourite Romantic language.

I have been asked if I really felt love for him at this stage, and the answer is yes. I fell head over heels in love and experienced a heady, giddy euphoria. Call it infatuation if you like but I called it love, and I remember thinking that nobody should ever settle for anything less. It chills me now, though, to read the text message relating to Mark buying me an Audi car where I say 'This is insane … but it is fun! This is like fiction', because never once did I stop to consider that it might actually be insane, or contemplate that it really could all be totally fictitious or realise that I had I hit the nail on the head when I told him that he was 'mighty dangerous'.

The following morning, I had a text from my friend Anne.

> How's the adventure going?

>> Emotionally exhausting – not that I have seen anything of him. About 4–5 hours in total. Brother and sister-in-law and friends worried. This is unlike anything in regular life as you and I know it. Had a bit of a wobble last night but talked to him and felt reassured (and very stupid). The next step requires a great leap of faith, but I feel ready to jump.

On 2 February, Mark asked me to conduct a property search for us, saying that he had a budget of £2–3 million, but would pay more for something really good. He wanted a minimum of 6,000 square feet and stipulated that the property would have to have a new kitchen and bathrooms. He was also very keen to advise me on my banking, urging me to open accounts with Barclays, pointing out that I would earn a better rate of interest, and receive the very best service – after all, Barclays' chief executive, Bob Diamond, was a friend of his. It was madness, he said, to leave the money where it was, when it could be doing so much better elsewhere. Mark also told me I would need to get a euro account so that he could transfer money to me whenever I needed it when we were abroad. I'd need two offshore accounts, he added.

I listened to what Mark had to say, but having been with the same bank for thirty years I was in no hurry to change anything as, apart from anything else, I was still looking for my own house to buy and needed my money to be readily accessible. I had had an offer accepted on a property the year before, but the owners subsequently withdrew from the sale. They had just contacted me again though, to ask if I was still interested. So with my focus briefly turned to buying my own place, I went to view a second property as well. Mark did his best to dissuade me from tying up my money in either house, reminding me that now I was going to be spending time with him my requirements would probably change and it would be better to wait to see how things panned out.

Late on the night of 7 February, while 'waiting for a debrief', he bombarded me with questions and information about both properties, telling me that both were vastly overvalued, and convincing me to hold fire.

> In my position you can always win.

> Information is power my love.

The following day, he texted to say that he was making an appointment for me at Barclays to discuss opening some accounts there. He said he would go with me, but the day before the meeting in the bank our relationship faltered when he failed to either return or pay for a mink coat that he had taken on approval a couple of days before. I was absolutely livid with him for not keeping his word, and for putting my reputation with Kerry in jeopardy. I told him that if the coat was not returned as promised, that would be the end of our relationship. Mark claimed that his associate Paul Deol would have to fly the coat back from Switzerland, to which I replied saying that he had better get going. At 5.45 p.m. there was a knock on the door of the shop, and I experienced my first encounter with Paul Deol. Mark had told me that Paul was an ex-bank manager, so I was expecting someone who was probably retired, in their sixties, soberly dressed. It was dark outside, and I didn't invite Paul in, but he looked to be in his forties and had the stature and bearing of a night-club bouncer rather than a City gent.

'I don't know what all this is about,' he said in a south-London accent, offering me the coat.

'I'm sorry you had to get involved,' I responded, taking the coat from him. 'It's not your fault. It's not mine either.'

Amazingly, just a couple of hours later I was no longer angry with Mark and found myself texting him to say I had 'got my zing back', and that I loved him.

The following day, Mark failed to appear at the bank, but Paul turned up to accompany me to the meeting and help with the opening of two accounts. On 15 February, I transferred all my money to my new Barclays account.

The next day, Mark was with me as we drove to the bank in Cirencester. He took a phone call, and I heard him discussing a cash-flow problem. When I questioned him about it he explained that it was all to do with paying for renovations at our new home. West End Farm was long forgotten and we were now planning to move into Widcombe Manor, a property that Mark had recently bought, that I was aware had been for sale. It was a beautiful Georgian manor house, set in stunning grounds on the outskirts of Bath but with access to the countryside too. I loved the idea of living there.

'How much do you need?' I asked.

'Nothing much, around twenty-six thousand.'

'Well, I can lend it to you – after all, it's only sitting in the bank,' I told him, eager to prove my generosity, and that I trusted him completely.

'No, baby, honestly, it's no problem. I'll see to it.'

'No, please, I'd like to help. It's the least I can do – after all, it's for our new home.'

By the time we got to the bank we'd agreed that I would help out, but Mark told me that a smaller sum would suffice for now and I transferred just under £22,000 to Paul Deol, who, apparently, was dealing with all the contractors. This proved to be the first of seventy transactions, made on an almost daily basis via Paul over the next couple of months, totalling some £750,000.

A couple of days after the first transfer Mark told me he had to go away on a dangerous surveillance mission to Iran. He phoned me from the cockpit of the jet he was flying, as he sat on the taxiway before take-off, and I then spent one of the worst nights of my life, as I feared for his safety and wondered if I would ever see him again. But the following morning, as I was getting ready to go to work, I saw a car emerging out of the early-morning mist and making its way down the drive. It was Mark – he'd come straight to see me on his return from Iran.

He asked me to make him some coffee, then went upstairs, and from the kitchen I overheard him on the phone. He asked for a secure line, quoted encryption numbers and identification codes, then, addressing the person at the other end as 'Sir', he said that everything had gone well, and the mission had been successful. He must be talking to someone very high up in National Security, I told myself – maybe even the Foreign Secretary, William Hague, himself.

The following day, Mark presented me with the first of two loan agreements for the sum of £90,000, on the basis that £100,000 would be repaid to me on or before 6 April. I believed all the money was to be spent on renovations at Widcombe

Manor – a project that I could easily believe might cost hundreds of thousands of pounds – but how my original offer of £26,000 mushroomed into an agreement to lend him £90,000 and ultimately £750,000 over the next couple of months I am at a loss to explain. A third loan agreement for £375,000 materialised some years later, also with my signature on it. I had no recollection of ever seeing, let alone signing it, and it was subsequently confirmed that my signature had been forged. I have no idea what it was for.

With my banking sorted out Mark said it was time to deal with my security. Since we first met, he had consistently drawn my attention to CCTV cameras. Where I saw one, he'd find half a dozen. Everyone was being watched constantly, he told me, explaining how easily people's emails, voicemail and telephone conversations could be hacked into.

'Governments are at it all the time,' he said. 'They have their eyes on everyone – it's unrelenting. Nobody can have a private life any more, especially if they're careless about deleting text messages and emails. I told you I delete everything at the end of the day. You must do the same.'

I liked to keep some email correspondence, and also some text messages, but this exasperated Mark, and from time to time he would pick up my phone and delete things. It used to annoy me no end, but I did worry that if I kept messages, particularly ones from him, it would be putting us in danger.

Mark also pointed out suspicious-looking people in the street and told me that I had to be extra vigilant. There were a lot of people who would like to see him dead, he warned, and although he promised that my life was not in danger, he insisted that it was only sensible to do everything possible to maximise my security generally, starting with replacing my mobile phone and laptop. Mark provided me with a new iPhone and MacBook Air, telling me that he would have remote access to everything on both devices. It was for my own good, he said, because you just couldn't be too careful. Again, he stressed that it was imperative that I deleted everything from the phone and the laptop at the end of each day, just as he did. 'It's to protect us both.'

Paul and Mark explained to me all about 'high-' and 'low-viz' security. Back in Switzerland, Mark said, he often had an armed police escort, and his house there had security like I just wouldn't believe. He showed me a photograph of a modern, luxury mansion that looked like Fort Knox. In the UK though, they favour low-viz security – generally no armed escorts (although Mark did claim there were armed guards at the end of my drive one night) – but he would change his car and his phones regularly, and, he said, I might have to do the same. For now, I would be driving a Volvo XC60, the first of a number of cars that Mark provided for me.

During the month of February, alongside doing his day job in Geneva, moving his project along up at Kemble airfield, expanding his property portfolio, and undertaking a dangerous mission to Iran, Mark also claimed to be in 'cabinet meetings' in Madrid, said he had to go to Germany to protect the king of Spain's son-in-law on a corruption charge and, on one occasion, told me he was off to Whitehall to 'stop a war'. He also claimed to know Vladimir Putin and Hillary Clinton. I know it sounds incredible, and looking back on it I can't believe I fell for all his lies, but I did; he is a truly astonishing, pathological liar – and very convincing. His alleged comings and goings also dazzled and disorientated me, as well as making me fear for his safety.

Very early on we talked about marriage (as I recall, it was first mentioned when we were in the bank together one day), with Mark telling me that I would have to propose to him, as it was a leap year. I didn't see him on 29 February, but I prepared a card for him. On the front was a photograph of me, aged twenty-one, with a speech bubble saying, 'You Make Me Feel So Young!' – a reference to what he'd said on our first date about women and younger men. Inside it read, 'I love you. Will you marry me?'

I was feeling so happy, but my spirits were deflated later that day when I received an unwelcome text from my sister-in-law, Annalisa.

> Carolyn, we are v v v worried that this guy does not exist – think about the name. You are being marked for a con. No car/house/meal has materialised. If he was genuine he would be horrified that he was causing such a worry to all you know and would do something about it. We are sure you are going to be conned out of all you own and your identity stolen. Take action now to protect yourself from this. This con can happen v fast and may be underway. We can give you a genuine contact for investment. We very much hope that we are wrong but please listen to those who know and love you and care. Annalisa xxx

I look back on this message now and think, If only I had listened. But I know why I didn't. I remember reading the message and thinking, How totally ridiculous. She hasn't even met Mark and she's reacting like this. I'm being marked for a con? How utterly absurd!

I had always got on pretty well with Annalisa, but now, not only did I feel upset, I felt furious at what I considered to be interference. Why couldn't she just be happy for me, and wait until she'd met Mark before passing judgement? An email from Kerry in the same vein only made things worse, and rather than feeling that my friends and family were trying to help me, I felt under attack. A text message to Uma shows how I was feeling at the time:

> Just to let you know that this is the real thing. My
> instincts are right. This is mega, mega, mega. I am
> totally in love. Just be happy for me.

'Anyway,' I explained the next time I saw her, 'what's the worst that can happen? I'll have my heart broken. But a broken heart will always mend, and there are times in life when you just have to seize the moment and take a chance. It's worked for me before, and I know it will work again.'

The next morning, 1 March, Mark came to my cottage. I was so happy to see him, and I gave him the card I had made for him, together with a love letter. He opened the card and looked at me, smiling.

'You know I want to marry you,' he said as he kissed me.

We sat down on the sofa, and I then explained to him how our relationship was now causing problems with my friends and family. I showed him Annalisa's text message and Kerry's email and, in so doing, I fell into the classic trap of confiding in my abuser, forewarning him of potential problems. His eyes welled up.

'It just sullies everything,' Mark told me, as a tear rolled down his cheek. 'Your sister-in-law sees what you have and it just makes her jealous. And as for your boss, she's only thinking about herself and her business. Think of everything you've done for her. She'll never get anyone as good to replace you – that's all she's concerned about.'

What he said made sense to me at the time, and I felt closer to him than ever.

'It doesn't sully anything,' I told him. 'What we have is what we have, and nothing anybody says can change that. I don't understand, either, how people can be so suspicious. What sort of dangerous world do they inhabit? What vivid imaginations they have and what unhappy lives they must lead!'

What was happening might well be unusual, but surely the chance of experiencing love at first sight had to be far greater than that of meeting a dangerous conman in safe, sleepy Tetbury, I thought to myself. It was too ridiculous.

'I just wish people could be happy for us. I'm so sick and tired of all this doom and gloom – and they're so bloody heavy-handed,' I mused.

Suddenly, Mark picked up my phone, clicked on to Annalisa's text message and started typing a response.

'We've got to stop this right now,' he said as he held out my phone to show me what he had written.

> We have seen a car that we like and are waiting for the new number plate
>
> We have seen a house that we like which hopefully we will be in before Easter
>
> We have had several meals
>
> I do my own investments with my own bank
>
> Please let me get on with my life

'OK?' he asked me.

'Yes,' I replied, and he pressed 'send'. I didn't realise it at the time, but now Mark was taking control of my personal correspondence and beginning to undermine my relationships with my family.

In retrospect, I can see how he began to manipulate me. The staged visit to my cottage with Bianca was undoubtedly designed to showcase his loving, caring nature, as were the things he told me about Pedro. He continually stressed his honesty and integrity, his bravery, and the fact that he would always put others before himself, and I bought straight into it. I believe the extravagant display he made of returning my thirty-five pounds and telling me that I was going to have to get used to spending money was designed solely to make me feel mean (a character trait I hate), thereby conditioning me psychologically, so that I would be only too ready to jump in and prove my generosity – first by ordering and paying for a pair of Gucci shoes for him, costing £400, and trusting him to pay me back (he never did – when I told him they had arrived, he immediately thanked me for such a lovely present, and I didn't like to say that I had not intended them to be one), and soon after when he set the stage for me to lend him everything I had.

Instructions to transfer money usually came from Mark in the morning via text message, and I would make the transfer. Looking back, I am sure the telephone conversation about his 'cash-flow problem' that I overheard was staged and he was clever in mentioning a sum of £26,000 and then asking that I transfer just under £22,000 because it made me think that he would not take advantage of me – after all, in that first transaction he could have had another £4,000. The loan agreements were, of course, not worth the paper they were written on. As I tell my story, I can understand how astonishing people find it that I should have been taken in so easily, and looking back, I cannot believe I behaved so recklessly. But Mark is a conjuror – I was spellbound – and it is impossible to describe to anyone who hasn't met him just how convincing and manipulative he is.

In the course of a few weeks, I had gone from being totally independent and carefree to being totally dependent and manipulated. It shocks and pains me to remember how I would jump to attention when Mark called me – I, who had previously refused to let the phone interrupt anything I was doing, often going out without it or switching it off (I had chosen the most demanding ringtone I could find to identify his calls – a loud piano riff that rhythmically urged 'just answer the phone!' whenever it sounded). I also cannot believe that as someone who hates being controlled (as my reaction to Annalisa and Kerry's messages demonstrates), I allowed Mark to read my personal messages and to have access to everything on my phone and laptop.

I got in very deep, very quickly, and it was all because I had fallen head over heels in love. The letter I wrote to Mark on 28 February 2012 to go with the 'Marry Me?' card reveals how totally captivated I was by him.

Tetbury, 28th February 2012

My Darling Mark
The past few weeks have been the most amazing in all my life. I cannot believe how lucky I have been to have met you. Our coming together has been extraordinary and beautiful. I love you from the bottom of my heart, unconditionally and forever. You are my soulmate and the very air that I breathe. I really don't think I could survive without you.

It is very difficult to express adequately how I feel about you and the beautiful relationship we have. Looking back over some of the things I said to friends very early on (and it is still less than six weeks since we met), I realise that I knew from the very beginning, just as you did, that you were the one for me.

When we met for that drink I found you totally captivating and I was sure that we would have some sort of relationship. Because my guard was up I tell myself that I could never have imagined things would come so far so soon, but I did say to a friend in those first few days that it wouldn't surprise me if we got married the following week!

Darling, I am so excited. I absolutely adore you. You will recall that I told you on that first date that I am not interested in your money. Of course at that stage I had no idea of the extent of your wealth. I just want to say now that I look forward to enjoying all the treats that your money can buy. Money certainly makes all sorts of things possible and is to be enjoyed. I know it makes you who you are – to a certain extent. I really admire you for the way you have worked so hard to get what you have, but it is you I love, not your wealth.

I am sorry that I have, on a couple of occasions, been stupid and petty over my money (which of course is yours). I can only try to explain my insecurity by telling you that my ex-husband made comments to me such as 'marriage isn't a meal ticket you know', and 'when are you going to start pulling your weight?' All this when I was trying to create a loving home for my family and working really hard at raising my two beautiful daughters. Post-divorce I found myself in a relationship with someone who never had any money on him, demanded I paid half of everything (down to the last pence), and lied to me. I vowed then that I would always keep my independence and told friends that if I ever showed any inclination to even share an address with a man they should have me locked up.

I am telling you this only to try to explain my minor wobble early on. I am ashamed of it. I felt very stupid and I want you to know that deep down I have always trusted you absolutely and implicitly. The trouble is that you are the only person I can confide in about such things. Other people have felt compelled to give me the benefit of their advice and I have had to bear the burden of it. You have been the only person I could tell. I know it has angered you and I am sorry, but I would rather that than keeping things secret from you. I hope you can understand.

Really, darling, none of that matters. I have never had anyone in my life who really wanted to look after me. I have spent years with my guard up as far as men are concerned. It really is quite amazing that I have let you in so completely – and I have never had any doubt. I love you, adore you and trust you absolutely.

*Our love is the most beautiful and precious thing to me,
darling. I will be there for you always and I want to do anything
and everything I can to make you happy. I am so excited about
moving into our new house and learning all about you and telling
you about me. I have to say that I will really enjoy living in a
palace, but only as long as I am with you. If I had to choose
between a palace without you or a tent with you – well I might
have to think about it because you would be very grumpy in a tent
– and so would I. Anyway, darling, you know what I mean. I will
enjoy all the wonderful things that you have that money can buy,
but most of all I will just love being with you.*

*Please always talk to me about any niggles that you have. I am
bound to annoy you sometimes – please talk to me and explain
how you feel. I will do the same.*

*I love you so much. I want to become really intimate with you
physically and emotionally. I so look forward to getting to know
you inside out.*

*You were made for me – I have no doubt. I am the luckiest,
happiest woman in the world.*

Thank you for everything.

All my love,

Bubba xxx

How sick it makes me feel to read that letter now. To think that
I gave my love and trust so easily to such an evil man. To think
again about how, as I now believe, he planned to abuse me, even
before he met me. It makes me sick to see how I apologise to him
for being 'stupid and petty' over money, but that is certainly how
he made me feel. The letter also reveals that in spite of my independent nature, I liked the idea of being looked after and
cherished – but, after all, who doesn't?

By the end of February, I was blinded by love, and totally
under Mark's control.

4

THE LOVE BOMB

Bathsheba loved Troy in the way that only self-reliant women love when they abandon their self-reliance. When a strong woman recklessly throws away her strength she is worse than a weak woman who has never had any strength to throw away.

Thomas Hardy, *Far from the Madding Crowd*

Mark regularly needed to be in London and he would often pick me up and take me with him. I enjoyed having him trapped inside the car with me, as Paul drove us up and down the M4. I probably spent more time with him in the car than anywhere else – and he often had some surprise or other up his sleeve.

'I've booked you a hair appointment at Nicky Clarke's. He's a friend of mine. He won't actually be doing your hair but one of his best protégés will be looking after you. Do you know how difficult it is to get an appointment there? Life is so much easier if you know the right people. And you, baby, you've got to start getting used to having the best.'

When I emerged to meet him in Berkeley Square I had to admit my hair looked good; but then I had always received plenty of compliments when it was cut by my regular hairdresser back in Buckinghamshire.

'Darling, forget your old life. You're moving up a few notches. You look fabulous. It's so much better. You've got to forget your old ways. Now, let's go shopping.'

Being with Mark was really good fun. He took me to Harrods and Chanel and he remains the only man (with the exception of my father) I have ever enjoyed going shopping with. He was fantastic. He knew Harrods like the back of his hand, and he appeared to be well acquainted with some of the sales assistants. He seemed to know instinctively what would look good on me. He went through the rails picking out items for me to try, and when I came out of the changing room he was decisive and unhesitatingly gave his opinion.

'That's perfect, we'll take it … No, baby, not that: that was a mistake. It makes you look a hundred and fifty … Now that's really nice. What about a jacket to go with it? This is really quite easy because you're a perfect, standard size ten. I'll never have a problem buying presents for you.'

Mark knew exactly what constituted a capsule wardrobe, and I ended up with just that. A few beautiful key items: a classic Dior handbag for day, a small classic Chanel bag for evening, a beautifully cut pair of black trousers and jacket by Ralph Lauren, an Armani navy shift dress and tweed edge-to-edge jacket, two Chanel jackets – one a long-line navy blazer, the other a classic short navy knit – a Chanel dress, a couple of pairs of Tods loafers, Dior shoes to match the bag, a pair of Chanel pumps and a Montblanc pen to go in the bag.

'It's really important to have a good pen,' he told me, and I couldn't deny it.

Everything was beautiful – and to me ridiculously expensive – but I was going to have to get used to that. Along the way, Mark needed some cufflinks, a lead for the golden-retriever puppy he had shown me photographs of, and was having expertly trained, and most extraordinary of all, and obscenely expensive as far as I was concerned, a whole ham from Harrods' food hall costing £1,500. And whenever we went to pay, Mark just looked straight at me and I mutely produced my banker's card. But as we sat drinking champagne in Chanel, waiting for a pair of shoes to be brought over from another store, I thought I wouldn't mind getting used to this way of shopping.

On one of these mornings, when we had planned to go to London, Mark told me to meet him at Calcot Manor, a hotel a couple of miles outside Tetbury, as we did from time to time. He told me he had a surprise for me, and this time he arrived in a helicopter to pick me up and show me how he really liked to travel. I loved it. It was a beautiful morning and we flew over Stable Cottage, where I had lived when I first arrived in Tetbury, before gaining some altitude to fly right over the top of the cooling towers at Didcot power station. Then, spread out beneath us I recognised Turville, in the Chiltern Hills, and the familiar landscape of my past life. Finally, as we approached London, I picked out the business park at Denham where I had worked for ten years, before redundancy had acted as a catalyst for change. Thank goodness I'd had the courage to try some different things. And who would have thought it would lead to this? As we landed at Denham airfield, Mark told me that he was thinking that we would have to live somewhere where we could have a helipad, as travelling up and down to London by car was just getting too time consuming.

I loved the excitement of those early days with Mark, and within a couple of days I was sure I had met my soulmate. Mark reinforced this feeling by telling me he felt exactly the same (in fact, I remember thinking that he was even more infatuated with me than I was with him). This, I now know, is a big red flag in a relationship, but if you're not aware of it, you just think how lucky you are and plough headlong into something that becomes more and more toxic. And if, like me, you are a 'romantic' and believe in love at first sight, it is impossible to resist.

Mark completely swept me off my feet and taught me every dance he knew. And I loved the way he just got on and organised things. It was a novelty for me to be with someone so strong and decisive, someone who took charge (that had always been my role) and did things well. I had utter confidence in him.

His latest project was our wedding, and I was more than happy for him to get on with that. The morning after we had agreed to get married, he called to tell me to have my ring finger measured, which I immediately did. He told me he was having my engagement ring and our wedding rings made in Switzerland. The wedding rings would be crafted from the same piece of white gold to Mark's own design. He sent me photographs of very expensive jewellery, asking if I liked them: there were so many things he wanted to give me, he explained, but he didn't want to get me anything I didn't like, and was trying to gauge my taste. Next, he told me that he wanted us to be married in the chapel at Widcombe Manor, with an extravagant reception in the house itself. He would order seafood from Bibendum, the most beautiful flowers money could buy (there was a new variety of red lily he described to me that would be the focus of the floral decorations), Nicky Clarke himself would do my hair, there would be musicians, fireworks, *son et lumière* in the garden – everything anyone could want or wish for. It would be a magical, fairytale wedding – a real extravaganza.

I have always thought that second or third weddings should be low-key, but Mark made me feel like a queen and, as he painted a dazzling picture of it all, I got caught up and swept away in all the excitement,

'I've never done it properly before,' he told me. 'Please indulge me in this. I've received top military awards for bravery: we'll have a splendid guard of honour, and I'll be in uniform – a red jacket. You'll love it!'

Wandering through Harrods together, he took me through the china and glass departments pointing out things that he liked.

He told me we would be given some of the most beautiful things money could buy as wedding presents. He also took me through the security department, drawing my attention to numerous listening devices and security cameras, all for domestic use. I couldn't believe that such sophisticated equipment was so easily available off the shelf like that – in a department store.

'It's a treacherous world out there, baby,' Mark confided. 'You never know who's watching you. That's why we've got to be extra vigilant.'

Without consultation Mark made an appointment for me at Caroline Castigliano in Knightsbridge, to have my wedding dress fitted. He had hoped that we would be able to go to Paris for a couple of nights, to see Karl Lagerfeld, who was a friend of his, and to have the dress designed and made by him but decided there just wasn't time. He wanted us to get married as soon as possible and he wanted it done in style.

He accompanied me to my first appointment but soon left me sitting in the ornate mirrored showroom, drinking champagne.

'What's your budget?' asked the assistant, as she brought out a few dresses to see which styles I favoured.

'There isn't one,' I replied, recalling a conversation I had had with Paul (who was forever complaining about the amount of extra work he was having to do to get things organised for the wedding), when he had remarked that Mark liked to 'put on a bit of a show'. There was only one thing for it. I would choose the most glamorous wedding dress money could buy – glamorous and classy. I would look a million dollars.

'In that case I think I have just the dress for you.'

The assistant gave me a knowing look, disappeared and then re-emerged with a heavily beaded, corseted, very 'Hollywood', fishtail dress.

'I really think you should try this one,' she told me, and she led me into the changing room. I looked at myself in the mirror as I stepped into the dress and felt it tighten around me. I loved it, and I looked radiant as I held myself erect and poised, looking at myself from every angle. With its heavy beading the dress weighed a ton, but as I came out of the changing room and sash-ayed the length of the showroom floor, towards the giant floor-to-ceiling, gilt-framed mirror at the far end, I felt chic, elegant, confident and beautiful.

'You look fabulous in that dress!' crowed the sales assistant. 'Not everyone can carry that off. You've got to have supreme confidence to wear it well, but you can do it. Wow – the way you move in it! You came alive the moment you put it on – I can tell you love it.'

She was right, I did. I also chose a sheer, beaded, boxy, round-necked bolero that fastened at the nape of my neck but revealed my back, to go over it. Mark and I would make a very striking couple.

To relax, Mark took me to Babington House (one of his compa-nies had just acquired the Soho House group of hotels) and booked me in for a manicure and massage. He apologised that at such short notice that was all that was available, all the while drawing my attention to the way the staff were treating him.

'See baby: look how they jump to attention when they see me. They know who I am and they know I won't stand for anything but the best. The first thing I'm going to do here is get a new chef – the food is crap!'

He accompanied me to the treatment suite where I was going to have my manicure, and sat down beside me, chatting to me as the beautician settled me down and started on my hands. Then he got up, bent down to kiss me and told me he'd see me back in our room later on.

'Isn't he nice!' cooed the therapist as she removed the old polish from my nails. 'What a gentleman. You're very lucky.'

'I know,' I smiled. 'I just can't believe my luck.'

We were staying in a suite with an enormous green sofa in the sitting room, and a bed in a mezzanine at the end of the long room. But the next day, after we had walked around the grounds and I had admired the formal kitchen garden, Mark told me he had a surprise for me, and showed me into another room that looked out on to that beautiful garden.

'When we walked around the garden earlier and you told me how much you liked it, I thought you might prefer this room. Isn't the view lovely? And look, we've got a wood-burning stove.'

The room was indeed lovely. The sitting room was exceptionally cosy with the fire, and the sleeping area, which looked down on to it, was rustic with exposed brick walls. The bathroom was luxurious with a free-standing copper bath, and outside on the terrace there was a large copper jacuzzi.

'I thought you said the place was fully booked. What happened to the people in here?'

'They had to move,' he told me. 'Like I told you, I can have any room I want. Do you like it?'

'I love it!'

'You know I could quite happily live in a hotel,' Mark told me. 'In fact, I did once live in a hotel for a while. It would have to be a bloody good one though! Wouldn't you like to stay here until we move to Widcombe, rather than go back to that cottage of yours?'

'Absolutely not! And what about my cat? And getting to work?' I told him that I could never live in a hotel, however good it was. A hotel suite could never feel like home to me. I needed a place of my own, decorated to my own taste, with my own belongings around me. That was not to say that I wouldn't enjoy staying in a first-class hotel from time to time – and I was enjoying every minute of this.

Mark lit the wood-burner and we settled down in front of the fire. But he never relaxed for long as he always had some business or other to attend to, and he constantly seemed to be on one or other of his three mobile phones. Now he turned the television on and sat watching some investment channel, following the price of gold intently. Suddenly, he picked up a phone and instructed someone to buy (or was it sell?) a huge amount of gold. I couldn't really follow the conversation as it was conducted in a series of rapid-fire sound bites. Then the next thing I knew, the graph on the television had shot up (or was it down?).

'See that?' he said. 'I did that.'

I hadn't really been following what was happening, but I had seen the graph on the screen change dramatically, and what he said seemed impressive and totally believable at the time. In retrospect, however, I am sure it was just another illusion that he created on the spur of the moment, using whatever came to hand to conjure up a false picture. I recall another occasion later on, when we were living in Bath, when he looked out of the window and drew my attention to two police officers who were walking nearby in Victoria Park.

'Good,' he said, 'they've put extra officers on duty while I'm here. They said they would.'

I am sure now that the police presence in Bath that day was exactly the same as any other day, but that Mark just took the opportunity to create a backstory around the two officers. He is highly skilled at sowing seeds and painting pictures in people's minds, and very convincing. He did this throughout our relationship, either by twisting normal occurrences to his advantage, or staging events to back up his more fantastical claims. All the time he did this he gained more and more control over me and, as the relationship developed, he used these tactics to isolate me, make me fearful, rob me of all my confidence and, eventually, to strip away and suck out my very essence, so that I didn't even recognise myself – in the mirror, or in any other way.

*   *   *

Over the following few weeks, I went up to London alone a couple of times to have my wedding-dress fittings. One morning when I was in town, Mark called me to say that he had made an appointment for me to see a cosmetic surgeon in Harley Street. He had talked to me before about cosmetic surgery and had tried to persuade me to see Sarah Prescott, a woman he knew in Monkton Combe, just outside Bath, about having Botox. He had even made appointments for me.

'There's no way I'm having Botox – or anything else,' I had told him firmly. 'Not even for you. You'll have to put up with me the way I am – take it or leave it!' I felt mildly annoyed that he should even have suggested it.

'You're beautiful baby, but I believe in making the most of every asset. This woman is brilliant with Botox. You should see her – she looks fantastic for her age. Just go and see what she says.'

I had resisted so far, but this time, with an appointment booked just around the corner from where I was, I decided to go out of sheer curiosity. I made my way to the Harley Street clinic where Sarah Prescott practised in London and was shown into a small, windowless consulting room with a floor-to-ceiling mirror and very harsh lighting. Sarah invited me to come and stand in front of the mirror and show her the areas of my face that I was concerned about. I hadn't ever really been concerned about lines on my face, but now, standing under the unsympathetic lights, every imperfection in my skin seemed to be magnified. My face looked covered in lines, particularly around my eyes, and I could see a network of tributaries above my upper lip. I pointed them out to Sarah.

'To be honest, I've not thought about it much, but I suppose if I were going to do anything, I'd like to get rid of the lines around my mouth and the bags under my eyes.'

'Well, I don't think there's anything we can do for those with fillers or Botox,' Sarah replied, examining my reflection in the mirror. 'I'm going to ask our cosmetic surgeon to come and talk to you. He may be able to suggest something.'

Bloody hell! I thought, shocked that anyone should suggest I have surgery.

The consultant arrived and examined my face in some detail before repeating what I had already been told. There was nothing they could do with Botox or fillers.

'What you really need,' he stated authoritatively, 'is a full facelift. You might want to go away and think about it, but I believe that way we could achieve a really good result.'

Fuck! I thought to myself. What a bloody cheek!

I told him I would have to think about it, left the clinic and called Mark immediately.

'You won't believe what they told me at that clinic. They said I need a total facelift. Bloody cheek! They can forget about that – I've never wanted any kind of treatment like that. I've always suspected these people work on knocking your confidence. You should see the harsh lighting in the consulting room. It would make anyone look awful. Anyway, I'm not having anything done. I've never wanted anything like that. You can forget it!'

'Calm down, baby. I don't know why they suggested that. I thought they were supposed to be experts on Botox and other non-surgical treatment. I'll find out what's going on.'

Later that afternoon he called me back.

'Bubba, they specialise in surgery there, that's why they suggested a facelift.'

'Well, I don't know why you made an appointment for me there – or why on earth I went. I'm not interested in any of it.'

'OK, darling, that's up to you. I'll have Botox myself, when I need it, but what you do is up to you.'

Hmmm, I thought. But over the following weeks I found myself scrutinising my face in the mirror much more than was normal for me.

Now that we were getting married Mark wanted me to give up my job and continued to insist that I let my rented cottage go. I gave in my notice at the shop and then I spoke to my landlady at the Little Coach House. When I'd moved into the cottage the agent had told me that the owner believed it to be 'the house where dreams come true'. Previous tenants had experienced dramatic changes of fortune while living there, I was told. Now it seemed it had worked its magic again.

Mark also persuaded me to dispose of nearly all my belongings, telling me that I needed a complete break from the past.

'When you buy your own place, just think how you will enjoy furnishing it from scratch – and anyway, it's a complete waste of money paying to keep things in storage. You've already spent a small fortune keeping all your stuff.'

As for my clothes, he told me that if I was going to be with him, I would have to look the part and up my game.

'I wouldn't want anyone thinking I'm not looking after you properly,' he told me. So I decided that most of my wardrobe would have to go too.

Not long after the Babington House trip I was in London, waiting to meet Mark in Harrods' shoe department, when my phone rang.

'Baby, where are you?'

'I'm where we arranged to meet – in the shoe department in Harrods.'

'I'll be with you in a minute – but prepare yourself – and don't laugh!'

'Why? What is it?'

'I've been in a meeting with Nicky Clarke and Chris Evans. They said they'd make a big donation to charity if I agreed to let Nicky Clarke do whatever he wanted with my hair.'

'Oh God! What did he do?'

'You'll see in a minute.'

Mark hung up.

He appeared a couple of minutes later, and his hair had definitely been seen to. He had a spiky fringe and the hair on top of his head had been gelled up. It looked awful.

'What do you think?' Mark was running his fingers through his hair.

'It's bad, but I was expecting worse. It'll grow out. Actually, once you wash it it won't look so bad.' I was laughing. 'But I don't want to marry you looking like that, and I don't want Nicky Clarke anywhere near my hair if that's what happens!'

On another occasion Mark took me to Lucknam Park. It was one of his favourite haunts, and the first time we went there he'd told me he was negotiating a big business deal with the owner.

'I'm buying Colerne airfield. It's just down the road and ideal for wealthy guests to fly into. It's a no-brainer,' he'd said.

This time, however, instead of going into the hotel for a glass of wine and an espresso as we normally did, Mark disappeared into a small stone outbuilding near the spa and came out with a bicycle.

'This is for you,' he told me, before vanishing again and reappearing with a second bike. Both of them were too small, but we climbed aboard in any case and he led the way, at high speed, as I pedalled madly behind him. We arrived, breathless, at a wooden stable block.

'This is where I'm going to keep Bianca's pony,' he explained. 'She's going to have everything she wants. I can't wait for us all to be together. And isn't this fun, out riding bicycles together? Come on, I'll race you back!' And off we charged once more, laughing hysterically, as we pedalled away furiously on our undersized bikes.

But not all the time Mark and I spent together was so carefree. On one occasion, when we were in Knightsbridge, on our way to Harrods, Mark told me that it wasn't really a good place for him to be. He was too well known there, he explained. Paul said he thought it was plain stupid for Mark to be anywhere in the vicinity that day, because there was some demonstration going on nearby and he felt it was really risky. We went to Harrods all the same, but Mark seemed very on edge, and it wasn't long before he took a call from Paul and told me it was time to move on.

'Don't worry, Bubba, but we've got to get out of here quickly. Paul's waiting in the car outside. Come with me.'

He took me firmly by the hand and guided me swiftly through the store. Heads turned as we rushed past, now almost running. We reached the car, where Paul had the engine running. We dived in and made a quick getaway. It was all very unnerving.

'I think we'd better keep away from there for a while. That was a bit close for comfort. Exciting, huh?' Mark was talking to Paul.

'It's not exciting, mate. It's stupid. I told you not to come up here today, but you wouldn't listen. You're going to be in big trouble the way you're carrying on.'

Mark looked at me.

'Don't worry, Bubba. I'll never let anything happen to you.'

Later that afternoon, on our way back to Tetbury, Mark suddenly told me to make sure my seat belt was secure.

We had left the M4 and were driving along a narrow country lane when he said, 'There's a change of plan, darling. Paul's really got to put his foot down now. We'll be going very fast, but Paul's an experienced driver, so don't worry. I've been called back in. Hold on tight. OK, Paul – let's go!'

I was pushed back into my seat as Paul changed gear and slammed his foot to the floor. We were speeding along the narrow lane at eighty miles per hour and I was terrified, sitting there rigid, just praying that nothing came towards us from the other way. Eventually, Paul slowed down and we pulled into a dilapidated farmyard.

'This is where I have to leave you. They're sending a helicopter to pick me up,' Mark told me, and he kissed me before opening the car door and stepping out into the rain. 'Paul will take you home. I'll call you later.'

I felt totally bemused, and as Paul turned the car around and we drove away, I watched through the rear window as Mark made his way across the muddy yard and disappeared behind some farm buildings.

Now Mark told me that he was having doubts about us living at Widcombe Manor. I had loved the idea of living there. Previous talk about moving to Bath had worried me as I thought I would feel cooped up living in a city – it was not what I wanted at all. But Widcombe Manor didn't feel like a town house; it was a village manor house, but with Bath station and the attractions of city life all within walking distance it seemed the perfect compromise, as Mark couldn't stand the idea of living in the country. Not that I would be spending much time there, as Mark was a tax exile, after all. I told him I was never going to be a tax exile. I just couldn't understand why anyone would do it. Anyway, we were going to have a house in the UK for when we were together, and I would be only too happy to join Mark in Switzerland, Spain, Italy or anywhere else for that matter. In addition, I still intended to buy my very own home somewhere in the Cotswolds. I would have the best of all possible worlds.

But now Mark explained that there were problems with security at Widcombe Manor. Because of its Grade I listing the windows couldn't be fitted with bullet-proof glass, he couldn't fit a steel security door behind the original front door and the gates couldn't be changed. The property was too exposed, he said; and besides, he felt it was jinxed because a young girl had drowned in the swimming pool there some years before and he thought it was a bad omen.

I didn't understand the necessity for all the security, but he told me that there was a lot about him that I still didn't know – that I would not want to know – and that I must trust him. Once again, he assured me that my life would never be in danger, but emphasised that his was – constantly. That was why he changed his cars and mobile phone number on a regular basis, he reminded me. He couldn't risk anyone being able to identify him.

I sometimes wondered if I could cope with this kind of life-style. I loved my freedom and, despite what Mark used to say about my never having lived, I often thought he was the one who couldn't live properly. He had everything money could buy, but he seemed to have no freedom at all. A walk with me in the countryside or a trip to the theatre or cinema were out of the question.

'Theatres and cinemas are two of the most dangerous places for me,' he explained. 'Think about it: if someone comes after me in a place like that, it's almost impossible for me to get out without a lot of innocent people getting hurt. I'm not a selfish person, Bubba, I never have been. I will always put other people before myself, sometimes before us – you'll have to accept that. There are lots of people who would like to see me dead, darling. It's a fact of life. Don't forget, I infiltrated the IRA. They tortured me – you've seen the scars – but I got away, and they don't forget. You think all that's over, but it never goes away – believe me. But don't worry about it. I'm very good at surviving – I just have to be careful. And remember, you must never tell anyone about any of this. There is nothing more dangerous than careless talk. I shouldn't even be talking to you about it, but you're the only person I can trust.'

Mark had indeed shown me what he claimed were torture scars. He flashed an ankle and shin at me while we were driving along one day, with him at the wheel, so it was very difficult to see clearly. I did think I saw some marks that could have been made by the electrodes that he claimed had been used during torture, but in retrospect, I wonder if I imagined them, or just believed what he was telling me, even though I couldn't really see properly. He also showed the 'scars' to Rick Libbey, his contact at the Prince's Trust, and later to Martin Brunt, but neither of them was convinced there were any. It seems I was rather more gullible.

Meanwhile, plans were going ahead for the wedding and Mark continued to insist that we get married as soon as possible. He had it in his head that we would get married over the Easter weekend but the whole thing seemed impossible to me.

'That just doesn't give us enough time to ensure that the people we want to be there will be able to come,' I argued. 'People make plans for Easter. I can guarantee that hardly anyone I know will be able to come. Anyway, I'd like to introduce you to my family in a more informal way first.'

'Baby, everyone will be thrilled for you, and the ones who want to be there will make sure they are there. If anyone isn't there, it will be because they just don't really want to be. Then you'll see who your true friends are.'

'That's not right, darling. We're not all like you who let people down all the time. Some of us stick to our commitments. I know I do. Anyway, I thought you wanted to do everything properly and that takes time.'

'Just leave it to me, Bubba,' he said as he kissed me. 'I love you loads.'

'I love you too.'

On the day of my final wedding-dress fitting Mark had some bad news. There had been a plumbing catastrophe at Widcombe. There was water everywhere and ceilings and floors and whole rooms were ruined. God alone knew how long it was going to take to make good all the damage.

'I'm so sorry, darling. I was just in too much of a hurry to get it all sorted. I persuaded the plumber to take a risk and told him I would take responsibility if anything went wrong – and it went spectacularly wrong. Fuck knows what we're going to do now. I told you that house is unlucky for us.'

As I stepped into my wedding dress, my heart was heavy and I felt overcome with a sense of doom and disaster. I looked at the bride staring back at me from the other side of the mirror, wearing her beautiful dress, and I no longer felt I was looking at myself. What had happened to me? Where had that classy, glamorous, confident, beautiful woman gone? She had been here only a couple of weeks before, smiling radiantly in the mirror. Now I felt I was losing myself. Who was that expressionless ghost staring back at me? I felt incredibly sad, almost grief stricken, and had a sudden vision of myself years from now, still unmarried, a tragic figure in a beautiful but tattered dress. I felt the hairs on my arms stand up on end and I shuddered.

Later that afternoon, when Paul came to collect me and the dress, I questioned him.

'This wedding isn't going to happen, is it?'

'Mark has his own way of making things happen,' he replied, cryptically.

One morning, not long after, Mark called me declaring, 'We've got sheep!'

Once again, I was bemused, as he told me that he'd be with me shortly and would explain everything. He picked me up and we drove off towards Bath. As we approached the city, he stopped the car on a hill overlooking the countryside beyond and told me to get out.

'All this is yours,' he explained, surveying the scene in front of us and telling me that he was buying the whole estate. 'It's perfect,' he said. 'Much better than Widcombe. I know you love that house, but the security there is a nightmare. I got carried away with it because I thought you'd like it. I thought I could make it work, but that house is unlucky for us. This one is perfect. We'll never want to move again. I'm going to show you where it is, but I don't want to take you inside until it's ready. I shouldn't really show you anything yet, but I'm so excited about it and I want you to see where it is and be excited too.'

We got back in the car and drove on, through narrow lanes, to a small hamlet called Beach. Mark pointed out a farmhouse on the right that he said was part of the estate, and he stopped the car a little further along the road, at the end of a meticulously manicured drive. I couldn't see the house, but the boundary of the property had been planted with an immaculately trimmed beech hedge, behind which I could see discreet wire fencing.

'See that, Bubba? All high-tech security fencing and cameras. We'll be totally secure here.'

'But why didn't you tell me about it before? You've got to take me in,' I pleaded. I felt my spirits rising, and for the first time since I had been told of the concerns about Widcombe, I felt excited. This might be even better. The location was absolutely stunning.

'Come on, darling, you can't bring me here and not take me in. I don't care if work needs to be done. I want to see the house and garden now.'

'Darling, I told you I want it all to be finished first. It will be my wedding present to you and I want everything to be perfect.'

'Please, Bubba. Now. I want to see it now.'

'I've told you, darling, the best things in life are worth waiting for. You are going to have to be patient.'

I started to protest once more, but he put his finger over my lips and then kissed me.

'God, you're so frustrating!' I sighed. 'What about Widcombe? What's happening with that?'

'The insurance will cover the damage there. I'll get it all repaired and sell it on. I've got a buyer. It's not right for us, darling. This is much better. You'll see. Trust me. I adore you, baby. Everything's going to be just fine – I've never been so happy. And we'll make a very nice profit on the sale of Widcombe.'

A few days later Mark was on the phone to me, upbeat and excited.

'Get dressed, baby,' he said. 'I'm coming to pick you up to take you to Bath to see the house we'll be living in while the work's completed at Beach. I hope you'll like it. Put on that new dress I like – I want you to look a million dollars. I'll be with you in an hour.'

It was a beautiful spring day and I was trying to feel happy and positive. I did my hair and applied my make-up carefully, then put on my Chanel dress and my Dior shoes. It was important that I looked good for Mark – he obviously wanted me to dress the part when he showed me around this other house of his.

'People will be looking, baby. We'll be as discreet as we can but there are always people looking.'

I didn't like the sound of that. In fact, I didn't like the idea of living in Bath at all.

'I don't understand how it can be safe to live in the centre of Bath when you say it isn't safe to live at Widcombe Manor. Surely there are all the same problems with security – and the same restrictions – plus Bath is teeming with tourists, which must make it much easier for anyone hostile to get close?'

'Just the opposite, baby. Nobody would risk causing a commotion with all those tourists around, and there's always a strong police presence. Safety in numbers. In any case, there'll be extra security about when I'm there and I will be very careful. I know how to "appear" without attracting any attention, just as I know how to make a grand entrance, if I want to. Now, come with me. I want to show you this other place of mine. I really hope you'll like it.'

Paul drove us to Bath and we stopped in a street just off the Circus. Mark escorted me from the car and took me to the door of Number 1 Brock Street. Brock Street runs between the Circus and the Royal Crescent, both of which are regarded as among the greatest examples of Georgian architecture to be found in the UK. They are breathtakingly beautiful, built of honey-coloured Bath stone with tiers of columns and ornate façades in the classical style.

The Circus (from the Latin, meaning a ring or circle) comprises three curved terraces of equal length which form a circle, with three streets, Brock Street, Bennett Street and Gay Street radiating out from between the terraces, and a large grass circle with a group of enormous plane trees in the centre. The Royal Crescent, located at the other end of Brock Street, is vast and sweeping; it is 150 metres long and looks down over a large lawn to Royal Victoria Park. The Royal Crescent and the Circus are the two most prestigious addresses in Bath and Number 1 Brock Street, which has its front door situated in Brock Street, forms the corner of one of the three curved terraces that make up the Circus, looking out over it at the front and towards the Royal Crescent and Royal Victoria Park at the back.

Mark opened the front door and showed me in.

'I've done a deal with the people here and bought the place lock, stock and barrel. It's really cool.'

We were standing in a large hallway that must have taken up a quarter of the entire floor space. I looked at the grand staircase that wound its way along three walls up to the first-floor landing and then up again, around and around and around to the second floor and beyond. Mark led me into a room off the hallway.

'This is the study. Cool, huh? I bet you've never had a study like this before.'

That was true, but I felt uncomfortable. The study was dual aspect, looking out on to Brock Street in front of the desk on one side and the Circus on the other. Hordes of tourists were milling around the Circus. Indeed, there was a group right in front of the study window, looking straight in at us. It felt like being in a zoo. We moved through two sets of double doors into a dining room. The room was beautiful, decorated in fashionable metallic wallpaper, with luxurious floor-to-ceiling metallic curtains, lined and interlined and nicely furnished. But again, I was acutely aware of the throngs outside. I hated the lack of privacy, but I said nothing.

'Look, darling.' Mark was opening the drawers and cupboards of the sideboard. 'There's everything we need. I bought up everything I liked and I've had them get new stuff if I didn't like what was here. You won't need to bring anything with you. What do you think?'

'It's beautiful,' I replied quietly, trying to raise a smile. 'Show me more.'

We moved from the dining room through an inner hall into the kitchen. I liked the kitchen. The walls were painted blue, the units pale pink and blue, and the room had a feminine feel to it. It was very spacious, with a fireplace with a large overmantel mirror on the wall on the right, and stylish easy chairs on either side. In the middle of the room was a large granite island housing a modern halogen hob and a small sink, with a range of drawers and cupboards underneath, including the latest must-have kitchen appliance – a wine cooler. Along the left-hand wall were two built-in ovens, a steam oven, a warming drawer, a double butler sink and a range of cupboards including integrated appliances. At the far end of the room, in a large bay window, there was a white painted table and six chairs upholstered in pink and blue. It was quite lovely, but still I kept quiet. Mark took my hand and led me back to the hall and down a flight of stairs to a basement flat. The unpleasant smell of Jeyes fluid caught me in the back of my throat as we descended the stairs. Mark was talking again.

'Now this is really cool. It will be perfect when Lara and Emma come to stay. We've got two self-contained flats – this one and another on the top floor. They can come as often as they like and they'll be perfectly independent – friends too.'

There was a woman in the basement, ironing sheets.

'I've kept the staff on,' Mark explained. 'We'll see if they're any good. If not, we'll get our own.'

He took me into the bedroom, which led out to a pretty, but very small, courtyard garden, that I noted was overlooked by scores of windows from neighbouring properties. It made me feel claustrophobic and cooped up. There was no privacy here, no facility to just wander in the garden, let alone get out into the countryside, or even sit and have a drink outside in private. I feared I would find it very difficult to adapt to city life, albeit in a very beautiful city. Mark was guiding me back in, and he showed me the rest of the basement flat. It was all beautifully and stylishly done, but he seemed to be living in a different world to me, and this house felt more like a boutique hotel or an upmarket self-catering holiday rental than a home. It even had a regulatory fire exit sign leading to the back door.

'What do you think? Do you like it?' He pressed me for a response.

'Yes, it's all very nice, but isn't it a bit strange to have to go through a bedroom to get to the garden? Anyway, show me the rest.'

He led me back up to the hall and we ascended the grand staircase to the first floor. At the top of the stairs was a bedroom, relatively small but beautifully decorated and furnished (if you liked that sort of thing), with a photograph of Sean Connery as James Bond on the wall above the bed. At the other end of the landing was a beautiful curved door, with gilded mouldings, leading into the drawing room. This room was stunning, with a large floor-to-ceiling bay window overlooking the courtyard garden and across neighbouring gardens towards the Royal Crescent and Victoria Park. It was painted pale grey, had a large, open fireplace and was furnished with two large sofas upholstered in magenta crushed velvet and art-deco-style mirrored tables and chests. The Hollywood theme continued in here with large black and white photographs of Grace Kelly and Cary Grant gazing down from the wall.

Through spectacular double doors the drawing room opened into a music room-cum-library, overlooking the Circus, also with an open fireplace. This room felt very feminine as it was predominantly pink, with full-length floral print curtains framing the floor-to-ceiling windows that looked out over the Circus, and pink armchairs either side of the fireplace. With the massive double doors open, the two rooms became one, running the whole depth of the house. It was quite stunning and very beautiful and, as I looked at the photograph of Grace Kelly, I thought of my parents – my mother in particular, who was said to have looked like Grace Kelly in her youth – and wished they were there. They loved Georgian architecture and knew and liked Bath. They would have approved of this house and would have especially loved this room. I felt a sudden pang of loss as I remembered them.

There was a baby-grand piano in the music room and I was momentarily lifted up on a wisp of hope.

'Did you buy the piano?' I asked Mark eagerly, my spirits rising at the thought of being able to practise again.

'I'm still negotiating on that,' Mark replied. 'They are supposed to have moved all their shit out of here by now, but I'll have to double-check. They said they wanted to keep it. Cunts!'

'Well, try to keep it for us, will you? I'd love to be able to play again. I have a lifetime's collection of music and I'll have plenty of time to practise.'

'Baby, if you want a piano and they take this one, you can just get another one. Don't stress out about it. You can have whatever you want. Now, come with me.'

We went on upstairs. The first room we came to was a bathroom. It was luxurious with a freestanding bath in the middle, in front of an open fireplace, and a separate double shower at the far end of the room. It was dual aspect and looked out over Brock Street on one side and the Circus on the other. It led through to a dressing room which, again, was very feminine, decorated with bronze and pink floral wallpaper and a range of fitted wardrobes in powder pink. There was a mirrored dressing table between the two windows, and an easy chair and a small occasional table either side of the fireplace.

Mark led me back out to the landing to the other side of the house.

'And this is our bedroom, darling. Our very own bedroom – at last!' He led me in. 'Do you like it?'

The room was spacious and decorated in silver metallic wallpaper with a pink floral pattern. There was an enormous bed dominated by a rather masculine, highly polished headboard and bedside tables with a matching gentleman's wardrobe on the wall opposite. A vast, modern beige arc of a sofa dominated the bay window. I thought the furniture rather ugly. Marilyn Monroe gazed down from the wall above the bed; well, she didn't exactly gaze down – rather, she lay there naked, eyes closed, with a sheet artfully draped across her voluptuous body. The picture looked too small for the room.

'Darling, it's impressive but not quite to my taste.' I was looking at the dressing table which was very out of keeping with the rest of the furniture in the room, and from which the mirror was missing. It looked incongruous.

'It's our bedroom, baby. Just think of that. Our own bedroom! There's more. Come with me.'

He led me up another small flight of stairs to another flat in the attic and continued the tour, effusive as he talked about the house.

'I just love this place. What do you think? Do you like it?'

'It's a beautiful house, darling, there's no denying it. But the layout is a bit strange. It's not really laid out as a family home.'

'But do you like it? Just think, Bubba, we'll be living in the Circus – most people would give their right arm for an address in the Circus – and we have the whole of Bath on the doorstep. Do you like it?'

'It's a beautiful house,' I said again, flatly.

'I'm so glad you like it. I've been worrying that you wouldn't want to live here.'

He just didn't seem to be taking on board anything I was saying or tuning into my mood at all. He took my hand, chatting on enthusiastically as he led me back downstairs.

'Come on, baby, let's go for a walk.'

We went back outside and took a stroll. The stone buildings glowed in the spring sunshine and the city was looking its best, but my heart felt heavy. I had never wanted to live in a city – not even in a mansion in a beautiful city. I wanted so much to feel happy, but I just didn't. Even though this house was at least ten times the size of my rented cottage I already felt cooped up at the thought of living in it. It just didn't feel private at all. It was attached to another house, there were people everywhere, there was virtually no outside space, and it looked as though parking would be a nightmare. But there was no going back. I had already handed in my notice at the shop and the Little Coach House.

I hated the waves of doubt that were assailing me. Perhaps it was just pre-nuptial nerves and I would get used to city life. But then again, perhaps I wouldn't have to get used to it. After all, this was only a temporary address. And in any case, I would soon have a place of my own – a place I could think of as home; somewhere small but beautiful, out in the country. I was looking forward to that.

'You don't need to bring anything with you,' Mark told me. 'We've got everything here. Just bring your new clothes; that's all you need.'

'Well, I might bring some of my books and my photos, that kind of thing. I'll arrange for the rest of my stuff to go into storage.'

'That's crazy. You'll end up spending a fortune on storing stuff that, believe me, you won't want in the end.'

'But I'll need all my things when I buy my own house.'

'Bubba, you're crazy. Have a completely fresh start. Get rid of all your shit and start again when you buy your house. Think how you would enjoy starting from scratch and buying new furniture to fit it. You'd be brilliant at it and you would enjoy it. You're going to have more than enough money to do anything you like.'

'Perhaps you're right. I'll think about it. It's a shame Lara and Emma can't take any of it – but, talking about Lara and Emma, one thing I must do it is pay off their student loans. I told them I was going to do that a while ago, but I've been so preoccupied.'

'Darling, we've had this discussion before. I've told you I think we should do things properly. You know I have a couple of properties in London that I would like to give them – it would actually help me out as I haven't known what to do with them – but we need to set up a trust for them. I'll get my lawyer on to it as soon as I can. We have to do things in the proper way. You wouldn't want them getting a great big tax bill now, would you?'

'All I want to do is to pay off their student loans. It's quite straightforward.'

'Baby, let me talk to my lawyers about all this, will you?'

'OK, but I want it settled soon.'

'It will be, baby. Don't you worry. In the meantime, you'd better get organised and sort out exactly what things you want to bring with you. But if you take my advice, you'll get rid of most of them.'

I mulled it over for a while and in the end I agreed with him. It would be healthy to have a complete break from the past. I would keep my personal photographs and letters, and a few items that were of sentimental value to me, and some of my books, but I would get rid of the rest.

A few days before I left the Little Coach House, I went up to the yard where most of my belongings were being stored. I had told Uma that I would be having a massive clear-out and she was already there, waiting, when I arrived. So was Paul. My containers were opened up and I made the cull. The atmosphere was frantic and frenetic and I felt sick. Uma took possession of most of my things and Paul said he would deal with the rest. I was happy that many of my belongings found a new home with Uma and Antony, but at the end of the day, I felt exhausted and torn apart. It was as though I had bagged up my past life and given it away. Perhaps I shouldn't have done it all in one fell swoop like that, but that was how I was – it was all or nothing with me. Now I had to look forward – to living in Bath.

Love-bombing is a well-known tactic used by psychopaths. They disarm the victim by moving the relationship on at such a pace that they can hardly surface for breath. Events merge and become so confused that it is impossible to keep up with them, or to make sense of anything at all. The victim is so dazzled, disorientated and distracted that she doesn't realise she is losing control of her life.

I have been asked what Lara and Emma thought about this new relationship, and whether they expressed any misgivings. I don't recall that they did, but Emma has said that she remembers exactly when she was told that I was going on that first date because she was seized by a feeling of total dread. She also recalls expressing her concerns to me directly on several occasions but stopped when she could no longer cope with my response and realised that she was probably doing more harm than good. On 17 March, she emailed Lara a link to an article about a fake spy who had fleeced some poor woman, and although I don't really think she consciously thought that was happening to me, perhaps unconsciously she had some sixth sense of it. Early on, Lara also emailed a friend of hers expressing concern, saying:

Everything in my world is a bit crazy at the moment – my mum met a man 2 months ago and has now moved in with him (he bought a house for them) and is living the crazy life of a millionaire's girlfriend. And when I say millionaire I probably mean billionaire – this guy has yachts and planes and all kinds of houses (he actually lives in Geneva – he works for UBS). It's all a bit mad – in fact it's very mad, and I hope not ill-advised.

Then, a few weeks later, after she had met Mark, she responded to the same friend's concerns, saying:

Mum seems to be ok but I don't think she's really worked out what she's gotten herself into. I think it's soon going to dawn on her that this is problematic – none of her friends will ever see him, and when they do I'm not sure they'll like him. More to the point my mum can't sit around waiting for him to turn up, I'm worried that she's putting her life on hold for him. Plus he's brutal so who's to know what could happen. It's a bit worrying.

As I said, I don't recall them expressing their concerns to me, although having spoken to them about it more recently, I have no doubt that they did. It pains me very much to think that I took no notice of their fears and demonstrates what a hold Mark Acklom already had over me. They tell me that right from the beginning they were sure that it would end badly. How right they were.

As for Mark's attempts to get me to have Botox or cosmetic surgery – in retrospect this makes my skin crawl. I am sure his comments about Botox were designed to undermine my confidence. He tapped into an insecurity that I had revealed on our first date when I had told him that I thought being with a younger man would make me feel old. When I discovered the truth about what he had done to me, I felt I had lost my identity, and for years afterwards I didn't even recognise myself in the mirror; but imagine the impact if I had allowed him to persuade me to have surgery and found myself looking at someone physically transformed.

I didn't have much experience of romantic relationships, having only had one long-term boyfriend before I met the man I was to marry. My husband and I had a whirlwind romance, going out only a dozen times before he asked me to marry him, so getting in so deep with Mark so quickly was normal, in my very limited experience. The difference was that I had been acquainted with my husband for about a year before I went out with him, and I already knew a bit about him. I knew where he lived and worked. I knew his friends and I soon met his family. With Mark, I only ever met two-year-old Bianca, an encounter that was specifically designed to endear me to him. Psychopaths are very elusive about their private lives. Mark told me things about his family – some true, some false – but I didn't meet any of them or any friends, and he didn't want to meet any of mine. This is an enormous red flag, but I think that as I was enjoying a rather heady sense of freedom I didn't mind if, for the time being, our relationship only involved the two of us. I didn't realise, until it was too late, that that exclusivity gave him complete control over me.

Mark was particularly clever in the way in which he conducted both his business and romance scams. He provided 'evidence' not only of his wealth, but also of his connections. What his unsuspecting victims never realised was that it was all a very clever charade in which he used real people and played them off against each other. His life really was 'like a film', and he manipulated his characters like puppets. In his relationship with me, his MI6 cover, which he went to extreme theatrical lengths to convince me of, was the perfect way for him to avoid all the normal social conventions that usually surround a relationship. In his business relations, I suspect he used a 'business-bomb' technique in which everything happened at an equally furious pace, involving distracting diversionary tactics: associates would be called at all hours of the day and night with demands to do this, do that, come here, go there. Telephone conversations with him were often no more than ten-second sound bites.

Being involved with Mark – in whatever capacity – was like going white-water rafting: it was incredibly exciting, there was a hint of danger, everything happened non-stop at high speed, and the more turbulent the water got, the more you would try to cling on to the raft, not realising that a precipitous waterfall lay just ahead.

5

THE SPY WHO LOVED ME

[It felt] very sorrowful and strange that this first night of my bright fortunes should be the loneliest I had ever known.

Charles Dickens, *Great Expectations*

On 3 April 2012, I moved to Bath. I took with me only a suitcase of clothes, yet felt weighed down by a nagging headache of doubt and apprehension. My remaining belongings had already been taken to Paul's flat, just a couple of streets away in Cavendish Place. Mark told me that he wanted Paul nearby, so that he would know that I was safe. Mark was already at the house, and when he opened the door to greet me was in ebullient form.

'I just love this house, darling. Isn't it cool? Aren't you happy to be living in such a great place?' He walked into the study, drawing my attention to the sales brochure for the property that lay on the desk.

'Look after this for me, will you?' he said.

I am very good at making the most of things and forced a smile. I told myself that this was only a temporary measure, as before long, I hoped, the renovations at Beach would be completed; plus, once I had settled into married life with Mark, I would know what sort of property to buy for myself too. With the right attitude, I could enjoy it – after all, we had the whole of

Bath on our doorstep and a house with four very comfortable spare bedrooms where friends could come and stay.

Our first visitors were arriving the following Saturday: my daughters, together with their boyfriends, and Anne with her son (who is like a brother to my girls) and his girlfriend. My brother, sister-in-law and nieces would also be joining us for dinner. When I'd originally asked everyone to put the date in their diaries, I had thought we'd be living in Widcombe Manor and Mark had said he'd hire a private chef to cook us a gourmet dinner, but when the venue changed at the last minute, so did the plans. Mark cancelled the chef and I, who normally liked to cook, just felt too overwhelmed and out of sorts to do it myself. Even going to the supermarket would be a hassle here as parking and trying to unload were impossible.

Paul turned up and the three of us were in the kitchen.

'Well, baby, what do you want to do?' Mark asked me.

'Couldn't we take everyone out to dinner?'

'Well, if that's what you want, but I thought you wanted everyone to come to the house.'

'Yes, darling, but you've moved the goalposts. You've changed the venue and cancelled the cook and I don't want to do it.'

'Well, come up with a suggestion, then.'

'I have. I suggest we all go out to dinner.'

'We'll never get anywhere decent for that number of people – how many is it?'

'Thirteen.'

'Exactly. We'll never get a table for thirteen people at such short notice.'

I felt harassed and was wracking my brain trying to think of a solution.

'Well, what about ordering a takeaway from that Indian restaurant you own? The one you're always telling me about – the Mint Room, didn't you say?'

'You want an Indian takeaway? I suppose we could do that. Paul, organise that, will you? What time do you want it delivered, baby?'

I didn't really want a takeaway at all, but I felt stressed and was trying to make the most of the situation and get something organised.

'Eight o'clock?'

'Eight o'clock, Paul,' Mark repeated. 'And Paul, go out now, will you, and get some drinks? Let's get this wine fridge stocked up.'

When Paul returned Mark helped to fill the wine cooler, but then he announced that he had to leave.

'I'll see you on Saturday, baby,' he said as he kissed me. 'I'll try to pop in before then, but I can't guarantee it.'

I couldn't believe it. I'd moved into this place so that we could spend more time together and already I was alone. I wandered through the house, wondering if I could ever feel at home there. When I reached the music room my heart sank as I saw that the piano had gone.

Saturday came around quickly and I was really looking forward to seeing my family and friends, although a nervous apprehension continued to nag at me, tugging at my sleeve all day long. Mark was due to arrive at around seven o'clock that evening and I couldn't wait to see him. I felt a little nervous about how he would be received by my family and friends. He wasn't like any of them and I knew they wouldn't like his arrogance. I hoped he wouldn't be too nervous himself, as I thought it would be quite daunting for him to meet eleven of the most important people in my life in one go like that.

Lara and Emma were the first to arrive and I felt overjoyed to see them. I gave them a tour of the house and showed them where they would be sleeping. Lara had spent a summer living and working in Bath when she was a student and she knew the city well.

'I just can't believe you're living in the Circus. I used to walk through here every day on my way to and from work. I used to dream of living here – I just can't believe you actually are. It's amazing!'

Lara's enthusiasm was infectious and I began to feel my spirits lifting. When my friends arrived, I did the tour around the house again and began to relax a little. I felt fine until my brother arrived with his family, and Annalisa seemed to barely acknowledge me when she came in.

'The toilet doesn't flush,' she announced as she came into the kitchen to get a drink.

'There's a knack to it,' I replied. 'You have to be patient.'

I showed them around too. My nieces were thrilled by the house and Nick was courteous and complimentary, but I didn't hear a positive word from Annalisa.

'That chandelier needs dusting,' she observed as we reached the second floor.

Mark still hadn't arrived and the minutes ticked by with me willing him to appear. I tried calling him but there was no reply.

Paul delivered the food and I was putting it out in the kitchen when I heard the demanding ringtone that meant Mark was on the phone.

'Where are you?' I asked. 'Everyone's here and it's embarrassing that you're not. They're all waiting to meet you. We're just about to sit down to eat.'

'Darling, I'm sorry, but I'm stuck in Ronda. I missed my flight slot and now I don't know when I'll be able to get out of here.'

I remember it striking me as odd that he should be stuck in Ronda of all places. I had visited the Spanish town and it seemed an unlikely place to find yourself if you were travelling by plane to the UK, but my mind was so full of other thoughts that I didn't question Mark about it. I was wondering how I was going to explain his absence, and I could feel a hot flush of embarrassment rising up my neck.

'What? How could you do that to me? You know how important it is to me that you meet my family. And this was the day that you said you wanted us to get married. I can't believe you're letting me down like this.'

'Darling, I told you right at the beginning, you will be let down by me a million times until we can be together properly. I'm really sorry, baby. I'll try to get there tomorrow. Just enjoy the evening with your family and friends. I love you. I can't wait to see you again.'

'I love you too.' My voice sounded small and flat as I hung up, and with a fixed smile, I made Mark's excuses as we all sat down to eat.

'Well, what a surprise,' remarked Annalisa.

The evening was not going as planned and I felt horribly stressed and out of sorts. My nieces asked if they could stay the night and, in a move that was totally out of character, I said no. I hoped that Mark would show up the next day, but suddenly felt that I didn't want him to meet my family, after all. As I said goodbye to Nick, Annalisa turned to me.

'I always knew he wouldn't come,' she announced. 'But at least we know where you are now.' Her expression was hard as nails. I felt very upset and, if there is such a thing as a familial umbilical cord I could have reached for the scissors and cut it there and then.

The following morning, I made a big cooked breakfast for everyone and we were just clearing up when I heard the front door open.

Mark made his entrance.

He was dressed in his designer jeans, a crisp shirt, the Gucci shoes that I had paid for, and his Crombie coat. Everybody's eyes were upon him. He paused for a second, taking in the scene before him, then he kissed me, immediately demanded a coffee and lit a cigarette as I introduced him to everyone. We sat around the kitchen table and I felt unusually nervous as a few pleasantries were exchanged. Lara complimented him on the house, telling him that, as a student, she had dreamed of living in the Circus.

'Yes, well luckily for me I can have just about anything I want,' he responded. 'I love this house, but I have properties all over the world.'

It was the first time I had seen Mark in company and he soon took over the conversation. He held court, lording it over everyone, boasting about his possessions and putting everyone else down.

'I have my own collection of planes and I own probably the largest collection of Picassos in the world,' he bragged, taking a drag on his cigarette and sitting back in his chair. 'I like nice things. I had a load of gold bars once that I didn't know what to do with, so I put a sheet of glass on top and used it as a coffee table. That was cool.'

Mark wasn't just arrogant: he was rude and obnoxious. He sat at the table drinking espresso after espresso, and chain smoking. I was smoking too – something that my family had rarely seen me do before, and something that I knew they would hate. We sat in a fug of smoke and I felt wave after wave of embarrassment wash over me as Mark got into his stride. But I felt powerless to stop him or to steer the conversation in a different direction. I sat in stunned silence, willing Mark to be quiet, but he just wouldn't shut up. At last, Anne's son, Nick, managed to get a word in. I saw the colour rising in his neck and cheeks and I could tell that he was riled, even though good manners prevailed and he remained polite.

'So if you've got so much and can have anything you want, what motivates you?' he asked.

'Well, it used to be money, but now it's power and control. I could press a button and shut down the UK economy. There are only about five hundred of us in the world with that sort of power,' Mark replied. He picked up another cigarette. 'To get on in this world you have to be prepared to sacrifice everything. The way to make sure you beat the casino is to have more money than the casino. You have to be prepared to lose everything you have, then take your clothes off and be fucked in the arse. Not many people are prepared to do that.'

I sat motionless – shocked. Why was he being so unpleasant and foul-mouthed? And why couldn't I speak up and change the conversation? I felt completely disempowered and disorientated, as though I had no will of my own. Then Mark was talking again.

'You live in Kentish Town?' He was looking at Nick, his mouth curled up in what looked more like a smirk than a smile. 'I like Kentish Town. Too many blacks though. You take any other group and they work – the Jews, the Chinese, the Poles – but there is something genetically lazy about black people. They need to go away, educate themselves and come back in fifty years. I drove in London recently – never again. There are all these black guys that can't drive. There should be one lane for us – the politicians, the diplomats, the educated people – and another for the common people. That's why I get around by helicopter.' There was a second's lull in his verbal outpouring – just long enough for him to flip the ring-pull on a can of Coke and take a swig. Then he lit another cigarette and started again.

'All immigrants should be put on an island and pushed out to sea or shot. In Switzerland they would take the guy that didn't want to work and say you're out of the country. He'd soon take the toilet-cleaning job. God, I hate this country! Switzerland's great because everything works. I have absolutely no sympathy for poor people. I sleep three hours a day max. I don't eat lunch – eating makes your productivity nosedive. I live on coffee, Coke and cigarettes. I had a heart attack a few years ago. It was fun! I woke up in hospital, pulled the wires out and went straight back to work. If I stopped, I'd die. We need another war to make this country great. We need another Thatcher.'

What was happening? I had never seen Mark like this. True, his language could be a little ripe at times, but when I first met him, I had been struck by his good manners. Why was he behaving like this now? He had always told me that he was motivated by the desire to help others. Yes, he was wealthy and he liked his money; and yes, he had mentioned owning some Picassos. But what was this about 'power and control'? Somewhere in the distant recesses of my mind I heard a faint alarm bell, but the sound of it was drowned out by more ravings from Mark.

'I know a lot of things. I was there the day Princess Diana died. It was all planned. And I know what happened on 9/11. The important people all got a warning not to be there that day. It was a conspiracy dreamed up by the American government. The people who died were only medium- and low-skilled people.'

He ranted on and I felt as though I was in another world. It was like being in one of those bad dreams when you want to shout out, but you can't make a sound; when you want to run, but your legs feel so heavy that you can't put one foot in front of the other. Still Mark raved on.

'You know I used to go to the opera at Covent Garden, but I can't do that any more. I can't stand it. Last time I was there I sat in my box watching the idiots below drinking champagne. They don't have a right to be there. It used to be exclusive, but now it's just ruined – and people just wander about in jeans. No, I can't stand this country any more. The climate's terrible and the food is just about inedible. I import all my beef from Galicia, you know. The restaurants here are crap too. Luckily for me if I don't like the restaurants near my properties, I can just buy one.'

Everyone was too polite to say what they were thinking, but I could sense how uncomfortable they all felt. Eventually, someone suggested a round of crazy golf in Victoria Park. Thank God, I thought. I felt ashamed. My family and friends had been insulted and I had done nothing to step in and stop it. What was wrong with Mark? It must be because he was so stressed at work; that's all it could be. But surely he must be aware of the damage he'd done. Nobody there would ever want to meet him again. I felt terribly sad, and my usual optimism was overridden by an unusual feeling of confusion. I felt burdened with the weight of responsibility of trying to keep everyone happy – and knowing I had failed – and masking my own uncertainty. I was utterly miserable.

'Are you coming, Carolyn?' Anne was smiling encouragingly at me.

'I'll join you shortly.' I smiled wanly back. 'I'd just like to have a bit of time with Mark before he goes.' The others departed and Mark and I were left alone.

'I've got to go too, baby,' he said, as bright as a button. 'I shouldn't be here at all. You can't imagine what I had to do to get here.'

I couldn't bring myself to tell him how disappointed and let down I felt, and I couldn't raise a smile. He kissed me goodbye and left.

I looked blankly out of the window. I felt done in and on the verge of tears, but I knew I had to pull myself together and go and find the others in the park. I cleared away the coffee cups, half-empty Coke can and overflowing ashtray – Mark's calling cards – and picked up my keys. As I left the house, I heard a helicopter flying overhead and wondered if it was him. I soon found the others.

'We saw a helicopter,' remarked Anne. 'Was that him?'

'I expect so,' I replied. 'I'll ask him when he calls.' As I spoke, my phone rang. It was him.

'What did they think of me?' he enquired eagerly. I felt a lump rise in my throat.

'We haven't discussed you. I'll tell you later. We saw a helicopter. Was that you?'

'Yeah, did you see me?'

'We saw you,' I replied wearily.

'Darling, I'll try to see you tomorrow. I love you loads.'

'I love you too,' I whispered, fighting back the tears.

Nobody said anything to me about Mark, but I knew that the whole encounter had been a disaster. I experienced a pang of loneliness as I felt the cold, thin edge of a wedge embed itself between me, and my family and friends.

The following week, my old cat stopped eating. A visit to the vet confirmed that she had a tumour in her mouth. There was nothing they could do and so, to put her out of her misery, I had her put to sleep. When I returned to Brock Street later that day, I closed the door behind me and burst into tears. I had never felt more alone.

During the first few weeks in Brock Street I saw Mark most days, but he only ever stayed for an hour or so, usually turning up late morning.

He was busy expanding his business empire and told me about InOrg, a new company he was forming, for which he showed me an impressive-looking website. InOrg was an umbrella company involved in many lucrative and diverse ventures – InResidence, InMotorsport, InAviation, InMaritime, InConcert, InTheMedia – the list went on and on. And knowing what I know now, I believe that every subsidiary was a lure, designed to suck in a real, unsuspecting person to manage whichever part of the company was their passion, with Mark promising the investment for them to build their part of the InOrg empire. Additionally, Mark said that he was continuing his work with the Prince's Trust, and also taking responsibility for the fund-raising at Clifton College, Bristol. He showed me a promotional video, filmed at the Cotswold Airport, for a fund-raising event at Clifton, featuring representatives of the Prince's Trust, the Air Ambulance Service, Clifton College and various other sponsors. Mark was on camera, sometimes giving a voice-over. He also told me he was planning a Spitfire flypast as a highlight of the fund-raising event.

'You see, baby, I told you things would get better,' he said, as we sat in the kitchen, discussing all his latest ventures.

'We've seen each other nearly every day since you moved here.'

'But we still haven't even spent one night together – and you nearly always have Paul in tow. I thought that with the beginning of the new tax year you'd be able to spend a few nights here.'

It was true: Mark and I had had virtually no time alone together, and even when we had there were constant interruptions.

One afternoon, Mark led me upstairs to the bedroom. He started kissing me.

'Darling, for once do you think you could just turn your phones off for a while?' I whispered as I played with his hair.

'Baby, I've told you – I know it's going to really irritate you, but I have to keep them turned on and I have to answer them. I know it drives you mad, but you're going to have to put up with it for now.'

I sighed, but Mark soon distracted me. We were making love, and in my head and in my heart I was a million miles away from Bath. But I was soon brought back down to earth by the insistent ring of one of Mark's phones.

'Leave it,' I whispered. He was about to come, but I felt him falter. 'Just leave it, Bubba you can't stop now!' But he did. He withdrew and reached over for his phone.

'Fuck!' he exclaimed. 'This is important. I have to take it.'

He started talking to someone in Spanish and I played with him, determined to keep his mind on the business in hand.

'Stop it!' he mouthed at me, listening to whoever was on the other end of the phone. He tried to pull away, but I would not be put off. I was enjoying spending some time with him. This was a rare moment alone together, and even now I could hear the drone of the hoover from another part of the house as the cleaners went about their business.

Mark was trying to get away from me as he continued his conversation, but we were both stifling a laugh. Eventually, holding his phone behind the headboard, he hung up.

'Baby, what the hell are you doing? That was the king of Spain on the phone. Fuck, Bubba. I can't come when I'm talking to the king of Spain! He wants my advice. His son's in trouble and I said I'd help him. Sweetie, you've got to let me take calls without trying to make me come. I mean, I hope he didn't hear anything – I had to hold the phone down behind the headboard!'

I was laughing.

'Darling, I'm not going to play second fiddle to anyone – not even the king of Spain. But honestly, Bubba, it does irritate me that you can't even turn your phones off for a few minutes.'

'Don't fret, sweetheart. I'm doing everything I can. Remember – the big picture. I've told you, the best things in life are worth waiting for.'

Ever since moving to Bath I had woken up on my own, got up and pulled back the curtains on leaden skies and another wet day. I had never known rain like it, and with no job to go to I found it difficult to motivate myself to do anything. I hated the rain at the best of times, but at least in the country, even if you didn't venture out in it, it wasn't so depressing. It was just part of the scenery, and I had always enjoyed viewing the rural landscape at different times of year and under different-coloured skies. The same didn't apply to the town.

I looked out at the rain as it transformed the honey-toned Bath stone to drab grey, and I felt cooped up and depressed. I made myself walk into town every day, but although I had previously always enjoyed trips to Bath, now it was as much as I could do to tolerate the place. The hordes of tourists were unbearable. There were swarms of them in the Circus, often photographing my front courtyard or, worse still, peering into the study or dining room. Now when I was in the study, I closed the shutters and sat there in the semi-gloom. The tourist bus that drove around the Circus and along Brock Street to the Royal Crescent frequently stopped right outside the front door, waiting for a gap in the oncoming traffic, and on a number of occasions I found myself on the first-floor landing, face to face with strangers sitting on the open-top deck of the bus. I took to keeping the blind down on the landing window in order to afford myself some privacy. Likewise, when I was in the bathroom, I would keep the blind on the north side down, as I was sure that otherwise I could be seen from the windows of the house on the other side of the street.

One wet Saturday afternoon, the doorbell rang. Even though Mark had told me not to answer the door to anyone I wasn't expecting, I went to answer it. As I opened it, four people lost their balance and stumbled backwards into the hall. They had been sheltering from the rain in the doorway and one of them had been leaning up against the bell. I snapped.

'What the hell do you think you're doing? This is my house. Get out!' I slammed the door shut behind them, but the sound of the slamming only made me feel like a prisoner in my own home.

The day of that fateful encounter between Mark and my daughters and friends was the only other time the doorbell had sounded unexpectedly, and Mark had got up to answer it. When he came back he said it was the woman from the flat next door, complaining that there had been a lot of noise coming from the house the previous evening.

'What on earth were you all up to?' he had asked me. 'She told me she heard the scraping of chairs on the floor. Look what she gave me – it's a funny sort of house-warming present.' Mark held out some felt pads to put on the bottom of the chair legs. I couldn't believe it. It had been a Saturday night, we had been chatting, we had had dinner, but that was it. No loud music, no nothing – and it had all been over by midnight. It was not a good start.

I didn't know anyone in Bath and now, unlike when I had moved to Tetbury, I felt no desire to socialise. Perhaps more tellingly, despite living in a house that needed to be full of people, I didn't want to have my old friends to stay. The very idea of it filled me with dread, and although I initially made the effort to invite a few close friends over, after only a few weeks at 1 Brock Street I found myself spending nearly all my time in solitude, behind closed doors, often with the shutters closed and the blinds down. I felt my natural sparkle going flat, as I filled the hours reading and listening to the radio.

On 20 April, it was my birthday. My family loved birthdays and I couldn't remember a time when I hadn't celebrated mine with my daughters, but this time I spent the day alone, with no plans to see them. I had hoped that Mark and I could be together, but I hoped in vain. I waited all day for him, but it was evening before he appeared, much to my dismay with Paul in tow.

'Happy birthday, darling.'

Mark kissed me cheerfully as he swaggered in. He was wearing his usual Crombie coat over jeans and a pink shirt with a frill down the front, and he was carrying a bottle of Cristal champagne, which he put down on the kitchen table. Paul was carrying a cake. Mark handed me a present and a card and then walked over to the kitchen bin.

'We called in at your cottage on our way over, to collect any post. There was a card for you. I opened it. It's from Dickhead.' Dickhead was the name he used for an ex-boyfriend.

'I hate to admit it,' he continued, 'but the card he sent you is better than the one I got you. Can I bin it?'

'Please do.'

I was sick and tired of this unwanted attention from an ex, but at the mention of my cottage I felt overwhelmed by a feeling of deep homesickness. I had been so happy there. Mark tore the card in two and put it in the bin.

'Now, are you going to open your card and your present from me? Paul, open the champagne and put out the cake, will you? It's a token gesture, Bubba. I haven't had time to go shopping. I had to send Paul out to get it.'

I felt my heart sink, but I forced a smile. I opened the card. It was from Marks & Spencer and was perfectly ordinary – not at all what you would expect from someone who owned a collection of Picassos. Inside, in his distinctive spidery scrawl, Mark had scribbled, 'To My Darling Wife, I wish you the best birthday ever, I adore you. Yours, Mark. xxxxxx' Then I opened my present. It was an iPod. True, I had expressed a passing wish for an iPod, but this wasn't the romantic, personal sort of present I had hoped to receive on my first birthday with Mark – just something that he could send anyone out to pick up (and did). I smiled and thanked him and the three of us sat at the table with the champagne and a Marks & Spencer birthday cake.

'What do you think of the champagne, darling? I only ever drink Cristal. I keep a few bottles up at the Priory, just to make sure they've always got some.'

'It's lovely, thank you, but I can't drink the whole bottle by myself.'

'I love it when you drink. You're funny. Have some more. And have a cigarette.'

The champagne was good. I love champagne and usually find it makes me feel bubbly myself, but not this time. I felt decidedly flat. It was not long before Paul reminded Mark that it was time to go. They left and I sat alone, feeling sad and very lonely. I poured another drink and lit another cigarette. It was the worst birthday I had ever had. I consoled myself with yet another glass of champagne and another cigarette. And then another. But if I thought this was bad, things were about to get much worse.

A couple of days later, there was a strange voicemail on my phone. It was from a female police officer – PC Harding from Cirencester police station – saying that she had been to my cottage looking for me. She said that she had met my landlady who had told her that I had moved to Bath, and she asked me to contact her. I immediately returned the call, but PC Harding was out, so I left a message to say I had called. I wondered what on earth it could be about. It must be something to do with a complaint I had recently made to Barclays Bank, I thought. Some money had gone missing from my account and I had been furious. Mark told me that the same thing had happened to Paul and he had written a letter of complaint too. Still, it seemed strange that the police should be involved. Oh well, I would just have to wait and see. But when Mark turned up later that day, I told him about the phone call.

'I mean I don't understand why they turned up at my cottage. It's a bit embarrassing; I'm sure my landlady won't have liked it. I mean nobody likes the police appearing on their doorstep.'

Mark was frowning.

'I don't like the sound of this, baby. Someone's keeping tabs on you and they'll be trying to unsettle you and fuck us up. Let me know when you get another call from them. This needs to be sorted out now. Listen, Bubba, we've got to get married. Once we're married, they can't come between us. We'll go to the church I go to when I'm in London. I have a marriage licence, and the priest there will marry us. All I have to do is give him a few Cuban cigars – he does like his cigars! Baby, did you get a copy of your decree absolute like I told you to? You'll need to bring it.'

'Yes, darling, but I don't want to get married like that – in some sort of Romeo-and-Juliet-style wedding. This is all turning into a nightmare.'

'You love me, don't you, darling?'

I nodded. 'You know I do.'

'You've got to trust me, baby. Those cunts will do anything to come between us. We've got to get married as soon as possible. We'll go and see the priest as soon as we can.'

A few days later I put on my navy Armani shift dress and the edge-to-edge tweed jacket with the silver thread running through it. Mark arrived with Paul to pick me up and we set off in the car for London. Mark was wearing a designer suit under his Crombie coat. As always, he was impeccably groomed and his fingernails were manicured. When we got to London Paul dropped us off at the Church of the Immaculate Conception, a Catholic church in Farm Street, Mayfair. The rain was torrential, and we were drenched in the time it took to get across the pavement from the car to the door. We walked inside. Mass was taking place and we took our seats at the back. Mark crossed himself and kneeled down to pray. I sat staring ahead of me, quite overawed by the gilded splendour of the interior of the church, but impassive, watching, while the congregation, including Mark, took communion. When the service ended Mark turned to me.

'Do you like the church? I love it here. I always come here when I'm in London. My faith is very important to me.'

'Well, as you know, I'm an atheist.'

'Bubba, we've got to get married as soon as possible, and I want to do it here – today.'

'Well, you'd better see what your priest says. I need the loo.'

Mark showed me where to go. He went to speak to the priest, and when I returned he was waiting for me.

'It's all arranged, baby. We'll come back this evening and he'll marry us.'

It all seemed so bizarre. I didn't know what to think. This wasn't how I wanted to get married. But I said nothing and decided to see what happened when we returned that evening. Mark continued talking.

'Let's go and get some lunch. I'm starving.'

He guided me back outside where Paul was waiting in the car.

'We'll drive over to Pimlico. I've got to call in to see my boss this afternoon. I'm in trouble.'

The rain abated and we ate a light lunch at a small café. I was cold because we were sitting outside so that Mark could smoke. I was smoking too. It was about the only thing we did together. Mark continued to smoke Marlboro Reds, but they were too strong for me, so he had taken to keeping me supplied with Camel Blues.

'We'd better go, darling. Paul's going to drive us over.' We settled down in the back of the car and were just about to drive off when my phone rang. I stared at the screen.

'I don't recognise the number. Perhaps it's the police.'

'Baby, this is really important. I'm in a lot of trouble about this. Answer the phone. Put it on speaker. We need to hear what's going on. I'll tell you what to say. Paul, hang on a minute, just stay put while we take this call.'

Paul turned off the engine and I did as I was told. I put the phone on speaker and picked up.

'Hello?'

'Hello, is that Carolyn Woods?'

'It is.'

'This is PC Harding. I left a message on your voicemail. I need to speak to you about something.'

'Yes, I know, I returned your call, but you weren't available. Can you please tell me what all this is about?'

'I'm afraid I can't talk about it on the phone. I'd like to come and see you in person. I met your landlady; she told me you've moved to Bath.'

Mark was shaking his head vigorously and scribbling a message on a piece of paper.

No! No meeting!

'I'm between houses at the moment. I still have my cottage in Tetbury, but I spend most of my time in Bath. But why can't you tell me what this is all about now? I think I know what it's about anyway.'

'I'm sorry, but I need to meet you face to face. I can come to Bath or meet you at your cottage in Tetbury. Whatever's easier for you.'

Mark was scribbling again.

NOT Bath. Tetbury. Delay. Say you're going away.

'OK, can we meet at my cottage? But I can't do anything for a week or so.'

'Well how about a week on Friday? Would that be any good? About eleven o'clock?'

Mark was nodding.

'Yes, that should be fine. I'll see you then.'

'Thank you. I'll see you a week on Friday, then.'

'Goodbye.'

'Goodbye.'

I hung up. Paul and Mark were both staring at me.

'Thank you, Bubba. Well done. That was great.' Mark took my hand. 'I'm in deep shit about all of this.' There was obvious relief in his voice.

'Well, do you know what it's all about?'

'No, darling, but whatever it is, it's drawn attention to you and therefore to me. I've been called in. We've got to go there now.' My phone rang again.

'It's her again.'

I looked at Mark.

'Answer it.'

I picked up.

'Ms Woods? It's PC Harding again. I've spoken to my supervisor about this and he says I *can* discuss the matter with you on the phone, after all.'

'I'm so glad you've called back. As I said, I think I know what this is all about.'

'We've been contacted by Barclays Bank in Cirencester who are concerned about unusual activity on your account. Are you aware of this?'

'Well, yes, that's what I thought it was about. I've written a letter of complaint to Barclays' head office. Some money went missing from my account.'

'The bank is concerned about a number of payments that have been made from your account to a Paul Deol. Are you aware of these payments?'

'Well, yes, of course. I made the payments. I have to say that I don't understand why the bank called the police about that. Why hasn't the bank contacted me in the first instance, if they've got any concerns?'

'Where the bank has a particular concern, they do sometimes contact the police. So, you're saying that you're aware of all these payments that have been made to Paul Deol? There have been very substantial sums of money transferred to him.'

'Yes, I'm aware of those transfers. As I said, I thought your call might be related to some sort of wrongdoing at the bank. I understand that Paul Deol has also had money gone missing from his account, and my concern was that there might be some sort of fraud going on at the bank.'

'I'm not aware of any of that, but if you say you are aware of the transactions between yourself and Mr Deol, I don't need to take this matter any further.'

'And you won't need to see me a week on Friday?'

'No, there's no need. Thank you for clarifying the situation.'

'Thank you. Goodbye.'

'Goodbye.'

I hung up again. Mark was looking at me and as he did so, another wave of relief seemed to wash over him.

'Thank you so much, Bubba. You've saved me. You were brilliant.'

I was bemused. What the hell was all that about? And I was furious. What on earth did the bank think they were doing contacting the police? They should have contacted me. I wished I'd never moved my banking to Barclays. When Mark repaid me, I would put my money back into NatWest, where I'd been a customer for thirty years.

'We'd better go. We don't want to keep Little Sister waiting,' said Paul.

He started the car and we drove off towards Vauxhall Bridge. The MI6 building loomed ahead. We drove away from the river and passed along the south side of the building. Then we looped around, eventually turning into a side street past some brownfield wasteland. The landscape here looked pretty desolate. We rounded another corner and Paul stopped the car. Ahead I could see what looked like the entrance to an underground car park. Two armed guards were on duty, dressed in black, wearing flak jackets and carrying what looked like machine guns.

'Wait for me here,' ordered Mark, opening the car door. 'They're expecting me, they'll be watching. I'll be as quick as I can – it shouldn't take long.'

He got out of the car and walked towards the guards, and then past them, unchallenged, into the building. I was left alone in the car with Paul. We waited, and about twenty-five minutes later Mark reappeared, smiling and looking relaxed. He got into the car and lit a cigarette.

'Thank God! I'm off the hook. You were brilliant, Bubba.'

The relief he was experiencing was palpable and infectious and I felt my spirits lifting. Mark continued talking.

'They played back your telephone conversation – they'd been listening in – and what was it he said, what was the word he used? He said you were staunch. Staunch, that was it. You'll meet him one day – my boss. You'll like him. Luckily, he likes me. He's had problems himself because he's married to an Iranian. Can you believe it? Imagine the trouble that caused! Thanks, Bubba, you were brilliant. Let's go and get a coffee somewhere and then we'll get back to Farm Street.'

Later that afternoon we made our way back to the church at Farm Street, but the traffic was terrible and we were snarled up for what seemed like an eternity. When we arrived at the church another service was in progress. Mark was beside himself.

'Fuck! We're too late. We've missed him. It's too late now. Fucking traffic! Come on, darling. We've got to get out of here now. I'm sorry.'

Thank God, I thought. I felt out of my depth and confused. The phone calls from the police, the bank, MI6, an aborted clandestine wedding, it was all too much for me. Thank God we'd arrived too late at the church. I didn't want a Catholic wedding. I didn't really want a church wedding. I wasn't even sure that I wanted a wedding at all. I would have to tell Mark – but not now. Just now I wanted to go home, except that I didn't really feel I had one.

* * *

The visit to my cottage by the police remained a mystery for a very long time. My landlady confirmed that two police officers had indeed come to the cottage and spoken to her. For years, as I tried to work the whole thing out, I believed that the visit by the 'police officers' and the subsequent telephone call were staged by Mark to test my loyalty to him, and to frighten me, but more light was to be shed on this later on.

The MI6 visit I am sure was staged to convince me that Mark was an MI6 agent. Who the armed men were, I have no idea; neither do I understand how anybody who wasn't a bona-fide armed guard could get anywhere near the MI6 building, and if they were real guards, how could Mark walk straight past them unless they were expecting him? It was all utterly convincing, and once I believed that Mark was a secret agent, everything was so outside my realm of experience that I took whatever he said about it on trust. It never crossed my mind at the time that the whole thing was staged, but I now know that this type of theatrical performance was typical of the way Mark acted out a number of charades to test me, or to back up some of the more extraordinary claims that he made.

Back in February, after we discussed marriage for the first time, Mark told me to make sure I had my divorce papers as I would need them in order marry him. Whether he ever spoke to the priest that day I don't know, because he supposedly did so when I was absent, but the abortive attempt at a Romeo-and-Juliet-style wedding was no doubt designed to convince me of his strong intention to marry me, and everything else that happened was to prove that what he had told me about his MI6 work was true.

The following morning, Mark phoned to tell me he was on his way to pick me up.

'We'll go out somewhere,' he told me.

He turned up, as usual, with Paul in tow. Why did Paul always have to be there? I longed for some time with Mark on his own.

'Come on, Bubba, let's go.'

As we drove away from Bath towards the M4, Mark suddenly told Paul to stop the car at the little toll-house café at the side of the road.

'Let's go and have a coffee here,' he said. 'I've always wanted to see what this place is like. It reminds me of when I was a kid and I used to go out with my grandmother. She was always going to places like this for tea. She liked to go out on a Sunday.'

We ordered coffee and a sandwich. Mark seemed to like it, but I didn't and thought it a strange choice of venue; Mark did behave quite bizarrely sometimes. As we left, he told me he wasn't feeling very well.

'I just threw up in the toilet. God knows what was in that sandwich. Are you feeling OK?'

'I'm feeling fine.'

'God, I feel rough. That was a mistake. Where shall we go?'

'Well, we could go back home.'

'No, let's do something to take my mind off things. Let's go somewhere else. Where can we go?'

'How about Babington House?' I suggested. 'You like it there and it's away from Bath.'

'Perfect! Paul, take us to Babington House – you know, that place in the middle of nowhere.'

On the way there, Mark stretched out in the back of the car, groaning.

'God, Bubba, I feel rough. Fuck knows what's wrong.'

When we got to Babington we ordered a Coke and a glass of wine and sat in a small lounge. Mark closed his eyes and appeared to fall asleep. I sat quietly beside him, holding his hand and staring into the middle distance. When Mark awoke, he said he was feeling like death, but it was time to go.

'Darling, you'd better see a doctor if you don't improve tomorrow.' I was worried. I'd never seen Mark the slightest bit under the weather.

'I'll be OK, baby. I'm as strong as an ox. I'll be fine by tomorrow. Let's go.'

As usual, I was dropped off at Brock Street. Whenever we arrived back in Bath Paul would do a circuit of the Circus and the neighbouring streets, before pulling up outside the front door, just to make sure that the coast was clear.

'But I don't understand,' I protested. 'Is it safe for me to go out or not? Is there any threat to me? I wouldn't know if I was under surveillance or if I was being followed.'

'You're quite safe, baby. It's just when I'm around that you need to be careful and we don't take any chances. We're always vigilant.' As usual, he couldn't stay, and I kissed him goodbye.

'I hope you feel better soon. Call me tomorrow and let me know how you are.'

I spent a restless night worrying about him and his health, which led to more worries about my money. What if anything should happen to him? I'd be left with nothing. I must talk to him about this, I thought. I couldn't believe I hadn't considered it before.

Mark called me the following afternoon.

'Hello, Bubba, how are you?' I asked, thinking about how ill he had seemed the day before. A voice I barely recognised rasped down the telephone line in response.

'God, Bubba I'm sick. I can't talk properly, it's too painful.'

'What's happened to you? You sound dreadful.'

'Those bastards have it in for me. I'm in a military hospital in Malta. They fucking well poisoned me.'

'What? Who poisoned you? What are you talking about?'

'Those cunts at MI6. They're punishing me for drawing attention to myself and for being in a relationship with you. They want me to end it. Baby, you've got to stand by me. I'll never give you up, but those cunts will do everything they can to come between us. They think you won't be able to stand the pressure. I know you're strong, Bubba. I've got to know that you'll stick by me. I always told you it was going to be hard and that it would take time.'

'I can't believe they'd poison you. You're one of their best agents.'

'Yes, and they don't want to lose me. This is my punishment for being with you. They know I've had enough of it all.'

My mind was in a spin. Surely this couldn't be happening!

'You don't know a fraction of it, baby.' Mark was straining to talk again. 'Those bastards are as bad as anybody else anywhere in the world. Don't think that they don't use torture and every other fucking trick in the book to get what they want. I can't talk any more, baby. It's too painful.'

'But darling, are you going to be all right? Are you being looked after properly?'

I was terrified.

'Yes, baby. Don't worry. They just want to frighten me. I should be better in a few days. I can't wait to see you again.'

'I'm scared.'

'Don't worry. I'll be fine. It will all be fine. Trust me. Just be strong for me and think of the big picture. Baby, I really can't talk any more. It's too sore. I'll call again tomorrow. I love you loads. Bye, baby.'

'Bye-bye, darling. I love you too.'

I hung up and sat where I was for a very long time. What could I do? Nothing. That was the problem. I found myself in a situation where I was totally disempowered. What did I know about MI6 and espionage? Absolutely nothing. There was nobody I could talk to about any of this except Mark. He had told me I mustn't talk to anybody else about it. It would put him in even more danger and, although he had told me that I wasn't at risk, I wasn't sure that I believed him. After all, if these people would go to any lengths to get what they wanted, they would surely not hesitate to dispense with me? Once again, I felt the hairs rise up along my arms. I didn't exactly feel afraid, but I felt alone – very alone.

The only friends I really felt comfortable seeing were Uma and Antony, and I frequently went up to Tetbury to enjoy their company and hospitality. One day Uma called me. She sounded anxious and upset.

'Carolyn, there's something I've got to tell you. I've been agonising over it for days now.'

'Well, what is it?'

'I feel so bad about it. You see, when you started seeing Mark, I was worried about you. You remember I asked you for your brother's telephone number, in case anything happened to you?'

'Yes, I remember.'

Well, I phoned your sister-in-law. I'm so sorry, Carolyn.'

'What? Why on earth did you contact her?'

'I was worried about you. I called her up to discuss the situation. You told me they'd been worried too. She's phoned back a couple of times. Luckily, Antony answered the phone – I haven't spoken to her again, and I'm not going to. I just wanted to tell you, Carolyn. She was telling me things about you and your family. I feel I betrayed you. I'm really sorry.'

I was furious. Why were these people interfering in my business? Why on earth had Uma taken it upon herself to contact Annalisa? And what was Annalisa doing, talking to a total stranger about me and my family on the phone? I didn't know what to think. God knows what they had been saying! I felt betrayed. They had gone behind my back, but at least Uma had 'fessed up.

'God, Uma. What were you thinking?'

'I'm sorry, Carolyn. It's just that everything was happening so fast and I was worried about you.'

'Well, I have to tell you I'm really pissed off about this – but thanks for telling me. At least you had the courage to do that.'

'Well, let's get together soon, shall we?'

'Yes, sure. We'll speak again soon.'

When I got off the phone I was fuming. Always one to strike while the iron is hot, I immediately picked up my phone again and dialled my brother's number at work. I was shaking, and I felt my voice crack under the strain as I spoke.

'Nick, I've just had a call from my friend Uma. She told me that she contacted Annalisa – God knows why! – and she tells me that Annalisa has been discussing our family, among other things, and she seems to think it appropriate to talk to a total stranger on the phone about all this. She's completely out of order, Nick. I'm telling you this because our relationship has been strained enough. She always thinks she knows what's best for everyone and it's bloody annoying. Anyway, I'm simply not prepared to put up with any more of it. I have to tell you this because I know it will affect you too.'

Nick remained calm on the other end of the line.

'Carolyn, we have been very worried.'

'Well, all this really doesn't help. I don't deny that Annalisa can be very kind and helpful, but this interference has to stop. I'm sorry to phone you at work about this, but I had to let you know how I feel about it all.'

I came off the phone exhausted. My fury with Annalisa was unabated, but I felt deeply saddened at the thought that my relationship with her and my brother was now unravelling. The whole infrastructure of my life seemed to be falling apart and I wondered where it would all end.

* * *

Over the course of the next few days, I spoke to Mark daily. He remained in the military hospital in Malta and his thin, raspy voice croaked faintly at the end of the line. I was beside myself with worry. Somehow, I got through each twenty-four hours, but the days remained stubbornly grey and wet, and stretched ahead with a dull monotony that I hadn't known since my board-ing-school days. The isolation I now felt was chronic, but luckily, I had learned in those unhappy boarding-school years how to deal with solitude. People always used to say that boarding school taught you to stand on your own two feet. That was true enough, but I sometimes thought that I had become far too self-reliant. I had been brought up to think that I must take responsibility for my own life and sort things out for myself, and I found it very difficult to accept help, even when it was offered, and virtually impossible to ask for it. Now I was going to have to call upon my own strength of character more than ever before.

It is very difficult to convey to someone who hasn't met Mark, just how convincing he was, even at his most outlandish. This is another hallmark of the psychopath: he will saturate you with love and adoration, constantly reminding you how lucky you are to have found each other, constantly reinforcing the bond you feel with him, using charm, flattery and other emotional-manip-ulation tactics, always presenting himself as the perfect partner. Talking about psychopaths in his book *Without Conscience*, Robert Hare says, 'Everyone, including the experts can be taken in, conned, and left bewildered by them.' If the experts can be taken in, what hope is there for a love-bombed target?

Once in the psychopathic bond, you are transfixed – you don't want to break it, even though, when the perpetrator has gained power and control through the love-bombing technique, he will go on to replace the non-stop love, with hot/cold behaviour, so that you find yourself on an emotional roller coaster. He will begin a calculated assault, starting to blame and devalue you.

This he will alternate with profuse showers of affection, grooming you back into submission before blaming you all over again.

Mark started this phase when he constantly told me how his relationship with me was putting him in danger. Then he staged a punishment (the poisoning), effectively blaming me for it. This was just one of a number of faked events, all of which were deliberate moves designed to make me feel guilty and fearful and, at the same time, to strengthen my resolve to stand by him. After all, if he was suffering all that to be in a relationship with me, the least I could do was stand by him.

6

HALL OF MIRRORS

'I'll tell you', she said, in the same hurried passionate whisper, 'what real love is. It is blind devotion, unquestioning self-humiliation, utter submission, trust and belief against yourself and against the whole world, giving up your whole heart and soul to the smiter – as I did!'

Charles Dickens, *Great Expectations*

It seemed like an eternity until I saw Mark again, but it was, in fact, only about a week before he appeared in the kitchen one morning. He seemed as right as rain.

'I told you, baby, I'm strong. Physically and mentally. Anyway, they were only teaching me a lesson.'

'Well, I think it's terrible,' I protested. 'I just can't believe that government organisations in the UK behave like this. I thought this sort of thing only happened in films.'

'Believe me, you don't know a fraction of it. But I've been thinking, Bubba. It's impossible to fight these people single-handed, but I've got a plan that I think could get me released early from my contract. They want me to go and operate in Syria. It's very dangerous but I think I can do what they want. I'm going to see if I can do a deal with them, so that if I'm successful, they'll let me out early.'

'God, darling, but that sounds really dangerous. I don't want you to go to Syria. I've been so worried about you as it is. That night you went to Iran was the worst of my life. You seem to think you're invincible, but what if you get killed, or badly injured? And what about me? You've got all my money. I'd be left with nothing.'

By now, the demands for money had stopped, but I had only about £15,000 left in the bank. At this stage, I wasn't worried that Mark would deliberately not repay me and was in some ways quite relieved that I didn't still have an enormous sum of money sitting in my bank account. This was something that had worried me greatly in the prevailing financial climate when I had sold my house back in 2010, having witnessed the run on Northern Rock and its collapse a couple of years before. I was, however, seriously worried about not being repaid should anything happen to Mark.

'Darling, there is no need to worry about that. Do you honestly think I would allow that to happen? I look at my will every month. If I die, you'll be a very wealthy woman. OK, Bianca gets the most, because she needs it – sorry, but that's just the way it is – but you don't need to worry about a thing.'

'Well, I'd like to see some evidence of that. I do worry. I have no control over anything any more. I don't like it. I was expecting to have been paid back by now.'

'Don't you trust me?' His voice had a sharp edge to it. 'Because if you don't, tell me, and we can draw a line under everything here and now, and both go back to our old lives. I thought we had absolute trust between us. It's what makes us special.'

'You know I trust you. It's just that when I say I'll do something I do it right away. You're different. You've told me yourself that you get things done "eventually". Eventually isn't any good in this sort of situation. I need to know that my interests are protected.'

'Darling, I just need you to be strong. Let me go and do this shit. I'm really good at my job – the best – and if I'm successful, which I will be, we can be together properly in just a few months.'

There was nothing I could say or do to change anything. He had made up his mind, and a couple of days later he told me he would be leaving for Syria in the next twenty-four hours. He promised to contact me whenever he could, to let me know he was OK, and he said that Paul would be bringing me a new, more secure phone.

Life became hell for me. I couldn't sleep at all and I was on tenterhooks, day and night, waiting for the ping of a message. Often, Mark would text me in the middle of the night. His messages were brief and to the point.

02.14 Down. All good.

And I would respond equally briefly.

Be careful. I love you.

Sometimes, if I hadn't heard from him, I would be unable to resist the urge to contact him, especially when my mind was in turmoil, in the middle of the night:

Please let me know you're OK.

And if I was lucky, I would get the only response I really needed:

Alive

These days and nights were interminable for me. I would get up in the morning feeling exhausted. It took me longer and longer to get ready to face the day, and although I still forced myself to get out of the house every day and walk down to the centre of Bath, it was becoming a terrible effort. On one occasion, walking back to the house and not having heard anything from Mark for over twenty-four hours, I found myself unable to control myself, and broke down in tears, sobbing on the pavement. The fear and suspense were unbearable.

Then, suddenly, one morning, with no warning, Mark appeared in the kitchen. His arm was neatly bandaged and held in a sling. I ran up to him and kissed him.

'What's happened? You're hurt!' I was so relieved to see him, but terrified too. My eyes welled up.

'Yeah, I got shot. It's really grim out there. Don't cry, baby.' He kissed me. 'Now, get me a coffee, will you?'

'Well, I hope you won't be going back there. Tell me that's the end of it.'

Mark was trying to sit down, very gingerly, but he stood up again.

'Fuck! I've got grazing on my lower back and buttocks. It's really uncomfortable trying to sit.'

'Darling, tell me you won't be going back there. I can't bear it.'

'I've got to try and finish the job they sent me out there to do. I've got to do it, Bubba. Then I can say goodbye to this shit for ever, and we can be together. You know I used to love my job; now I hate it.'

'But you can't go back there now. You're injured. You can't even sit down.'

'Don't worry. I'll be fine. You'll see. I can't stay long today. Paul's waiting outside to take me back to London. I just had to see you, darling. I'm doing all this for you. You only know a fraction of it. One day I'll tell you just what I've done for you. Then you'll understand. But you've got to bear with me. It will all be worth it in the end.'

It seemed he had hardly arrived before he'd left again. My heart sank. I felt weird. Not like myself at all. I had started to feel I was losing myself when I'd looked in the mirror at my last wedding-dress fitting. Now I felt even more estranged – a shadowy, ghostly reflection of my former self. I looked miserable. There were dark circles under my eyes, despite my carefully applied make-up. The woman I saw in the mirror looked lifeless and stared back at me impassively.

I poured myself a glass of wine. I didn't normally drink during the day, but it was all I could think of to do. I was drinking every evening now too. It helped to numb my senses. I sat down at the kitchen table and stared across the inner hall, through the dining room and out through the windows looking out on to the Circus, where the usual throng of tourists was milling around. I could hear chatter and laughter. There is life out there, I thought, and I was overcome by an overwhelming sense of longing – for my old job, my cottage, my belongings and, most of all, my family and friends.

I felt so insecure and I just wanted everything to be as it used to be. I sat almost motionless in the kitchen for nearly two hours, only moving to raise the bottle to the wine glass, the wine glass to my lips, until both bottle and glass were empty.

Mark went to Syria three more times and every time he left I thought his chances of coming back diminished. But three more times he appeared again in the kitchen, and each time I rushed up to him to kiss him and hold him.

'Thank God you're alive! Bubba, I thought I was never going to see you again. It's been awful.'

'I know, darling. I've felt it too. Things got so bad this time. I was shot again – in the leg. I feel my luck's running out. I can sense these things, you know. I can't finish this mission. We'll have to find another way.'

'Well, of course you can't. You've been shot twice now. They can't expect you to go again.' I remained outwardly calm, but inside I felt hysterical and didn't know if I could keep a lid on it.

'Don't worry, darling. I've told them I'm not doing these dangerous missions any more. They're going to put me in a desk job at the MOD. I'm going to hate it, but that's the only option. It's going to be much more difficult to see you too. I'd like us to be able to move into Beach. I know you're not happy here – though God knows why. I don't understand it; you're living in the Circus, for fuck's sake, but you were happier in that cottage of yours. It's insane!'

I felt such a sense of relief when he said he wouldn't be going back to Syria that, for a moment, I almost felt happy.

'Yes, darling, but I thought we were going to be together here – at least one or two nights a week. I had no idea it was going to be like this. We still haven't spent a night together and I don't want to go out on my own. I thought we'd be doing things together.'

'And we shall be, eventually. I'm not a selfish person, Bubba, never have been and never will be. I've tried all my life to do things for the greater good. I never put myself first. Not ever. You're going to have to put up with that and I know that you will because it's why you fell in love with me. It will all work out in the end. It will be worth all the heartache, I promise.'

Mark continued to build his InOrg business empire. Now he was sponsoring a promising young racing driver, Dino Zamparelli. He took me to the Cotswold Airport to show me the first of twenty-six racing cars he had ordered. It was being painted with the InOrg logo, and he told me that David Coulthard was going to drive it for a publicity stunt. He also said that he was composer Ennio Morricone's agent. He became obsessed with Facebook 'clicks', texting the numbers to me day and night, and telling me that he would make millions from the advertising revenue they would generate. He seemed almost manic at times. I saw less and less of him and, as usual, when I did see him there were constant interruptions.

He also confided in me much more than he should, often voicing his grievances about how he was being treated by the security services.

'You're the only person I can talk to, Bubba, the only person I can trust. I want to tell you everything about myself, but at the moment I can't, and you mustn't repeat anything I do tell you to anyone. Information can be powerful, but it can also be dangerous. There's something I've been wanting to tell you, but you must never tell a living soul.'

'You know you can trust me. What is it?'

'It's about my background – my parents. I'm actually the illegitimate son of George Soros. You know, the guy who brought down the Bank of England? I learned everything I know about finance from him. It's been a great education.'

'So you see him? You're on good terms with him?'

'Well, not exactly. There's a pretty strong rivalry between us. One day soon I'll be better than he is at everything he's taught me. He knows it, but he doesn't necessarily like it.'

When Mark left, I googled George Soros. I knew his name and I remembered Black Wednesday, but that was about it. Could Mark really be his son? As I looked at the photographs of Soros on my laptop, I could see a resemblance. They had that same supremely confident, almost arrogant air about them and there was a similarity about the line of the nose and the set of the mouth. And Soros was a philanthropist; Mark was always telling me about how much he himself had done to help people less fortunate. He must have inherited that quality from his father. My God, I thought to myself – it's all so bizarre.

I loved Mark, and I loved the way that, however scared and uncertain I might be feeling, as soon as I spoke to him he was able to allay all my fears. Even if it was on the phone, he was always able to reassure me. I just wished he was around more. I was feeling so isolated and my loneliness seemed to increase by the day. Anyway, thank God, he was alive, and now he wouldn't be going away any more. Despite what he said about it becoming more difficult for him to see me, I hoped it would prove otherwise and that he would have more time to spend with me, but I knew that he would hate doing a desk job and I hoped he wouldn't resent me for it.

But towards the end of May, over the course of a week I didn't see Mark at all. He called me every day and said he was sorry, but he couldn't get to Bath just yet. He hoped we might get away the following week for a few days' holiday though – somewhere warm and sunny.

'Pack your suitcase, darling,' he told me. 'You must always be ready to take off somewhere with me, and I've earned a break.'

I really hoped the holiday would materialise. When I first met Mark he had told me that I must always carry my passport with me and be ready to travel at a moment's notice, but the sad fact that I had only ever travelled as far as London with him weighed heavily on my mind. I needed to have a proper conversation with him, but it seemed impossible. He always sounded deflated these days, and when I tried to talk to him he didn't really seem to be listening to what I was saying. Then one day, he didn't call. I was beside myself. I wasn't sleeping and I felt terrible. My life seemed like a void and I could see nothing clearly. I couldn't confide in anyone, and there was no one I really wanted to see. I had to protect Mark and I was sure my friends would realise that things weren't right if I saw any of them. That would lead to questions, and I couldn't cope with that.

But why hadn't he called me? I tried his number, but it went to voicemail. That night I didn't sleep a wink and at five o'clock the following morning, I gave in and got up. Things had been going around in my mind all night. I had to tell Mark how I was feeling. I went into the study, picked up my Montblanc pen and started writing.

Brock Street
26th May 2012
5.00 am

My Darling Bubba
I have spent another restless night in a state of such emotional turmoil that I feel I must write to you to try to explain how I am feeling. Of course if I felt there was any chance of saying this to you face to face, over the next day or two, I would wait to have the conversation, but our encounters seem to get fewer and fewer and to be of such a short duration that I have no confidence at all that such an opportunity will present itself. You have not even found time for a phone call over the past 24 hours.

Before I say anything else I must tell you, again, that I love you with all my heart and soul. I pray that things are going to work out for us but, as I sit here writing this, my mind is full of doubt.

When I met you, darling, I fell for you instantly. I find you devastatingly attractive physically, but I was drawn to your aura of positive energy and intellectual prowess just as much. I think you may have recognised similar qualities in me. Anyway, there is no doubt that there was, and still, is a very strong mutual attraction, and I knew that my life was going to change for ever. I thought that, although our relationship would not be conventional, we would still be able to spend time together, opening each other's eyes to a different way of looking at things, seeing things from a new perspective, having interesting, challenging conversations and having a wonderful physical relationship that would allow us to express our love for each other like never before, and bind us so close that we could never be undone.

I know that events took a course that I couldn't possibly have foreseen, and maybe you couldn't have either, I mean in terms of the pressure put on you by certain people regarding your job, and I have certainly found these weeks to be some of the most terrifying of my life. I have never before gone to bed night after night in such a state of dread that I would never speak to or see you again. It has been a living hell. I remember the first time I became aware of the type of work you did, when you went on a dangerous mission. I felt that was the worst night of my life. You might think that I would get used to it and it would become easier to cope with, but if anything the opposite is true. Every time you came back only seemed to make it more likely that the next time you went out you wouldn't return.

What I am trying to tell you is that over the past few months I feel as though I have lost myself. I feel as though I have aged a good ten years and I have lost all my confidence in everything. I hate myself because this is not me! I am a naturally attractive, positive, energetic, vivacious human being but I have turned into a reclusive, unconfident, middle-aged wreck of a woman who spends her days drinking, smoking and crying. I honestly feel as though I am dying a horrible drawn-out death. I have tried to keep my mind on the 'big picture', but now I just stare at a blank wall.

Bubba, I know how much you have done to try to change things for us and I really do appreciate it but I have to say that the past week has brought both joy and despair. Joy because you are alive – what a relief – thank God! Despair because you are now doing a 'desk job' and I wonder how you will cope with that, and I have seen virtually nothing of you. Not only that but there has hardly been time for a phone call.

You told me that things would get easier when we were living together and I put all my trust in you and jumped and came to Bath. Bubba, you will laugh, but I actually believed we would spend a night or two together – each week! I told myself that if you had 90 nights in this country that is what would happen. I don't now think that is ever going to happen.

You know, darling, the past few months have been a roller coaster of promise and disappointment. Descriptions of a beautiful house with acres of garden, a planned wedding with fireworks, light shows, music, etc. Promises of holidays dashed and dashed again. Will we get away on Monday? I doubt it, and I am almost beyond caring. What I do have to do is sort myself out and that brings me to the next point.

I have told you that I feel disempowered. This is partly to do with not working, not being independent and that kind of thing. Although I understand it I resent being tied to a mobile phone. I also don't think you should feel justified in reading my text messages and emails or opening post addressed to me. It is not that I have anything to hide but everyone has a right to privacy – you cannot deny it.

Also, when I helped you out with your cash-flow problems I did think that it would only be a matter of a few weeks before the money was returned to my account. You talked about it a number of times. I may well have misunderstood and I was, and still am, happy that I was able to help, but what you don't seem to understand, despite my attempts at explaining, is that I feel trapped and a lot of this feeling of disempowerment has to do with the fact that I have no financial options.

You know that I wanted to pay off the girls' student loans and you tell me you have set something up to pay them off at the end of the year. You are missing the point, darling. I told them I was going to give them a sum of money each. I am their mother and I should be able to do that in my way when I want to. You do things 'eventually'. I am different; if I say I'm going to do something I do it there and then. I really do feel that I should be able to give Lara and Emma the money now, myself. You didn't even discuss your arrangement with me.

You know, Bubba, perhaps it is as well that my bank account is empty. If I had £800K sitting there I would be sorely tempted to buy myself a country cottage. I don't actually think that would be a good idea, but I hope you can understand that if the possibility was there I would feel less trapped and less like running away.

At Christmas last year I decided that if I hadn't found a house and moved into it by June I would leave Tetbury and go and spend the summer working in France. I actually thought about contacting my [former] employers the other day. I am at the end of my tether.

Bubba I know this will sound like a self-centred rant. It is not meant like that. I love you so much and I really want things to work out and I will work really hard to get there. The thing is, darling, I need to share things with you: time, hopes, fears, ideas, bodies, experiences – everything. The problem for me is that I am not sure that we want the same things. I know I cannot survive if I never wake up at your side.

You know darling, I have not been able to look at my wedding dress at all since I brought it here. That day when I was having the final fitting and Widcombe (or Beach – who knows?) had flooded, I remember saying to Paul, 'There isn't going to be a wedding, is there?' When I was being fitted I felt like Miss Havisham in Great Expectations. A terrible sense of dread overcame me. I cannot bear to even think about that dress, and for the first time ever I have felt a niggling doubt about getting married. My heart feels broken, Bubba.

I am sorry my darling. I have tried to be strong for you and put on a brave face but I am very unhappy. I know you have moved heaven and earth to try to change things so that we can have a life together and now you find yourself in a job that I fear will be a living death for you.

You have told me I haven't lived. You know what, I think it is you who is missing out. You can't even go to the theatre or take a walk in the park. There is more that I would like to write here, but it is too dangerous.

I hope we can work things out. I never would have believed that love could be so painful. I read something in a book recently that struck a chord:

'But here she is, all mine, trying her best to give me all she can. How could I ever hurt her? But I didn't understand then. That I could hurt somebody so badly she would never recover. That a person can, just by living, damage another human being beyond repair.'*

I love you, Bubba, but I need time with you and I'm not sure you will ever be able to give it to me. At the beginning of all this, when we decided to 'live together' (Ha!), I thought it was a win-win situation. I had been on my own, quite happily, for nine or ten years. Even if I didn't see you very much, when I did see you that would just be a bonus, I told myself. How wrong I was. When there was nobody I wanted to be with and develop a relationship with I was happy to be on my own. Now I am just lonely – probably for the first time in my life.

I love you Bubba.

Bubba

I folded the letter and put it in an envelope. The next time I saw Mark I would give it to him. The hours passed slowly that day, which seemed especially long due to the five-o'-clock start, but early in the afternoon I heard the insistent, demanding ringtone that meant Mark was on the line. I picked up. He sounded really upbeat.

'Hello, Bubba, how are you? Sorry I didn't call you yesterday. Things have just been crazy.'

'Actually, I haven't been feeling very good. I had a terrible night last night. I got up early and wrote you a letter,' I explained.

* Haruki Murakami, *South of the Border, West of the Sun.*

'There's so much I want to talk to you about, but we never seem to get the chance.'

'Well, talk to me now. Tell me what's in this letter of yours.'

'Let me give it to you when I see you, so that you can consider it properly.'

'No, Bubba, tell me now: read it to me – I need to know.'

I took the letter out of the envelope and read it over the phone. When Mark finally spoke, his voice was as cold and sharp as steel.

'Destroy it,' he ordered.

The next day, I was expecting to see Mark, but by early evening he hadn't shown up and I hadn't heard from him. I tried to call him, but he didn't pick up, so I texted him asking him when I could expect him. Eventually he responded.

27 May 2012

7.39 pm

> Darling I am in a meeting and shouldn't be texting.
>
> I will call when I can
>
> What time I get there will depend on what time I finish
>
> I never have planned an hour ahead let alone 5
>
> I would rather not live than to live that … English life.
>
> You know I would be dead had I lived … that way.

8.00 pm

If you knew even 1 percent of the stress I suffer

It's hell on Earth

You are not the only one who is under stress.

I am not going to argue by text.

It's pointless.

I agree.

You obviously have your view and I have mine.

He went on to say that among other things, he'd destroyed a three-year-old's life to be with me, a career he loved and a life he cherished. He said that he had come back to a country he despised, and that he was now stuck in a job that he couldn't get out of without dying.

I am responsible and I live with that.

I love you but please don't compare situations.

How dare he blame me for destroying Bianca's life? I felt furious as I texted back.

Now I am really angry.

My phone was ringing. It was Mark, but I was so angry I ignored him.

The ringing stopped and another series of text message pinged in, like rapid gun-fire.

> Re getting angry I have no idea why.

> … Not taking calls when I have just left a meeting …
> isn't clever.

> I am on massive pain killers so … grouchy … I
> apologise.

I couldn't stop thinking about what he had said about Bianca, so texted back:

> **Don't ever hold me responsible for destroying a
> child's life – especially when I think what I was
> prepared to do for her.**

Mark responded by saying he knew what I was prepared to do for her:

> I will always love you for that.

Then he ended by saying he hated his life as much as I hated mine.

> But they are not comparable.

8.20 pm

> **Now I am going to throw both phones out of the
> window!**

I was like Mark now, carrying two phones around with me. I hated it. I hated everything about my life. Mark called me again, but I was not going to speak to him.

8.59 pm

Please Bubba call me.

9.41 pm

I love you.

Still I didn't respond. I loved him so much it hurt, but his comments hurt me too. He seemed to have no idea how much I had sacrificed for him. It struck me that this was our first row – and we'd had it via text message. I'd always despised that sort of thing. But I was not going to capitulate now and text him or call him back. I went to bed that night feeling sad and alone. I tossed and turned, only drifting off fitfully, until, in the early hours of the morning, I heard the ping of another message.

28 May 2012

04.02   Alive and down in Italy.

Love you.

Will call first thing.

I was wide awake. Italy? What was he doing in Italy? Surely he wasn't off to Syria again? Sometimes I felt as though I was going mad and I remembered the film *Gaslight* that I'd seen on television when I was very young. I couldn't recall the detail, but it was

Me in 2010 before I met Mark Acklom.

Mark Acklom the fraudster, posing outside no. 1 Dulwich Oaks in 1991. At 16, he conned victims out of millions posing as a fake stockbroker.

The image of Mark Acklom used during the police investigation that featured in the Crimestopper's 10th anniversary campaign in 2016.

Mark Acklom in Gloucestershire in 2012.

Mark Acklom in a sports car in 2012.

Mark Acklom in the Royal Enclosure at Ascot with his wife,
Maria Yolanda Ros Rodriguez in 2012.

Mark Acklom (*right*) photographed outside a café in Geneva in 2017.

CCTV footage of Mark Acklom and me in January 2012,
in the shop in Tetbury, the evening we first met.

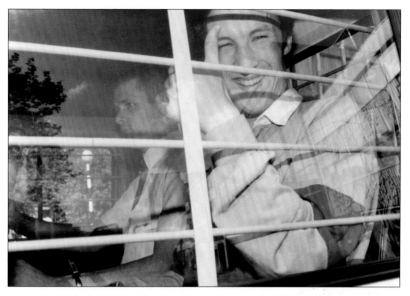

Mark Acklom leaving court in 1991, 'celebrating' his
4-year prison sentence.

Mark Acklom in court in Spain in 2015.

A police mug shot of
Mark Acklom in 2019.

Me, happy in
Gloucestershire
in 2014.

Me appearing on *This Morning* in October 2016.

Me taking a selfie in Scotland in September 2020.

an old black and white film about a man who convinced his wife that she was going mad. He played psychological games with her, turning down the lights, which unnerved her, and then telling her that she was imagining it, all the while gradually taking control of her. All those years ago that film had really frightened me. Now I sometimes felt that Mark was gaining control over me, but I forced myself to scrub these thoughts out of my mind as soon as they surfaced. What a terrible thing to think about someone. It was just that he was so strong and he expected the same from me. But he had been trained to withstand all sorts of stressful situations and all manner of assault, physical and psychological. I hadn't. I had lived in a safe world where people were generally kind and well-meaning. I'd been brought up to be honest and truthful and I expected the same of everyone else. Up until now my life had been pretty straightforward. But with Mark there were things that just didn't add up. He worked for MI6 though – of course nothing was going to be straightforward. And although he said I was the only person he trusted, that didn't mean he always told me the truth. Well, he couldn't, could he? I was now living in a world where none of the normal rules of engagement applied.

It was 1 June: Mark's birthday. I hoped that we would be able to celebrate properly, but I didn't even get to see him on the day. I made him a card and baked him a cake, even though I was sure he wouldn't eat it. We seldom ate together. In fact, he didn't seem to eat at all, but I knew that he couldn't possibly survive on a diet of caffeine and nicotine.

He assured me we would see each other the next day. 'I'm really sorry, Bubba. These bastards won't let me off the hook. I'll be there tomorrow. I know it's impossible for you to understand. I'm good at a lot of things, baby, but one thing I'm not good at is keeping people informed about what's going on. Often, I just can't. I'm sorry, sweetie.'

The card I had made was with one of my photographs. I regarded my camera as a barometer of my state of mind and happiness and the fact that I had hardly taken any photos since arriving in Bath was very telling. The one I had chosen to make into a card for him was of the arched window and balcony of a neighbouring property. It overlooked the courtyard at the back of the house. A pink rose climbed up to the balcony and the scene was romantic, reminding me of the balcony scene in *Romeo and Juliet*. After our failed attempt at a Romeo-and-Juliet-style wedding, I thought it rather appropriate. The caption underneath the photograph read: 'Wherefore art thou, Bubba?' Inside, the card read 'HAPPY BIRTHDAY SEXY!' which was a rather forlorn attempt at levity from a spirit that felt severely deflated.

Mark arrived late in the afternoon the day after his birthday. I gave him his card and presented him with his cake.

'Darling, I thought I'd see you yesterday. I'm finding all this very difficult. I hardly saw you on my birthday and didn't see you at all on yours. Can't we celebrate. Can't we go out to dinner, and couldn't you stay the night, just once? We've known each other for four and a half months and we still haven't even spent one night together.'

'I know, darling, but I told you right at the beginning how it was going to be. You know I'm doing everything I can. You have no idea what I've done for you.'

I felt bad. I was being selfish. What he said was absolutely true; I had agreed to wait for him. I was just going to have to run the course.

'Baby, look at this. I wasn't going to show you – but come and take a look.' He was looking at something on his mobile phone.

'Where's that?' I was looking at a photograph of an enormous room. It had a kitchen at the far end with what looked like a Kandinsky on the wall. In the foreground was a large table, seating about a dozen people.

'That's our kitchen at Beach. Isn't it insane? I turned the ball-room into the kitchen. The architect told me I was a genius. Look, see there?' He was pointing at a small picture on the wall at the far end of the room.

'What is it?'

'It's a picture of you – you know, one of those Warhol-type ones. Isn't it cool?'

'Well, I can't really see it properly. Where did you get the photo?'

'Off your computer. I told you, baby, I can get anything I want off your computer.'

'And what's the large picture?' I asked him.

'A Kandinsky.'

'I thought so. Bubba, when are we going to move there? I don't like living here. Couldn't we just go there now, I mean it looks as if it's all done.'

'Not yet, darling. I want it to be perfect when I take you there. I told you it's really important to me that it's all done properly. But it won't be long. It's nearly finished and you're going to love it. It will be my present to you.'

All through June, Mark continued with his empire-building and took me to the Chew Magna Manor House estate, another impressive property development of his. He offered me two reno-vated houses there, that he said I could run as a business and rent out, but I wasn't interested. All I wanted was to choose a house for myself – when he paid me back what he owed me. He prom-ised days out at Ascot and Wimbledon, but didn't show up, and on both occasions, I was left in limbo all day. He then told me that we would be going to Marbella, where he had just bought a luxury villa, La Villa Ermita, along with the Marbella Beach Club. He told me to have my case packed, ready to go, but we never went. In the meantime, some chairs were delivered to Brock

Street. Paul came to take them upstairs, but was suspicious of the delivery, and told me that he had checked they were not bugged.

I was becoming more and more isolated, not sleeping and sinking deeper and deeper into depression. One evening, during a telephone conversation, when I tried to explain how terrible I was feeling, Mark responded with four words: 'My dad just died.' This was one time that I remember seriously doubting him, but I didn't dare question such a statement, and he made me feel selfish and demanding. I did, however, ask him which dad – was he talking about George Soros? He told me he was referring to 'the man who brought me up'. I was finding it increasingly difficult to make sense of anything, and I couldn't believe our continuing bad luck.

At last, one day around the end of June, Mark called me and said we would be moving to the estate at Beach and I should start packing. I felt euphoric at the thought of a fresh start and moving to a quieter location. I packed my belongings, but they remained boxed up for six weeks. Paul, who was to have moved them, was out of action, as his son, I was told, had cancer. I told Mark that I would call a removal company, or move myself, but he said that it would be dangerous, and that I must not do so. My boxes were piled up in the study and he insisted that I kept the shutters closed at all times, because he didn't want anyone knowing our business.

During this period, I became obsessed with spy dramas. I was addicted to *Homeland* and spent hours watching box sets of *24*. I also read *Agent Zigzag*, a non-fiction account of a wartime double agent – a maverick with immense charm. In my mind's eye, I likened Mark to *24*'s Jack Bauer, *Homeland*'s Brody and the real-life double agent Eddie Chapman.

Late one evening, I was in the top flat, where I would go to watch television. It was still light outside and through the large bay window I could see colourful hot-air balloons rising up from the Royal Crescent. Normally, I would have been tempted to go for a stroll on this rare, fine summer evening, but I remained indoors and turned on the television to watch another episode of *Homeland*. I was lying on one of two chaises longues, engrossed in the action, but somewhere in the back of my mind I registered an unfamiliar sound. I turned the sound down and listened acutely, but everything was quiet. I must have imagined it. But a few seconds later, there was no mistaking the sound of the door brushing over the carpet. I looked up and gasped as Mark entered the room, dressed in full desert combat gear. As he came to sit beside me and take me in his arms I felt the tears welling up. He too looked as though he might cry.

'Darling, I shouldn't be here, but I had to come and see you. I can't stand it when you're upset. I've left a group of men I'm supposed to be training for action in Syria. I can't stay long. You've got to keep strong for me. I'm doing my utmost for us – one day you'll understand just what I've done for you.'

He stayed no more than ten minutes and, as usual, I felt reassured by his presence and what he said. When he left, I stood by the landing window and watched as he jogged around the Circus towards Bennett Street. I wondered who was waiting for him there.

A dismal summer was drawing to a close. Mark called one day, saying that my car needed servicing. The following morning, Paul came over to pick it up, and that afternoon Mark was on the phone to me again.

'Darling, what on earth have you been doing with the car? It's fucked.'

'What do you mean, it's fucked? I haven't been doing anything with it. I hardly ever go out.'

'Well, it's fucked. The brakes are lethal. Baby, it worries me – it looks as though it's been tampered with.'

'Tampered with? Do you mean someone wants me to have an accident? Who would do that? I thought you said that I wouldn't be in any danger.'

'Well, that's what I thought, but now … I just don't know. I wouldn't put anything past those cunts.'

I now began to fear for my life.

During this phase of our relationship Mark displays typical psychopathic behaviour, reminding me that everything he is doing is for me, but then making me feel guilty about it. At this stage I remember often trying to stand up for myself, pointing out that I was making sacrifices too, but as the text-message row demonstrates, he reprimands me for even thinking my sacrifice is comparable to his, trying to make me feel responsible for the destruction of Bianca's life; and then, just to make me feel even worse, he tells me he is on medication, thereby making me worry about his wellbeing, before finally putting the boot in when I don't respond to him, using two of his favourite words, telling me he is 'alive' and 'down', so that I immediately think he must be on another mission. How selfish of me to act so petulantly when he is risking his life for the greater good!

At this stage, he is also using tactics to make me fear for my own safety. Having managed to make me acutely conscious of CCTV cameras so that I feel that I am constantly being watched, he now tells me to keep the shutters closed and has chairs delivered to the house that Paul checks for bugs. Now I start to wonder if the whole house is bugged, and I am too frightened to even keep a diary. My obsession with spy stories, real and fictional, demonstrates my state of mind. I thought again about the old film *Gaslight* that had scared me when I watched it as a child and wondered if I was going mad – I certainly felt as though I was. At this stage I was unaware of the phenomena of 'gaslighting' and 'ghosting', but I now realise that Mark used both tactics to sap my confidence, frighten me, and further isolate me. To 'gaslight' somebody is to psychologically manipulate them so that they start to doubt their own memory, ability to do things and eventually their own sanity; when you 'ghost' someone, you disappear out of their lives (virtual or actual), leaving them feeling lost, confused, worried and abandoned. In retrospect, I can see how Mark used both techniques on me.

Mark's appearance late at night when I was engrossed in *Homeland* was particularly lucky timing for him, and only reinforced my feelings of fear and admiration for him. The combat gear was probably army surplus, and I later recalled that he was wearing black boots, which I think are wrong with desert combat gear. The story he told me about the brakes on my car having been tampered with was another lie, designed solely to make me even more fearful. I didn't see that car again and my car was subsequently changed three times, which I assumed was an extra security measure. Drawing my attention to the Warhol-style picture of me (that was impossible to identify) and telling me he had taken the photograph off my computer was another attempt to reinforce the idea in my mind that nothing I said or did was private, and that he could access everything. Looking back, I can see how Mark really piled on the fear and the guilt and the extreme stories, as his contempt for and power over me grew. How he must have enjoyed hearing me read my letter to him and to learn how lonely, sad and disempowered I was feeling. Psychopaths feed off humiliating their victims, so the more confused and miserable I became, the more superior and grandiose he would have felt. I now understand how, on numerous occasions, he groomed me back into submission, and whenever I saw him he would stare deep into my eyes and convince me that everything would be all right in the end.

7

SLEEPING WITH
THE LIGHT ON

It seemed to me, especially when I was going to sleep, that some octopus with supple and cold tentacles was stealing up to me, coming straight for my heart, so I had to sleep with the light on.

Mikhail Bulgakov, *The Master and Margarita*

It was the end of August and my phone was ringing. The demanding ringtone made me jump to attention.

'Darling, where have you been? I've been calling you all afternoon.'

There were no missed calls on my phone.

'I'm at the house. Where are you?'

'I'm on my way to pick you up. I think you deserve a treat. How do you fancy going flying?'

'Flying? I'd love to. Where?'

'Kemble. I'll be with you in thirty minutes.'

'Fantastic. I can't wait.'

Mark picked me up and we made our way slowly out of Bath, in the rush-hour traffic, driving on to Tetbury and eventually arriving at the Cotswold Airport in the early evening.

I was excited as I climbed into the 1936, silver Ryan STA that I had spotted on my first visit to the hangar. It had a romanticism that appealed greatly to me. I would literally be flying with my head in the clouds. I had assumed that Mark would take me up, but it turned out that the pilot was to be his business associate James Miller. He was very courteous and kitted me out with a jumpsuit before helping me into the front cockpit, strapping me into my parachute and then into the aeroplane itself. Then he climbed into the back cockpit, started the engine and went through the safety drill with me. Mark was pacing up and down outside the hangar, speaking to someone on one of his phones. Occasionally, he stopped and took my photograph.

James was talking to me. 'I'll just have to let the engine warm up for a few minutes, then we'll be off. Are you OK?'

'Fine, thank you.'

Ten minutes later we were taxiing to the runway, and as the aeroplane gathered speed and we took to the sky, I wished I could fly away and leave all my worries and cares behind me. The sense of freedom and exhilaration was incredible, and I didn't feel anxious at all.

'Wow, this is fantastic!' I exclaimed, talking to James through the radio.

'I'm glad you like it.'

'Everything looks so beautiful. I'm trying to work out where we are. I used to live in Tetbury, but things look very different from up here.'

I settled down and we flew over the Gloucestershire landscape in companionable silence. Looking down, I began to pick out some familiar landmarks and I thought back to my first year in Tetbury. I had been so happy and proud of myself for having made such a success of the change in my life. When I met Mark, I thought all my dreams had come true, but the dream had turned into a nightmare. Suddenly, I saw Stable Cottage, my first idyllic rented cottage, just outside Tetbury, and I felt a terrible pang of sorrow and regret. How I would love to be able to go back there now. How I wished I had kept my own address, my job and my independence.

My daydreaming was interrupted by James talking to me through the radio.

'Would you like to do a roll?' he enquired.

'What's that?'

'Imagine the aeroplane doing a manoeuvre a bit like a corkscrew; it's very gentle.'

'OK,' I replied. I was experiencing a sense of freedom and excitement that I hadn't felt for months now, and I was always keen to try something new.

'Are you ready? Here we go.'

I felt the nose of the aeroplane lift up suddenly, and then I didn't know where I was. The whole world was spinning and I was screaming. I could barely keep my eyes open. Then, as abruptly as it had begun, it was over.

'Are you OK?' James asked.

'Yes, I'm fine. I'm sorry, but I just couldn't stop screaming.'

'Yes, I heard you, I had to turn the volume down!'

'But it was so exhilarating!'

'Would you like to do it again?'

'Yes, please!'

'OK, we need to regain some height first. Up we go!'

We climbed, and a moment later, I felt the nose of the aeroplane lift once more, and we were rolling again. I still couldn't control my screaming and, again, I could hardly keep my eyes open. The sensation of the world spinning around me was thrilling, and we did it a third time. It felt so adventurous and as I screamed and screamed, I felt myself letting go of months of pent-up emotion and anxiety. But all too soon it was over and we had landed and were taxiing back to the hangar. I unstrapped myself and climbed out of the cockpit. James was already on the ground; I jumped down from the wing and spontaneously kissed him enthusiastically on both cheeks. For the first time in months, I had felt free – but the sensation was tinged with regret and I felt a sharp pang of loss as I thought again about the life I had given up so readily to be with Mark.

'Thank you so much. That was just fantastic. I can't tell you how much I enjoyed it.'

'Any time.'

Then it was Mark's turn to go up. His flight was much shorter than mine and he didn't do any aerobatics. I was surprised that he didn't take the controls himself, but back in the car he explained why.

'Those vintage planes can be tricky to fly and I'm used to flying super-fast jets. Anyway, I wanted to see how James handled the plane. I really wasn't at all happy with him doing those aerobatics with you. It was highly dangerous. I would never have done anything like that. He was flying far too low. Some people like to cut it fine, but it's just not worth the risk. He shouldn't have done it. I told him not to do anything like that while I was up there – and he'll have to rein it in a bit if he wants to keep flying my aircraft.'

A few days later I was in Cornwall for a week's holiday with Lara, Emma, Anne, Nick and Claire. It was such a relief to get away – I'd been so looking forward to experiencing some sense of normality. We arrived in sunshine and I couldn't wait to get to the beach, smell the sea air and take in the beautiful surroundings. The sense of freedom was totally exhilarating. I loved being with my daughters and I was looking forward to catching up with Anne. I felt bad because I had let her down a number of times over the past six months, something that was completely out of character for me.

The weather was set fair, so the day after we arrived, we decided to cycle the Camel Trail. We did this every year. We would walk along Daymer Bay to Rock where we would take the ferry across the river estuary to Padstow and hire some bikes for the rest of the day. The ride was gentle and peaceful and we would stop off at the pub or the vineyard or the tearoom along the way. Today, we had brought a picnic lunch and were going to stop off at the vineyard later in the afternoon.

As we were eating lunch, my phone rang. I heard the familiar, demanding ringtone sounding in my pocket.

I got up and left the picnic table to take the call.

'Darling, there's something I have to tell you,' Mark told me. 'I'm driving down to Marbella, but I've had an accident.'

'What sort of accident?' I was alarmed. 'Are you OK?'

'Yes, Bubba. I'm OK. I just thought I should let you know. I've got a nasty gash on my head. I've sent you a photo, as with everything else that's been going on, I didn't think you'd believe me otherwise. I'm in Barcelona. I blacked out last night and fell down a flight of stairs and hit my head on a table at the bottom. It's a pretty nasty cut. Anyway, it'll be OK. It's all stitched up, but it gave me quite a fright.'

'Thank God you're OK! Is there ever going to be an end to all this? Sometimes I feel as if I'm going mad; I mean nothing's worked out as we hoped – nothing!'

'It will all work out in the end. Don't worry, darling, I'm fine. How are you getting on, anyway?'

'We're fine, thanks. We're out cycling. You'd hate it!'

'Darling, I'll call you later. I've got to go. I love you.'

'I love you too.'

I hung up and opened my text messages. There was one from Mark with a photo attached, as he'd said. It showed a big gash on his forehead, a couple of inches long, at a right angle to his right eyebrow, slicing right through it. It looked really nasty. I missed him and now I found myself worrying even more. Had he really fallen down some stairs or had someone pushed him? All sorts of wild scenarios began to form in my mind.

It was so lovely to be away with my daughters and friends and to be in a natural environment that soothed me, and in which I could feel some sense of calm. Anne and I had known each other since our twenties, when we had worked together, and our children had been brought up together. We had been on holiday together when they were very young and were so happy that they still wanted to come away with us – with boyfriends and girlfriend in tow too, sometimes. As well as enjoying blustery cliff-top walks, strolls along the beach with the sand between our toes, swimming, surfing and cycling, we all loved our food. Days out were punctuated by picnics, barbeques, pasties and ice-cream, and we all took it in turns to prepare a delicious evening meal. And perhaps the best thing about these weeks away was that we all reverted to a time when the children were small, a time of much silliness and general larking about – a time of self-abandonment and having unself-conscious fun.

The week in Cornwall was the calm before the storm. When I returned to Bath, I was eager to see Mark. He had continued driving down to Marbella after his accident and had spoken to me from our new villa, telling me how great the weather was and how fantastic it would be when we were there together.

'I'd hoped you could just fly out and join me, darling, but I have to come back to the UK to get my head looked at. I went to the hospital in Barcelona but you-know-who wants me to have a complete medical back in the UK. I've been getting some really bad headaches. Anyway, you're going to love it here. Your stuff's all here – your dress and that box you sent over. You're going to need that dress as soon as you get here. We'll be going to one of my concerts. We're having it filmed for my internet music channel and I want you to look a million dollars.'

When Mark returned to the UK at the end of September I saw the nasty gash over his right eyebrow for myself. He continued to make light of it, but I was worried. He was always telling me how strong he was, but he had blacked out and fallen down a flight of stairs. It felt like another bad omen – and sure enough, as we sat having coffee in the kitchen at Brock Street not long afterwards, Mark delivered more devastating news.

'Bubba, they've found a tumour. On my brain. I've got to have an operation, and they want it done as soon as possible. Look at this, I've got the scans here.' He held out his phone, showing me something on the screen.

I couldn't believe what he was telling me. I stared blankly at an image of his brain on his mobile phone.

'You see that? That's the tumour. It's around the front, but they want to go in somewhere on the side. This is what caused me to black out and have that fall. Really, baby I was lucky. Things could have been a lot worse – I could have died – but this has got to be seen to.'

I was incredulous. 'Why is all this happening to us? I'm not normally superstitious, but I feel we're jinxed somehow. Everything we touch goes wrong. And this all sounds so dangerous and risky. Where are you going to have the operation? I hope they'll let me come and visit you. It's just not right the way they try to keep us apart. It's cruel.'

'I'll be OK, baby. Don't you worry. You know how strong I am. I'm hoping they can operate down here – in Bristol.'

He took my hand and gave it a squeeze.

The following week, I went to have lunch with Uma and Antony. Uma was a very good cook and she had invited a few friends over that day. Strangely, none of the guests had their partners with them. How independent everyone is these days, I thought to myself. Perhaps what I thought of as an unconventional relationship was actually becoming the norm.

It was good to be in company. I was in a relatively good mood and was pleased to be out of Bath. There were two men at the table and four women. The chat was informal and lively and everyone was relaxed, eating, smoking and drinking. The lone male guest seemed to take a shine to me and was mildly flirtatious, telling me that if I wanted a change of scene, I would be welcome at his place any time.

'In fact, what are you doing this evening?' he enquired jovially.

Thankfully, I didn't have to think of a witty reply. I was saved by the insistent ring of my mobile phone.

'I'm sorry, do you mind if I take this?' I was looking at Uma. 'It's Mark.'

I rose from the table and left the room to answer the call.

'Where are you, baby?' Mark was talking.

'I'm in Tetbury, having lunch with Uma and Antony and some friends of theirs. I'm really enjoying myself. Actually, someone's just asked me out. It cheered me up.'

Mark's voice sliced back at me, cold and razor-sharp.

'And you think that's the correct way to behave when I'm about to go into theatre to have brain surgery?'

I felt stunned and belittled.

'Darling, I didn't know you were having surgery today. You didn't tell me. Of course, if I'd known I would have come with you, but I had no idea. Where are you? Do you want me to come now? I really should be there.'

'I'm in Bristol. At the hospital. They won't let you anywhere near me right now, but I'll find a way around it. Anyway, I've got to go now. I just wanted to talk to you before the operation and let you know the situation.'

'Darling, I'm sorry. I didn't mean anything by saying I'd been asked out. It was just nice to get a bit of attention. I've seen so little of you recently. Sometimes I worry that when we do eventually get together we won't even be compatible.'

'Well, I have absolutely no worry on that score, but I have more urgent things on my mind just now. Look, I have to go. I'll call you later and let you know how things have gone.'

'Is there a doctor I can talk to? What's the name of your consultant?'

'I can't tell you that, baby. I've got to be really careful. I'm surrounded by security. These cunts are worried that once someone starts delving around in my head I'm going to start spilling state secrets. It was bad enough in Barcelona after that fall. Fucking bastards!'

Before I knew it Mark had hung up. I had been enjoying myself at lunch, but now, after my conversation with Mark, I felt like a burst balloon. I rejoined the table, but I had lost that fleeting sense of joie de vivre. It had evaporated like early-morning mist as I listened to Mark scolding me for my bad behaviour. It's not fair, I thought to myself. It's all so unfair. I felt my eyes prick as I suppressed the tears. I picked up a bottle of wine, topped my wine glass up to the brim and took a large mouthful.

'Is everything all right, darling?' Uma had her arm around my shoulders and I came to with a jolt. I had been deep in thought. 'You've been rather quiet since Mark called. Are you OK?'

'Yes, I'm fine. It's just that he called to tell me he was about to go into theatre to have an operation – to remove that tumour.' I had mentioned to Uma that Mark wasn't well. 'I didn't know anything about it until he called, but I feel bad for not being with him – not that I could be.'

'Well, I think it's much better that you're here. You have no life with Mark, Carolyn. You hate it in Bath and you hardly ever get to see him. You need to see your friends or you'll turn into a hermit – and that's not you.'

'It's been a lovely afternoon, Uma. Thank you. You and Antony have been so kind.'

It was true. I had spent many Sunday afternoons with them. I had eaten their food and drunk their wine. They had been a lifeline for me. I'd been feeling closer and closer to the edge. But the edge of what? The edge of life or death? No, I felt I was teetering on the edge of reason. I had always thought that whatever happened, however much I lost, nobody could steal my mind. Now, however, I wasn't sure. I felt I was losing my grip on everything – and it frightened me.

Mark's operation was a success. I thanked my lucky stars. I didn't believe in God, but every day now, under my breath, I would say a little prayer to anybody or anything that might be listening.

'Please let everything be OK.'

When I spoke to Mark, a couple of days after the surgery, I was beside myself with worry and couldn't wait to see him.

'I need to see you,' I told him. 'Surely they've got to let me come and see you.'

'They won't allow it, baby. You haven't signed the Official Secrets Act. And they're worried sick I'm going to start spouting state secrets now. They think this will destroy us, but don't worry, I'll figure something out. I need to see you too. I'll call you again when I've got a plan.'

A few days later, Mark called sounding excited.

'Darling, I've worked out a way for us to see each other. Come to the hospital tonight at half-past six. Park in the car park near the neurology unit and text me when you get there.'

At six-thirty I was driving around Frenchay Hospital trying to find the right car park. I felt stressed. The hospital had seen better days. Like me, it looked careworn and tired. At last, I found what I thought was the right place. I drove in, parked the car and texted Mark. I sat there, motionless, not knowing what to do. The minutes ticked by. Then I thought I saw him. Two men were walking towards me. It was Mark with James Miller.

When they got to the car, Mark opened the passenger door and climbed in. James walked back towards the hospital buildings. I was so relieved to see Mark at last. His head was heavily but expertly bandaged and some sort of tube appeared to be coming out of the side of his head. I felt my emotions spinning out of control.

'Bubba, I'm so pleased to see you. I can't tell you how worried I've been. But surely you shouldn't be walking about in the cold. And what's that?' I was pointing at the tube.

'I've got a hell of a headache, Bubba. You're right, I shouldn't be out in the cold. That's a drain. They have to drain the fluid off my brain.'

'And how long are you going to be here?'

'Fuck knows. They like it because they've pretty well got me under lock and key here. I've managed to escape for a few minutes, but all hell will break loose if they find out. I had to get James to come and help me.'

'Darling, I just want everything to be OK. I don't know if I can take much more of this.'

'You know one of the things I love about you is your stiff upper lip. You're old school, darling. I love that about you. Keep strong. It will all be OK, you'll see. You've just got to keep your head for a bit longer.'

'I'm doing my best, but it's such a strain, and I'm so lonely. I have no life, Bubba. I've always been an optimist, but recently I have been feeling hopeless. When will it ever end?'

It was two weeks before I was able to see Mark again. Once more I found myself waiting for him in the hospital car park and just as before, he emerged out of the gloom, walking from the neurology unit towards the car park. He climbed into the passenger seat of my car. Although his head was still heavily bandaged, he was showing signs of recovery.

'Baby, kiss me will you?' He was undoing his flies.

'A blow job? In a hospital car park? There are cameras everywhere, are you mad?'

'Go on baby, I need you to.'

'Put it away.'

'Shit, we haven't been together for ages and now you're refusing me!'

'I'm not doing anything in a hospital car park – but I'm pleased to see that you're feeling better. It's about time you came home and we spent our first night together.'

'I know, sweetie. Maybe at Christmas. It would be nice to have Christmas together.'

'I would love that.'

He kissed me, opened the car door and was gone.

I was desperate for company, but I was so frightened, both by what was happening to Mark and my own fragile emotional state that I hardly dared see anyone. In any case, the only friend I felt I wanted to see was Anne. I had tried to meet up with her a number of times since we'd returned from Cornwall, but every time I made an arrangement, I'd had to cancel it because Mark wanted me to be available.

During October, however, I did have one visitor. Christmas was on the horizon and I decided to hold out an olive branch to my sister-in-law, with whom I had had no contact since that fateful evening back in April, the weekend after I had moved into Brock Street.

Annalisa was working nearby and I decided I would text her and ask if she would like to pop in for a drink on her way home. I would have to swallow my pride, but I felt that if I didn't make a move now to try to enable the family to get together at Christmas, nobody else would, and things would just get more and more difficult. I had only seen my brother once over the summer, when we had met briefly one Saturday afternoon in Victoria Park, and I had felt the bond between us unravelling a little bit more.

Annalisa accepted my invitation, and when the doorbell rang that evening, I put on my broadest smile as I went to greet her. Annalisa looked straight at me and didn't even say hello before asking for a visitor's parking permit, which I didn't have. I told her she'd have to buy a ticket from the machine, but she said she had no change. I was already beginning to feel riled, but told myself to keep calm.

'I've got some. Just hang on a minute.'

I fetched my purse, went over to the parking meter and purchased a ticket.

Back inside the house, I offered my sister-in-law a drink.

'Would you like a glass of Prosecco – I'm opening a bottle?'

'Thanks, that would be nice.'

'With some Chambord?'

She declined, but I added some to mine as I prepared the two drinks, before leading the way upstairs to the drawing room. The tension was palpable.

'So, how are you?' I enquired as we sat down on the velvet sofas, the colour perfectly echoing the hue of the raspberry liqueur in my glass. Annalisa started to tell me how wonderful life was for her family. Her younger daughter had graduated in the summer, so that had been cause for celebration, and her elder daughter had got top marks for her Masters dissertation, so that was another celebration.

'You know Nick's started a new job, don't you? That's going really well too. Yes, everything's great. You've missed out on so much!'

'Annalisa, I hope we can resume some sort of a relationship,' I responded. 'I'd like us to at least be able to get together as a family at Christmas, but I want you to know how upset I was over your behaviour the last time I saw you.'

'You mean that evening when nobody showed up?'

I felt my hackles rise.

'I seem to remember there were twelve of us here.'

'*He* never showed up, did he? I knew he wouldn't.'

I tried to bite my tongue but as I listened to what she was saying I felt sparks of anger ignite and flare up in me, until I could contain myself no longer.

'Bollocks!' I exclaimed, feeling my heart thumping in my chest, fury flashing in my eyes.

Annalisa was staring at me, coldly, but she didn't raise her voice.

'You know, Carolyn, I used to like you. I used to like you a lot. Anyway, I'm a very busy person. I can't sit around here any longer.'

I was fuming. I felt the adrenalin surging through my body, but I was determined to control myself. I just hoped I could speak in a normal voice.

'Well, in that case I'm sure you won't mind showing yourself out.'

Annalisa put down her glass, got up and left the room. I stayed where I was and felt myself shaking with rage as another nail was driven into the coffin containing the few dry bones that were all that was left of my relationship with my brother and his wife.

It was only mid-November, but Christmas preparations seemed to be going on everywhere. Some people in the Circus already had their Christmas trees up. I hated the way everything happened so early now. Really, by the time Christmas came everyone was fed up with it.

It was a Saturday afternoon. My phone rang.

'Darling, get into the car and drive to that hotel in Bristol where we've met before. I'm being allowed out of hospital for a couple of hours. James will drive me over. I'll see you in an hour.'

I wanted to see Mark, but I didn't relish driving at this time. Both Bath and Bristol were heaving with Christmas shoppers and it was an hour and a half before I found myself in Bristol, sitting in the Hotel du Vin. There was no sign of Mark. I waited patiently, anxiously looking around, hoping to find his face. Eventually, he appeared. He looked ashen. His head was no longer bandaged, but his hair had been shaved above one ear and he had a large dressing over the wound. Once again, he was accompanied by James Miller. Mark asked James to get us a Coke and a glass of dry white wine and then, at last, we were alone together.

It was the first time we had been able to sit comfortably together since he had told me about his brain tumour. As I snuggled into him, I felt the tears welling up. I tried to control myself, but I started to cry.

'Baby, don't cry. Look at me, I'm fine.'

'Well, I'm not sure that you are. You don't look well. I want to speak to your consultant. And look at me, I'm not fine either.'

I was trying to suppress all the emotion that was about to boil over inside me, but I could hear the pitch of my voice rising and the pace of my speech quicken and I tried to regain control of myself.

'I've tried so hard to be strong for you, but everything is such a strain,' I sniffled. 'I just don't know what to do. I can't talk to anybody. I hardly ever see anyone because they'll see I'm not myself and their questions will just cause me even more stress. I don't know if I can cope any more. And, darling, I need money. I've been really frugal, but I'm up to my limit on everything and Christmas is coming. The bills on the house have crippled me. At this rate, I won't even be able to buy food.'

'Sweetheart, you've got to keep calm. You've seen what I've been through and the one thing I don't need just now is any added stress. It could be fatal. You know I'm doing my best for you, but it never seems to be enough. It's been impossible for me to keep my eye on things with everything that's been going on, and those cunts are watching me the whole time.'

'I know, darling. I don't mean to complain, but I just don't know what to do. Lara and Emma are coming for Christmas and I don't want them to worry. My nieces are coming over too. I need to buy presents and be able to offer everyone food and drink. They'll think it very odd if things aren't just as they have always been. We have certain rituals at Christmas. I just want everything to be normal.'

'And it will be, darling. Don't worry.'

'But I do worry,' I sobbed. The tears were streaming down my face now, 'And I worry more than anything about you.'

'Darling, I've told you before, worrying is a waste of time and energy. And I don't know why you're crying. It doesn't help me or you.'

'It's a human response.'

I felt utterly wretched. It seemed as if the whole world was tumbling down around me. Mark held my hand and looked into my eyes. As usual, I felt consoled when I was with him, but something was changing. I couldn't quite put my finger on it, but I no longer felt one hundred per cent reassured. I had lost my blind faith in him. I had always thought him so strong and capable, but now I wasn't sure. I'd been reading up on brain surgery and there were many things that concerned me – not least that Mark's personality might be affected and his mental capacity diminished. I had to be prepared for that. It worried me that he didn't seem to have a normal emotional response to events. Was that because of the surgery? His training? Or was he simply devoid of normal human emotion? I felt confused. Sometimes he seemed so cold; but then I had, on a couple of occasions, seen him in tears, and there was no doubting his feelings for me when we had first met. Uppermost in my mind now, however, was the return of my money – because as things stood, I was completely helpless.

James had returned to take Mark back to the hospital. He looked at me and I felt embarrassed because I was sure he could see I'd been crying.

'Hello,' he said in his gentle manner. 'How are you?'

'As well as can be expected – under the circumstances,' I responded, struggling to force a smile.

Then Mark and James departed, and I was left to drive back to Bath, alone.

November gave way to December and as Christmas loomed, for the first time in my life, I found myself dreading it. I had only a couple of hundred pounds' credit left and literally didn't know what I was going to do.

One morning in mid-December, I lay in the bath, fretting. I could no longer take a shower, as it was broken. Added to that, there was water leaking into the house in three places. I hated not being on top of things, but there was no way I could pay for the repairs. I already had outstanding utility bills and more would be arriving in the new year. I was on automatic pilot, washing myself as I lay there, but not really paying attention to what I was doing. Then I suddenly stopped, stock-still. What was that? Everything about me froze: my body, my expression, my thoughts. Tentatively, I felt again, and then more firmly. There was no mistaking it: there was a lump in my breast.

I felt sick. My mother had had breast cancer and my father had died of prostate cancer. Now it was my turn. It was the one thing that I had always dreaded. How was I going to cope with this, on top of everything else? I climbed gingerly out of the bath, as if anything other than the most delicate movement would cause me to shatter, but I could feel myself quaking. I had to get to a doctor, but I hadn't registered with one in Bath. Never mind, I thought – I could register now and get an emergency appointment.

I pulled on my dressing gown and went downstairs to the study. Behind the closed shutters, I opened my laptop and looked up the nearest surgery to the house. There was one just around the corner; I picked up my mobile and keyed in the number.

I spoke to a receptionist who explained that if I needed to see a doctor urgently, I would have to go to a walk-in centre. When I got to the walk-in centre I waited for two hours before being told that there were only nurses available and that I should have gone to see my GP! By now, I was on the verge of hysteria, and the nurse must have sensed something because she then said she would see if she could find a doctor.

My emotions were in turmoil. One minute, I felt numb, the next, I thought I would pass out. I was barely coping, and it wasn't just the physical symptoms – I felt as if I was going mad. This couldn't be happening. Surely I was going to wake up soon and find that all the events of the past few months had just been a bad dream? Please let me wake up, I thought. Suddenly, I was aware of the nurse standing beside me, talking.

'Sorry, what did you say?' I asked.

'You're in luck. The doctor's still here and can see you. Come with me.'

I was shown into a consulting room where a female doctor was sitting at a desk. She looked friendly as she greeted me and asked me to take a seat. After examining me, she said that under the circumstances she would refer me to the hospital for tests. She explained that I should be seen within two weeks, but that with Christmas and the New Year holidays it might take a bit longer.

'How is your health generally?' she enquired.

'Normally I'm pretty fit, but I haven't been feeling well for some time now. My partner's been very ill and I haven't been able to see him much. He had a brain tumour. It's been operated on now, but I think it's all got too much for me. I'm usually very strong in a crisis, but this is just the last straw.'

The doctor was looking at the form I had filled in when I arrived. 'I see you're drinking quite a bit and you smoke.'

'I know. It's only been like this over the past few months. The drinking helps to numb my senses and the smoking makes me feel closer to my partner – he's a chain smoker. It's horrible, I know, but that's just how it is at the moment. It makes me feel closer to him.'

'Do you have friends in Bath?'

'No.'

'What about family? Do you have any family nearby who could help you?'

'No. My brother's not far away, but I've fallen out with him and his wife, so I can't talk to them. My daughters are in London and I don't want to worry them. They're worried enough as it is.' Tears were now streaming down my face as I spoke.

'You poor thing.' The doctor seemed genuinely concerned. 'You really must try to get some help. Register with a doctor today and make an appointment. Tell the doctor you've been here. I'll get you a referral to the hospital to get this lump checked out, but you should explain to your doctor exactly how you're feeling. You need help.'

'Thank you so much. I haven't been able to talk to anybody. It's such a relief just to be able to let it all out for a moment.'

'I know. Now, you take care of yourself. Good luck.'

I felt profoundly grateful to the doctor for her kindness and compassion. I took her advice, and on my way back to Brock Street I registered at my local surgery and made an appointment to see a doctor.

The next couple of weeks, until I got a diagnosis, were going to seem like an eternity. That evening, when Mark called, I told him what had happened.

'Darling, it's nothing to worry about. Trust me, for a woman of your age in good health the chances are that it will be nothing.'

'Well, I do worry. My mother had breast cancer. I saw her go through it. She had a mastectomy. It was awful for her.' I didn't like Mark's response; he showed no compassion at all. All I wanted from him was a bit of sympathy, but he didn't offer any. He didn't seem remotely interested; on the contrary, he had news of his own.

'I'm not in Bristol any more, Bubba. I'm in London – at the Royal Free. I wanted a second opinion about having this other operation to remove air from my brain. Anyway, the consultant here agrees that it's necessary. I'm having the operation tonight. And you think you've got problems!'

Christmas 2012 was the worst of my life. I had to throw most of my decorations away because I'd stored them in the cellar and, although I'd put the boxes on racks off the floor, the damp had got to them, so when I opened them up I found nearly everything mouldy and ruined. The week before Christmas I still had no tree. I'd looked at some, but they were so expensive. Plus, most of my lights didn't work any more, as the damp cellar had ruined them too, and I couldn't justify spending money on a tree *and* new decorations. I'd think of something to say to the girls about that, but what about the food?

Then one afternoon, out of the blue, I received a phone call from James Miller. He told me that Mark had asked him to help me with the Christmas shopping and said he could take me to Waitrose that evening. I didn't know what to think.

'Well, yes, I do need food and drink, but I can't pay for it.'

'Don't worry about that. Mark's asked me to take care of it. And he says you need a tree.'

'Well, yes, that would be nice.'

'Perhaps we could go out tomorrow and get one. There's a place not far from you that has some nice ones.'

'I've been to have a look – but they're very expensive.'

'We'll talk about it later. I'll come and pick you up and take you to Waitrose. I'll be there about six-thirty. It should be reasonably quiet then.'

'Thank you.'

It was good to see James. I hardly knew him, but I liked his quietly spoken, calm manner. I felt rather self-conscious shopping with a near stranger, but I knew exactly what I needed and the trolley was soon full. James paid the bill and took me back to Brock Street where he helped me put everything away. Then he handed me a couple of hundred pounds, telling me that it was from Mark.

The following day, he called me to ask if I would like to go and choose a tree, but I felt this was too much of an imposition. It was only days before Christmas now and I was sure there wouldn't be any decent trees left anyway. And the more I thought about it, the less I wanted one. I was finding it difficult to keep up this charade of normality.

'Really, it doesn't matter about the tree,' I told him. 'I'll do without. To be quite honest, I've got more important things to worry about, and I'm sure you've got better things to do, but thank you anyway.'

I hung up.

A couple of hours later, my phone rang. It was James again.

'I hope you're at home. I'm outside the door. I've got you a tree – it's a nice one.'

'You really shouldn't have. I'm sorry I was a bit short with you on the phone earlier. I was sure the last thing you would want to do would be to come all the way down here.'

I went down and opened the front door, and James brought the tree in. He carried it up to the drawing room and put it up, ready for me to decorate it. I suggested we went down the road for a coffee. It was lovely to have some company and at least James knew something about Mark.

As we sat in the Chandos Deli drinking coffee, I felt the sudden urge to tell James what had happened and how I had lent Mark my money. I started talking, even giving an indication of the amount of money involved, but James didn't comment, and I ended up feeling disloyal to Mark for having mentioned it. I realised that the strain I was under was making me careless and made a mental note to be more cautious in future.

The following day, Lara and Emma arrived for Christmas. It was so lovely to see them, but I struggled to keep things going and they could sense something was amiss. On Christmas Eve they appeared in the drawing room dressed up for dinner, as was the custom, but I was still wearing my jeans.

'I'm sorry,' I said. 'I hope you don't mind. I'm just so slow at things at the moment. I can't seem to get organised. I'll dress up tomorrow.'

It was the first week of 2013 and as I left the Bath Royal United Hospital I felt elated. I had just been told that the lump in my breast wasn't cancer. Over the past few months, I had felt myself slipping further and further into a deep depression, but this feeling of near euphoria at being told that I didn't have cancer made me realise that, contrary to what I had been thinking over the past few weeks, I still valued my life.

I hadn't been sleeping properly for nine months now, and my insomnia had been getting worse. I would turn the radio on and off through the interminable silent nights, just to hear the sound of a human voice. Radio 4 and the World Service were the only company I dared keep. I was being troubled by nightmares and horrible recurring visions too. I often found myself deep in the ocean. I needed to breathe, but I was so far down. The water was clear and blue and I could see a shimmering disc of light, high above me where the sun hit the surface of the sea. I felt tired, and although I tried to swim, my legs wouldn't kick and I knew I was going to drown. Then I would wake up, gasping for air, hardly able to breathe.

At other times I would lie in bed, fully conscious. I could feel my heart racing and there was a terrible weight pressing down on my chest. I felt as though I was being crushed and suffocated. As the weight bore down upon me from above, an equally powerful force pulled at me from below and I felt sure I would be sucked through the mattress into the fathomless void beneath it. It was terrifying. I would reach out to turn on the light and put the radio on and lie there until my heart stopped racing and I could breathe again. If I was lucky enough to drift off to sleep, I was often woken again by a ghastly vision of Munch's *Scream*, metamorphosing into the figure of Death, coming to get me.

I was having suicidal thoughts and spent hours on the internet, obsessively working out how best to do it. After two particularly terrifying nights, although I hardly ever went to the doctor, I made an appointment with my GP and told him what had been happening.

'What you've just described to me are typical symptoms of a panic attack,' the doctor replied. 'I see you came to see us last month. You said you were depressed. Did the counselling service contact you?'

'Yes, but I decided against counselling. Please could you just listen to my heart and check my lungs? I'm sure there's something wrong. I'm not someone to make a fuss about nothing.'

The doctor listened to my chest and took my blood pressure.

'There's absolutely nothing wrong with your heart or your lungs,' he reassured me. 'Everything's quite normal. Are you sure you don't want to reconsider having some counselling?'

'Quite sure, thank you,' I replied.

I walked the short distance back to the house with my head bowed low. I didn't want to be seen and was now barely recognisable as the smiling woman who used to stride confidently about

Tetbury with her head held high. The doctor's words whirled through my head. 'Everything's quite normal'? He didn't know what he was talking about. Absolutely nothing in my life was normal any more.

The emotions I experienced on learning that I didn't have a tumour in my breast lifted me out of my depression just enough for me to stir myself into action. I had to get out of Bath. I couldn't bear living in Brock Street any more. I knew it would be the death of me, literally, if I stayed there any longer – but where could I go? I wracked my brain and eventually an idea began to take shape. I had friends who divided their time between Australia and the UK. They had a flat back in Buckinghamshire, near where I used to live, and it occurred to me that it might just be empty.

So a year to the day since my first encounter with Mark, I emailed them, asking for help. My luck was in and I soon received a reply telling me that the flat was free for me to use until the end of April. Mark had told me that he was selling the house in Brock Street and that the completion of the sale would take place on 3 April, so if I could just keep going, financially, until then, and Mark repaid me what he owed me, as he promised he would, everything should be resolved. I felt hugely relieved with a renewed sense of purpose, and I immediately phoned to arrange for my few remaining belongings to be taken into storage. The earliest the removal men could come was 25 January, so that was the day that I resolved to leave Bath for good.

Meanwhile, the news from Mark was not good. He had had the operation to remove air from his brain, but he told me that he had then been taken to the MI6 building where, he said, he was being forcibly held. He told me that he was being coerced back into operation and was expected to resume flying.

'They just want to blow my fucking brains out. Either that or they want me killed in action. They're forcing me back to Syria.'

I knew that there was nothing I could do to influence what was happening to Mark. Now I had to concentrate all my efforts on self-preservation, and so I told Mark that I would be leaving Brock Street.

'And how do you think that's going to help? You're crazy!' The anger flared up in his voice. 'You just get these ideas into your head and go off on one. Why didn't you discuss this with me?'

'There's nothing to discuss. I've made up my mind. It's all arranged. I move out on Friday.'

Moving day – 25 January 2013 – was cold and grey. It even started to snow, but it was a slushy, dirty brown, not crisp and white. The men arrived to pack my few boxes into a container, and Mark was on the phone constantly.

'Are they there? How long's it going to take? Honestly, baby, I don't know why you're doing this – and I hope they don't take all day over it. I don't want people knowing our business. It's dangerous. Why you have to behave like this is beyond me. You're so fucking headstrong.'

After a couple of hours, the men had finished. I went to get my car and pack up the few things I was taking with me. I couldn't wait to get out, and I felt the chains of responsibility slip off my shoulders as I closed the door on 1 Brock Street for the last time. At last, I had taken back a bit of control and drawn a line under life in the Circus.

At this stage in the relationship Mark continues to blow hot and cold, all designed to make me feel guilty and ashamed of my own behaviour (going on holiday, having lunch with friends), when he is suffering and so ill. I remember thinking that in all our sexual encounters (except the first), which were very few, the sex was rushed and perfunctory, and I can see that he was only ever after some quick self-gratification. I now thank my lucky stars that they were so few. When I expressed my concern to him, about our lack of intimacy, he said that he always had to be battle-ready, and couldn't risk being softened by lovemaking. He wanted to wait until he was free of MI6 and then do everything properly – 'with a hundred candles' and 'all the time in the world'. I now realise that he quite simply got bored with me. I suspect his comment about needing to 'come three times a day' may be true, and I believe he found other willing and equally unsuspecting women to help satisfy that need. Promiscuity is another hallmark of psychopaths.

I don't know whose brain scans he showed me, but I doubt they were his, and I later discovered that he was never a patient at Frenchay Hospital, although the gash on his head was genuine. The lengths Mark went to with the bandaged head and the clandestine meetings at the hospital were pure theatre, and to me they were utterly convincing. Knowing what I now know, I suspect that his bandages were applied expertly by a doctor at the hospital that I know he was in a relationship with and was also fleecing for money. I was totally convinced that he had undergone brain surgery, and I was worried sick on his account. His seemingly poor state of health also meant that I didn't feel I could press him about the return of my money; and my belief that he had had a brain tumour and had undergone brain surgery not only explained away any odd behaviour during the whole of our relationship, but also the callousness and cruelty he exhibited towards the end.

8

FALLING

The ice of self-command which had latterly gathered over her was broken, and the currents burst forth again, and overwhelmed her. A darkness came into her eyes and she fell.

Thomas Hardy, *Far from the Madding Crowd*

I was back living in Amersham, but I felt I was in a no-man's land. Everything seemed wrong and I avoided going anywhere near my old house. I confided in a couple of close friends, telling them that I had lent Mark all my money and about his claim to be working for MI6, his brain tumour and surgery. I think I was probably having some doubts about his integrity and was looking for reassurance, and although they were amazed at my story, the fact that Mark was in touch with me daily, made them think – as I'd hoped – that he was honourable, and would return my money. Looking back on this now, I have to say that I think there is a very strong desire in all of us to believe what we want to believe, and when hope is all we have left we cling on to it for dear life.

I was being hounded by the utility companies for payment of the outstanding bills on Brock Street, and I owed over £10,000 on my credit card and overdraft, so now I cashed in my small pension in order to pay off some of the debts and to keep going.

I was clinging to the hope that the sale of Brock Street would go through as planned on 3 April, and that by my birthday, Mark would have paid me back and I would be able to start looking for my own house to buy. I didn't dare raise my hopes too much, however, because the latest news from him was alarming. He had been injured again in action in Syria. He told me he had been shot and sustained very heavy blood loss and that he'd had to have a number of blood transfusions. He was recovering in a military hospital in Athens but confided in me that he no longer trusted the British authorities. On the night of 2 April, I was like a live wire as I lay in bed thinking that this time tomorrow all my worries could be over. I couldn't sleep and lay awake daydreaming. I closed my eyes and imagined myself in a new home of my own, with my daughters and friends around me. If only, I thought – telling myself that I would never take anything for granted again.

The following day, I was like a cat on hot bricks. I couldn't settle to anything and every hour or so I checked my bank balance. By the end of that day, I felt sick to the core. Mark hadn't called, I hadn't been able to get through to him and not one penny had been added to my account. When I retired to bed late that night, I was wrecked – and still no call from Mark. I lay there in the deafening silence, eyes wide open, staring into the void once more.

The next morning, I heard the demanding ringtone on my phone that meant Mark was on the line. I picked up. I could feel the adrenalin rush in my body and my own voice sounded strange to me, high-pitched and faltering, verging on hysteria.

'Where's my money? Nothing went into my account yesterday, and you didn't even call me.'

'Darling, I've told you, everything will be sorted out. It's just a minor hiccup.'

I felt tears pricking at the back of my eyes as my voice crackled with anger.

'You told me you had a cash-flow problem. You told me you would repay the loan in just a few weeks. That was over a year ago. Then you assured me it would all be repaid on 3 April, when Brock Street was sold. That was yesterday, and still nothing. I just don't know what to believe. My life has been hell for the past year, and you don't even seem to care.'

'Darling, calm down. If you knew what I have had to do to try to organise things so that we can have a future together you wouldn't talk like this. You think you've had it bad? It's nothing compared with what I have been through. We've discussed all this before. I told you right at the beginning I needed to be able to rely on you. You knew it was going to be tough, but you gave me your word. Now I've got problems with my lawyers. They tell me I owe them a shedload of money and I disagree. They're a bunch of fucking thieves. They are holding on to the proceeds of the sale of Brock Street while we sort it out – and it *will* be sorted out.'

'That makes absolutely no sense at all. That wouldn't be legal – unless you owe them millions. Sometimes I think you have no intention of repaying what you owe me – and I want my bank balance restored to what it was when I met you. I've used up every last penny, cashed in my pension and am still up to my eyes in your debts. I don't know how you can say you love me and treat me like this.'

'Darling, do you realise how insulting that is? We're in this together. You're being hysterical. If I had just been after your money, I would have disappeared a long time ago. Use that beautiful brain of yours. Think about it. You're the one who's talking nonsense! Anyway, this discussion is just a waste of time and energy. Let's just stop it here and now. I've got to call my lawyers now and try to sort this mess out. It's a fucking nightmare. I'll speak to you again later.'

No money materialised, and at the end of April 2013, after another solitary birthday, I moved out of the flat and went to stay with a succession of friends, before settling with my friend Angela for a few weeks. Time had no meaning for me now. Sometimes the days dragged by, but I lost almost all sense of the passing of time, feeling that I was just floating in limbo, my whole life like flotsam and jetsam on an unpredictable sea. I had had virtually no control over my life for over a year now; there seemed to be nothing I could do to influence events and with this feeling of disempowerment came another feeling that was even more terrifying. I felt as though the whole of my being was gradually being erased, as though my very essence was evaporating. I had no sense of the future or of who I now was. I could remember what I used to be like, but that independent, happy person had been all but obliterated by the strain of keeping my word to Mark, and everything that went with it. All that remained of my former self was the very powerful love I felt for my daughters. That was the only thing that kept me going. 'The big picture' was a blur. I could no longer envisage a future with Mark and, looking back, I know that the only reason I stayed in touch with him at all was to get him to repay what he owed me.

It was now over four months since I had last seen him and the eighteen months that I had promised to wait for him would soon be up. I still felt some obligation to keep that promise, but I know that if I'd had my financial independence I would have bought myself a house long before then. I continued to hope against hope that he would repay me the money he had borrowed; then I could get my life back on track. I had to keep on hoping. But if he failed to do that – and he had failed to deliver on just about every promise he had made – what then? I had often wondered how people ended up on the streets, homeless. Was that what was going to happen to me? Carolyn, the bag lady? I couldn't bear to think about it.

I'll cross that bridge when I get to it, I thought to myself, but even the thought of it, passing fleetingly through my mind, made me sick to the core with fear and dread. I just didn't know what to do.

Ever since I had returned to Buckinghamshire I had been in close proximity to my old home, my parents' house and the house I had been brought up in as a child. Often, as I lay awake in bed through the long, lonely nights I would revisit chapters of my past life. Sometimes whole decades would flash through my mind and I wondered if I was about to die. That was how it felt; a high-speed train, pulling all the carriages of the various land-marks in my life came thundering through my consciousness, belting past the platform of my memory. I feared seeing the last carriage disappearing into the distance, for when that happened, I was sure I would die.

I continued to have panic attacks at night, but each morning, somehow, I was still there, as dawn broke and daylight slowly filtered into my room. I would hear the dawn chorus starting up outside, and then the drone of traffic and the clank and rumble of the Metropolitan and Chiltern Line trains, as everyone else went about their daily routine as usual. I felt a tremendous sense of disconnect from everything and everyone. It was, indeed, as though the rest of the world, all 7 billion people, were buzzing around, milling about, getting on with their lives, and I was completely isolated and on my own. I felt utterly cast out.

Every day Mark would phone me. He told me that he had escaped from hospital and the British authorities and was now in Italy, that he hoped to be able to do a deal with the Italian govern-ment and that it would only be a matter of time before we were together again. He told me he was looking at flights and that I must come out to be with him – we could meet in Spain; in Barcelona perhaps, or Alicante, or Italy somewhere, or maybe France? Nice would be good. What about that? He would book the tickets right away. But every day the tickets failed to appear, until I couldn't stand it any longer. Mark just seemed incapable of organising anything any more and not only did that terrify me, it irritated me too. One day I snapped back at him.

'You've been telling me the same thing for days now. Nice, you say? Well, I can see there's a flight to Nice on Wednesday that would suit me. I think I could get a lift to the airport. Why don't I just book it myself? All this procrastination is doing my head in.'

'That'd be great if you can do that, darling.'

'And you're sure you can get to Nice on Wednesday? I'm talking about the fourteenth, the day after tomorrow.'

'Yes, baby, it'll be great. Book it. I can't wait to see you. I've missed you so much.'

I booked my ticket, despite the fact that, once again, I was close to my credit limit. As I packed my case, I felt none of the excitement that I had experienced when I had first met Mark and we had talked about all the places that we would visit together. I felt nervous about seeing him after all this time, but also anticipated the sense of relief that I hoped I would feel when we finally met – if he showed up. I knew what he was like, keeping people waiting for hours on end and then perhaps only turning up for five minutes, juggling his mobile phones and giving nobody more than a brief sound bite and a few hurried instructions. I had no confidence that he wouldn't do the same to me now, even though it was now six months since we had last seen one another.

On 14 May, Anne picked me up and drove me to Luton Airport.

'Just get your money back,' she said as she dropped me off. 'That's the most important thing. Even if you only get half of it, at least you can get your life going again. Good luck.'

She gave me a big hug.

'Thanks, Anne.'

I smiled weakly, then turned, pulled myself together and strode purposefully towards the terminal building.

I hate airports. To me, they feel like no-man's-land. Everyone is in transit, either leaving to go or having just arrived from somewhere else, not belonging anywhere yet. I am not a natural traveller and find the whole business stressful.

Now, as I found myself in the easyJet queue, I wondered what had happened to all those promises of first-class travel and private jets? The queue today – just one long one for half a dozen flights – was worse than I ever remembered. What the hell was going on? The check-in hall was like a cattle market, as hundreds of passengers were all herded and corralled into a zigzag maze of barrier tape, shuffling along like zombies.

Thank God I don't have to do anything once I get there, I thought. At least Mark should take care of everything then.

I wondered if he would still find me attractive – and me him. Would he be sympathetic and understand how the events of the past year had taken their toll on me? But surely he must have suffered the same? I wondered how he would look? He had looked dreadful the last time I had seen him, and he had been through the gates of hell since then, too.

The flight to Nice was uneventful and before I stepped out into the arrivals hall, I went to the Ladies, cleaned my teeth, touched up my make-up and brushed my hair. Despite everything, I wanted to look just as good as I possibly could when I met Mark again. As I passed through the doors into arrivals, I drew my mouth into a smile and tried to hold my head high.

I felt as though I had walked into an ants' nest. People were rushing this way and that in a seemingly haphazard and random way. I stood still, looking around at the sea of faces, trying to find the one I wanted. It would be easier for him to find me. He must be there somewhere. Where was he? Time seemed to stand still. It must only have been a few seconds, but I felt as though the world was passing by in slow motion, and that I had been standing there for aeons. Again, my eyes scanned the sea of faces before me. There was no sign of him. I couldn't believe it. He simply wasn't there.

Suddenly, a blinding flash of light jolted me out of my stupor. The Cannes film festival was on and some celebrity or other had just arrived and was being pursued by paparazzi. Cameras flashed through the arrivals hall. My knees began to buckle. I felt dizzy. I had to try to find a seat and sit down, otherwise I was sure I was going to pass out.

Someone stood up and I dropped into the empty seat – a cut of raw meat landing on the butcher's block. I felt barely alive and so disconnected from this tide of humanity that I didn't know what to do. I got out my mobile phone to see a string of short messages from Mark.

14:43   Ibis promenade des anglais

         359 promenade des anglais 06200 nice

         0033493833030

         Love you

         Faster I can't drive!

I tried to call him but there was no reply.

15:57   Where are you? Don't understand messages.

         I cannot pay for hotel – or even taxi.

         Where are you?

         I am seriously pissed off

Suddenly, my phone rang. Thank God! It was Mark.

'Baby, I'm sorry, I'm doing my best to get there. Go to the hotel. I'll meet you there.'

'I can't believe you're not here. After everything we've been through! I don't have any money. I thought you were going to be here and take care of things.'

'How much do you have?'

'Fifty euros.'

'That will be enough. Take a taxi. I'll see you there.'

'I want the hotel paid for – up front.'

'OK, darling, calm down. Call me when you get there.'

I felt sick. It was as if I was on a fairground ride that was spinning me around. I wanted to get off, but the ride kept going, faster and faster, spinning out of control while the organ grinder played his sinister tune. I approached the taxi rank and gave the hotel address to a driver. Another flurry of text messages rattled in like machine-gun fire.

16:43 Hotel is paid

Thank God for that.

When will you arrive?

What name?

Caroline Woods

It's Carolyn not Caroline, I thought. Why can't he even get my name right?

I'll go there

> I do love you

I was so upset, I couldn't return the sentiment.

> **If you're not there tomorrow I'm going back**

> Understood

> I will be

> Before breakfast

> **I've heard it all before**

> **I'm sick of it**

The taxi stopped at the bottom of an escalator by the station. At the top I could see the sign for the Ibis hotel. I stepped on to the moving staircase and was assaulted by the stench of stale urine as I was carried up to the foyer. Hardly the stairway to heaven, I thought. At the reception desk I gave my name, told the receptionist that I had a reservation and that the room had been paid for. I didn't like the hotel one bit, but I was exhausted and felt sick and needed to lie down. I certainly couldn't start trying to find somewhere else. I waited for the key.

'There is no reservation,' the receptionist said. 'Someone called. We have your name but there is no room.'

I couldn't understand what was happening. But I had to keep calm. I would phone Mark. Please let him answer the phone. When he picked up I couldn't contain myself.

'I've just got to the hotel. I spent twenty-five euros on a taxi. Now they tell me there is no reservation, and they have no spare rooms. What the hell is going on?'

'Let me speak to them, baby. Give them your phone.' I handed my phone to the receptionist.

I heard her telling Mark that there were no rooms. It was the Cannes film festival and everywhere was booked solid. Then she handed me back my phone.

'I told him I will try to find you a room at one of our other hotels, but I don't know if I can find anything. Nearly everything is booked up this week.'

'Thank you.' I smiled, but my smile felt as thin and ghostly as my washed-out, faded sense of self.

Mark was on the phone again. 'What are they doing? Is it all sorted?'

'They're working on it, but I now have only twenty euros left.'

'Don't worry about it, baby. It'll be fine.'

'I want the hotel paid for in advance.'

'OK. Let me talk to that cunt.'

I winced. Why did he have to be so foul-mouthed all the time? I offered my phone to the receptionist once more and heard her explaining to Mark that she had found a room in a sister hotel in Nice, but it was a little more expensive.

'OK, *oui, oui, d'accord.*'

She handed the phone back to me again.

'It's all arranged,' she told me. 'You will stay at the Mercure hotel. Look, I show you on the map.'

I looked. The hotel was only a few blocks away. Normally, I would have walked it, but just now, and with my suitcase, I didn't have the energy.

'I need a taxi, but I only have twenty euros,' I explained.

'I'll see what I can do. That should be enough. If you want to take a seat, I'll tell you when the taxi is here.'

I sat down and thought of my niece, Natasha, who as a little girl had gone into a piano exam to find that she did not understand anything the examiner was saying to her.

'I sat there and didn't know what to do,' she had explained to me. 'It was scary, but I just said to myself it's not life-threatening.'

The trouble was that everything now seemed life-threatening to me, and the more I thought about it, the more I thought what a wonderful release death would be. A voice drilled down into my consciousness as I was jolted out of my reverie.

'Madame, your taxi.'

'*Merci.*'

I went to the door and descended the escalator, my senses once again assaulted by the foul stench of stale urine. I explained to the taxi driver where I wanted to go, showing him on the map that I still held in my left hand, and told him that I only had 20 euros. Then I climbed into the back of the taxi. A text message pinged in.

17:52 Any luck?

Will let you know when I get there. Nightmare

OK

18:04 Update ???

Still in taxi

18:05 ??

18:06 ??

The question marks ricocheted in like flak. A brief respite, and then another flurry.

18:16 ???

Now the taxi driver seemed to be going in the wrong direction. I challenged him.

'There are roadworks,' he told me. 'If we go the direct route it will take us longer. I know a way around it.'

I was on my guard and frightened. I seemed to be in a car with the taxi driver from hell. I gave in and responded to Mark's continuing volley of question marks.

> **18:17** **This is a bloody nightmare. Still in taxi going all round the bloody houses. I feel sick and unhappy**

> **18:20** Fuck

> **I can't live this sort of life. I hate it**

> **We are back at the fucking station**

> **Back where we started**

I was beginning to feel hysterical. Fear was bubbling up inside me. I had to try to keep it under control or it would consume me. Mark was still texting.

> **18:24** What was easy is now complicated

> Call

I tried calling but we were now stuck in traffic in a tunnel, and my phone wouldn't work. I felt cut off from everything. Twenty minutes later, we arrived at the hotel. Every nerve in my body was jangling and my mind was fizzing. A journey which would normally have taken me about ten minutes on foot had taken nearly an hour by car. I was sure the taxi driver had deliberately tried to scare me. I found him menacing. Under normal circumstances I would have thought that things could get no worse and my natural optimism would have got me through, but now I felt devoid of hope. The one thing I had learned over the past year was that however bad things were they could *always* get worse. I climbed out of the taxi and handed my last 20 euros to the driver. Of course, that was what he'd been doing – driving me around until the meter clocked up 20 euros! I braced myself for whatever else was about to happen and entered the hotel lobby.

I stopped briefly to take in the hotel and its surroundings. It was on the sea front, which I liked. There were no foul smells and the whole place was definitely a good few steps up from the previous one. There was an air of calm in the foyer and I introduced myself to the receptionist.

'Ah yes, Ms Woods. We will need your credit card to guarantee the reservation.'

'I thought it was all paid for. That's what I was told.'

'I'm sorry, Madame, but no. There was a problem with the credit card. I cannot let you have the room until we have a guarantee.'

'Excuse me one moment. I have to make a phone call.'

I tried to call Mark, but I couldn't get through, so started texting instead. Fuck!

18:53   Problem with your credit card. I will call you now

Five minutes later a reply:

18:58   Send me by text their email address.

Tell them I will email them another card

I told the receptionist that I was sorting out the problem with the credit card and texted Mark the hotel's email address.

19:00 Perfect

I had no time or energy for pleasantries any more. I sat down opposite the reception desk and continued texting.

What a palaver

Tell me about it

All because you don't have 229 euros

Due to me

His short, sharp messages thudded in like bullets. Occasionally, I fired one back.

19:01 Precisely

All my fault

Now I have to call the guy who sorted the card

Will text soon

Sorry

Again

19:02   I will wait and hope I get the room. I have no credit
             on my card. No credit rating. Just debts. Interest
             accruing all the time

19:05   I know

             Please let me get on and sort card

Half an hour of silence passed before I sent him my own weak
volley of machine-gun question marks.

19:35   ??? I am done in

The seconds of the next ten minutes ticked by in my head as
though the weight on a metronome had been moved to the very
tip of an impossibly long pendulum. Ten minutes took what
seemed like ten hours to tick by, and still there was no response.

19:45   Please call

My voice sounded tiny inside my own head as I tapped out
another message – a tiny, mewling cry for help:

             You cannot leave me like this

I sat motionless in the hotel lobby. It took intense concentration
and the last few scrapings of my energy reserves to even remain
upright. I felt a desperate need to lie down. Another half hour
passed before my phone sprang into life again.

20:20   Its sorted in 1

Then the hotel receptionist was smiling at me.

'Madame? Your key. Room 203. Take the lift to the second floor and you will find the room along the corridor to your left.'

'Thank you.' I held back the tears as I took the key and made my way to the lift. I had been waiting in the hotel foyer for one and a half hours. I had tried to hold on to my dignity, but I felt acutely embarrassed.

I drifted in and out of consciousness all night long. A couple of times I got up and went to the bathroom. I felt sick and lay down on the bathroom floor. I was sure I was going to throw up. I tasted the bile rising up in my throat and then subsiding again. I hardly dared move, but eventually, I crawled back to bed where I lay still, pale and ghostly under the white sheet, like a corpse in a mortuary. Finally, I drifted into a fitful sleep, but awoke the following morning exhausted. It was nearly half-past seven. I had to decide what to do. I wanted to call Mark, but my phone bill was already going to be astronomical, so I texted him instead.

15th May 2013

> **07:24** Morning. Eta? I am trying to decide what to do. I haven't been very well

I waited twenty minutes before receiving a response. I had been hoping for some sympathy, some kind words and reassurance, but I hoped in vain. His message to me was hard and cold.

> If you did what I do you would not be ill

> Carry on feeling sorry for yourself

> It's a massive over-reaction

The only message I needed today was hello bubba, hope you're ok.

But I had no time for pleasantries. My sense of self-preservation was all that was keeping me going. I was trying to focus, but I felt overwhelmed by sadness and fear. My hand was shaking as I texted back.

I would never want to do what you do. You are cold and totally without empathy. If you are not going to be here this morning just let me know. It's so sad because I put all my trust in you and have truly loved you. You told me you had never loved or been loved. I offered you all my love and the opportunity to enjoy a beautiful loving relationship. I just don't think you know how to do it. Love is the only thing that really matters. Not power.

And with you needing money I had no choice.

I ate a burger from a bin yesterday.

You are the one feeling sorry for yourself. Are you anywhere near here? I have to be out by noon. Before I met you I had enough money and a job that kept me ticking over. The money was lent to you for a few weeks. It's been over a year. You've landed me in deep shit and don't care. You are a professional liar and I now believe you to be a compulsive liar. I hope that underneath it all you are honourable, as I have always believed you to be. Please restore my bank balance to what it was when I met you. It will take at least eight hundred and fifty thousand pounds. I will start afresh.

I am the most honourable person you have ever met.

I hope so. Are we going to meet today? Don't lie.

He told me I had two choices. I could go home again and feel sorry for myself or I could accept the facts, and that he would never meet me where everyone I knew knew where I was.

So? Come and get me and we'll go somewhere else.

That's what you never even realised.

You arrive and explode.

Instead of treating it like a game and saying where next?

We wasted what little we had on a craft hotel.

Mad!

You make it up as you go along. It's not a game. I hate it.

You don't trust me anymore. So there is no point.

True. But you lost a lot of my trust ages ago. You said you would win it back. Do you enjoy all this? As for the hotel it is nothing special. Just in an expensive place.

No I hate it.

I wanted you to arrive – get a train

Then I realised you have changed

Before you would have arrived and done that. Now no.

You want it all done.

You forget that I have to suck petrol to move.

I have a lot of spirit but I am old fashioned. I like a man who takes care of me.

I know. Me too. So you have two choices.

He said I could either go back to the UK and wait three months to get all of my money back or wait here and start helping him – and that if my attitude had been different the day before then I would have been with him by now by train.

Oh – and it would have cost less than the hotel!

You are being ridiculous. I don't like your attitude. I am actually terribly upset and sad about all this. I don't think this conversation is getting us anywhere.

I'll call you again soon.

I actually feel frightened. It is horrible.

I have been frightened since I left my job for you.

You made your decision just as I made mine.

So live with it as I do.

He then urged me to be happy and help him to make this work.

> **I'm going to pack. If you can be here by noon as you said you would be we can talk. I can't take any more dead ends. As I said I'm frightened, I have no money. I am not going anywhere without you except back to the UK. Call me again when you can.**

> I love you so much.

> **If you love me – or even if you don't – you will make it your priority to return my money so that I can get my life back. Then perhaps we can start again.**

> I have been doing so

> Baby we need to meet

> Give me an hour to work out how

> **Well you will have to come here soon. I am only going to one place from here: the airport.**

> Thanks.

> **As I said, I'm scared.**

I had had enough of the conversation. It was going nowhere and just wasting time. I dropped my phone on to the bed. I wanted to cry, but I had to focus. I had to find the strength to make a decision and follow it through. Mark had let me down time after time after time. Initially, I had believed everything he had told me, but latterly, I had just been believing what I wanted to believe

– because I couldn't actually face the possibility that he might have been stringing me along all the time. What if the whole thing had been pre-planned? What if Annalisa had been right all along and I had been targeted as someone who had money? Mark had always said it would take eighteen months before we could be together properly and I had given him my word that I would wait, but never in a million years had I thought it would be like this. What if it was all a scam and he needed eighteen months to complete his plan of theft and destruction? Was that why he was still in contact with me? None of it made sense. I thought back to when he had been doing business in the UK. He had dealt with respectable individuals and organisations – Clifton College, the Prince's Trust – and his InOrg company had appeared genuine. Was he really a spy? He had to be. I had seen him walk into a back entrance of the MI6 building, past two armed guards. Fragments of memories whirled through my mind like leaves dancing in the air on a blustery autumn day. Would I ever be able to piece the tree together again?

I pulled myself sharply out of my reverie. Focus, Carolyn! What are you going to do? You used to be so capable. Get a grip! Make a decision!

There was only one thing to do. I must get back to the UK where I had friends and was safe. I opened my laptop, logged on to my easyJet account and changed my return ticket. Fortunately, having foreseen exactly this eventuality, I'd ensured I had enough credit on my card to cover the small charge for doing this. I would fly back to the UK that afternoon. I called down to the reception desk, told the receptionist I would be leaving the hotel in about an hour's time and asked if she could print my airline ticket for me. Then I gathered my belongings together and packed my case.

Just after eleven o'clock I was at the reception desk asking for my ticket.

'Here you are, Madame. And if you could give me your credit card, I will settle your account.'

'Excuse me?' I couldn't believe what I was hearing. 'But everything has been paid for. My bill was settled in advance last night.'

'No, Madame. The booking was authorised, but no payment was made.'

'Well, please use the credit card details you were given and charge the room to that account.'

'I'm sorry, Madame, I can't do that.'

There was no point in arguing.

'Give me a moment please. I need to make a phone call.'

I had the metallic taste of fear in my mouth and I could feel the bile rising up in my throat once again. I dialled Mark's phone, but my call went straight to voicemail. I would have to text him again. This was just fucking unbelievable. This man who I had thought so commanding, decisive and capable couldn't even sort out paying a hotel bill.

Keep calm, Carolyn, I thought. Getting upset is not going to help. Try to keep a lid on it.

11:09 I now cannot leave the hotel as they say room was not paid for. Booking was authorised that's all. They cannot take payment unless someone calls and pays. I have never come across anything like it

The minutes ticked by as I waited for a response.

11:12 Calling hotel now

On it

5 mins

Another ten minutes passed in slow motion.

11:24   On phone

         To guy who paid

         Ok

The phone on the desk rang and I could hear one side of the conversation.

'Yes, the room for Mrs Woods? If you can give me your credit card number, please.'

The receptionist continued. 'And can you spell out your name for me, please?'

My ears pricked up. Who was on the other end of the phone?

'B ... R ... E ... S ... N ... A ... H ... A ... N. Thank you, sir.'

John Bresnahan. One of Mark's business associates. The one in charge of InResidence, who was involved with the development at Chew Magna. But why was he paying my hotel bill?*

I left the hotel and caught the bus to the airport where I texted my good friend and old neighbour, West, in whom I had confided since my return to Buckinghamshire. I asked him to come and meet me on my return.

Late that night, I stepped out of the arrivals hall into the chill of the midnight air at Luton Airport, hoping and praying that West was somewhere near. There was no sign of him and my phone was dead. I was making my way towards the pick-up point, scanning the car park and approach road as I went, when

---

* I have no way of knowing who was really on the other end of the phone. There has never been any proof that John Bresnahan was involved in any wrongdoing.

suddenly, I saw West's car drive on to on the roundabout ahead of me. I jumped up and down, waving madly at him. The sense of relief was overwhelming. As I settled into the passenger seat, I felt my shoulders relax. Every muscle in my body was raw and screaming, and hundreds of coiled springs inside me gave, just a little, as the safety blanket of true friendship was wrapped around me.

West looked at me. 'Things didn't go quite as planned, then?' he said, and I started to tell him all about it as he drove me back to Angela's.

That night, I slept for the first time in many months, but the following morning, I awoke feeling split in two. I still felt the overwhelming sense of relief I had experienced the night before when I had found myself back in England in the company of old and trusted friends; but the more I thought about the events of the past two days, the bleaker my future seemed. Neither logically nor emotionally could I make sense of anything that was happening.

I got out of bed, put on a brave face and went to say good morning to Angela who, I could hear, was already up. But my face began to crumple, and I felt the mask slipping. The corners of my mouth began to droop as my lips pursed together. I tried desperately to regain my composure, but there was the insistent flutter of a tic in my left eye as I fought back tears, and a searing pain lodged across my shoulders as my knees buckled and I slumped to the floor.

'I'm so sorry.' I was looking up at Angela. 'I thought I was OK, but I'm not feeling very well.'

I felt icy cold and my whole body was shaking uncontrollably.

'Go back to bed,' Angela told me in her firm but gentle voice. 'You're in shock. I'll bring you a hot-water bottle. Try to sleep.'

I crawled back into bed. The brave façade was cracking. I wanted to cry. I desperately wanted someone to hold me and tell me everything was going to be all right. I wanted to wake up out of the nightmare I was in and find myself back anywhere, at any time of my life other than any part of the past sixteen months.

'Please let it all be a bad dream,' I whispered to myself, over and over and over again, as I held the hot-water bottle tightly against myself, longing to slip into oblivion. What was I going to do?

Mark continued to call me every day and sent reams of text messages, which would ping in in their usual staccato, scattergun fashion. I was only just holding on to my sanity. For well over a year now, I had felt afraid, fearful of myriad things, too scared even to talk to my friends. I was sure I was being watched and that my phone and laptop were being monitored. I worried about Mark's state of health, and how it would impact the chances of me getting my money back, and now I worried about my own health too. I believed Mark to be in Italy, working for the Italian government – but then how could I believe anything? He told me he still had to be very careful and he seemed to be doing undercover work that involved driving thousands of kilometres, day and night. I got the impression sometimes that he was not alone; indeed, he had told me on more than one occasion that he couldn't talk to me because he was in a car full of men and was working. Our situation seemed dire.

Mark told me he had discovered that it was Paul, his associate and driver, who had stolen his money and managed to convince him that it had been seized by the British government.

'But surely he's not that clever – I mean to outsmart you?'

'Well, he hasn't outsmarted me, has he? I've found out what that cunt has done and he's going to pay for it. Baby, I've been under such stress over the past few months. I know I haven't been thinking clearly. But now I see what has happened. That bastard took advantage of everything that's been going on.'

'I told you I never trusted him.'

'I know, Bubba but, like I told you, we go back a long way. I did him a good turn and I really didn't think he'd let me down. I'm amazed he's got the balls to even think he can pull this thing off – just goes to show how stupid he is. But you're right, you can't trust anyone.'

'I don't think this nightmare is ever going to end.'

'It will, baby. We're almost there. Now I know what's been going on I can sort things out. I've got to go now. I love you.'

I thought about Paul. Was it really possible that he had managed to siphon Mark's money out of his bank accounts? I still didn't think he was clever enough, but Mark said he had been a bank manager, so he would know all about the workings of banks. Perhaps he had someone on the inside working for him. But how could he make Mark believe that his assets had been seized by the British government? I suppose he just took advantage of Mark's brain surgery and generally poor state of health, I thought. Perhaps there was now a glimmer of hope. If Mark could get his money back, I would get mine. But for now, I was stuck with nothing. I was being chased for bad debts on the house in Bath, and the future seemed so bleak that I couldn't even think about it. I just wanted an escape route.

By the end of May, I had moved on from Angela's and was cat-sitting for Anne when I received more alarming news. Mark told me that I mustn't use the car as Paul hadn't paid the insurance on it. I hadn't used it for weeks – unable to afford petrol, I had left it parked at the flat in Amersham – but knowing that it was now uninsured just gave me something else to worry about.

Mark's birthday came and went, but there was absolutely nothing to celebrate, and in a late-night exchange of text messages I told him that if we weren't together in a week's time, I would go to the police.

*   *   *

The following day, Lara and Emma were coming to join me for lunch and I was cooking their favourite meal – roast chicken. I had also invited West to join us, having confided in him again that I was going to tell the girls my worst fears about my money. I had intended to tell them something about it the last time I had seen them, on the May Day bank holiday. We had met at Richmond Station, bought the ingredients for a picnic and spent the day in Richmond Park. It had been an unexpectedly lovely day, warm and sunny. I had looked at my beautiful daughters walking beside me as we made our way to the park, and later as they sat basking in the sun. I loved them so much, and I was so proud of them. I just couldn't bring myself to break the spell and spoil the beauty of that early summer day by upsetting them with my fears. But now I felt I had to do it. I had to prepare them for the worst – and hope for the best. I knew that West would give moral support and help reassure them, letting them know that he was there for them if they needed anyone to talk to. Lara and Emma had known him all their lives and trusted him, and he had always cared very deeply for them. Neither of us underestimated the enormity of the shock they were about to experience.

Lara and Emma duly arrived, together with Lara's partner, Glenn. At least Lara had him to talk to, but I worried particularly about Emma, who I knew had taken a vehement dislike to Mark – and who could blame her after his appalling behaviour on the one occasion they had met? As I thought about it now, I wondered how on earth I could have forgiven him for that.

It was turning into a lovely early-summer day. The sky was blue and the sun shone down as though nothing in the world could be wrong. There was a cacophony of birdsong outside. I joined everyone in the garden for a drink and just wanted to enjoy this lovely afternoon. We sat down to lunch and as the first course came to an end, I knew I must break the spell and speak.

'There's something I have to tell you,' I started.

All eyes turned to me.

'I know you must have been wondering what on earth has been going on, what with me leaving Bath and moving around from friend to friend for the past few months. I know you've been wondering why I still haven't bought a house, especially as I got so excited about that one near Tetbury earlier in the year. Well, the thing is that a while ago I lent Mark all my money and he hasn't been able to pay me back.'

There was silence as the girls tried to take in what I was saying.

'You lent Mark your money?' Lara said, eventually. 'All of it? Including the proceeds of the sale of Eskdale Avenue?'

I nodded as Lara continued. 'I just can't believe you would do that.'

Emma and Glenn were looking incredulous.

'I know,' I said. 'I can't believe it either, but that's what I did. I'm hoping that he'll give it back to me, but I just don't know. I felt I must tell you because the fact is that I've had virtually no money since well before Christmas. I've had to cash in my pension to keep going. That's why I've been so careful about spending anything. I'm sure you must have been wondering.'

'But why did you do that? You've always been so independent. What made you do that?'

It was Emma now who was talking, wide-eyed and tearful. I swallowed hard, and tears pricked the backs of my eyes.

'We were going to get married. Mark had a cash-flow problem and I said I could help him. It was only meant to be for a few weeks, but here I am over a year later and he still hasn't repaid me. I hope that he will, but things have been so bizarre that I can't be sure.'

I watched their faces as the terrible facts sank in.

'You were going to get married? But why didn't you tell us? I can't believe you didn't tell us.'

This was Lara again.

'I know. Nothing went as we'd hoped, and our original plans had to be scrapped. Then Mark was away so much, and I just thought I'd wait until everything was settled before telling you. I've had a wedding dress hanging in the wardrobe for months.'

'Bloody hell, Carolyn!'

Glenn was looking at me, shaking his head in disbelief.

'Well, at least he's still in touch with you,' he went on. 'I mean it's not as if he's just vanished into thin air. Surely if he was just after your money, he'd have disappeared a long time ago. And you were living in his house in Bath. I think he'll come good.'

'I hope you're right. I really didn't want to worry you with all this, but I decided it was only fair to tell you. You know how worried and upset I've been with Mark having all that brain surgery and everything. It's been impossible for me to put pressure on him and he tells me he's doing everything he can to sort things out. Anyway, you know me – people always say I'm one of the strongest people they know, so if anyone can get through all this, I can. I'm just so sorry to have involved you all in it too. As you can imagine, I've been feeling terribly insecure, and I know that this affects your security as well. Since I moved out of the Little Coach House, I've felt so homesick – and I know you've hated not having anywhere to come back to. I'm absolutely determined now to get a place of my own.'

'But Mum, you've got no money.' Emma was looking pale and drawn.

'We've just got to hope that it will all be OK. At the moment there's nothing more we can do.'

'Have you thought about going to the police? I mean what if he doesn't give it back? How long are you going to wait?' Lara was questioning me again.

'Well, he told me the day we met that it would be eighteen months before he could be in a proper relationship. I gave him my word that I would wait for him. The eighteen months are up in July.'

'I think he'll pay you back.' Glenn talking again. 'Bloody hell, Carolyn. I just can't believe you did that though.'

It was time to try to lift the mood and enjoy what was left of this lovely summer day. Over the course of the afternoon, I spoke to everyone again and tried to reassure them that things would be all right. I had to be strong for them. Somehow, I had to keep going. I closed my eyes and felt the warmth of the sun on my skin and forced all other thoughts from my mind.

When it was time for them to go I felt a sharp pang of loneliness and a totally overwhelming wave of love that only a mother can feel for her children. I loved them so much and I felt ashamed at how I had let them down. I was worried about how they would cope with the knowledge they now had. I felt better for having unburdened myself of my biggest fear, but, although I thought it necessary, I felt bad for having passed it on to my daughters – and I hardly dared think about the consequences if Mark failed to sort out this unholy mess. How could I have been so stupid?

Looking back, although on one level I still wonder how I could have put myself in such a vulnerable position, I do know how it happened. I simply wasn't thinking straight. That's what falling in love does to you. It takes your eye off the ball and is a kind of madness in itself. A joyous, uncontrollable, intoxicating, irresponsible high. All Mark's talk of his massive wealth engendered a false sense of security in me. But why did I offer to lend him my money? Why didn't I just keep quiet and let him sort out his cash-flow problems on his own? I know the answer. Again, it was because I loved him, and he made me feel so bad about questioning his integrity. I felt demeaned when he erupted when I asked him to return the thirty-five pounds he owed me, making me feel mean and miserly. That was why I unquestioningly handed over my credit card for all those purchases in Harrods and Chanel. He said he would pay me back, and we do tend to expect people to behave just as we would, but now, as I started to think about his behaviour, it all seemed wrong. He should have paid for everything. And the bills on the house should never have been put in my name. It just wasn't right. Why hadn't I questioned him more? I'd tried but he had this knack of making me feel ungenerous and unappreciative. He should never have accepted my money – not if he was really honourable. Surely if he really cared about me, he would not have put me in such a vulnerable situation. I felt sick.

I had to shut the door on these negative thoughts. Mark claimed to be the most honourable person I would ever meet. I just hoped that was true – because right now I didn't believe it and I knew that time was running out.

The following morning, Mark called to tell me that as Paul had not kept up to date with the payments on the car it had now been reported as stolen. I tried in vain to contact my friends who had the key to it, to try to explain what had happened and to ask them to give the key to whoever turned up to collect it. They returned home to find a Thrifty van parked in their space and a 'POLICE AWARE' message on the car. Mark somehow sorted out the mess and my friends were spared a visit from the police, but I was acutely embarrassed.

'You lead a much more exciting life than we do,' exclaimed my friend Helen as I apologised for what had happened.

'It's not quite the excitement I had been hoping for,' I replied.

Over the course of the next couple of weeks, day after day, Mark said he was organising air tickets for me to come and see him. During the first week there were no tickets. Monday of the second week came, but no tickets came with it. They were promised for Tuesday. Tuesday came, but by mid-afternoon still nothing. Mark had been on the phone telling me it would all be

OK, but I had reached the limit of my tolerance. I still hadn't been to the police, but I decided that whatever happened I wouldn't go and see Mark. Even if the tickets did turn up, I no longer wanted to see him. I couldn't take any more bullshit, so I texted him.

11th June 2013

15:10   Forget it

> Quite remarkable
>
> We have both been through hell
>
> Now you will finally understand what I have suffered
>
> Both through living, and loving you
>
> Please just hang on

I felt sick. I had been hanging on for nearly eighteen months. I didn't respond.

15:46   Always the same

> Once critical you switch off

For four hours I sat, staring ahead, silent and unable to move. Then suddenly, I erupted, keying furiously into my phone:

19:44   Until I moved to Bath I was happy, confident, and enjoyed life. My life is now in ruins. I don't want it. I have been struggling with no home and no income

for over a year. I have been up to my credit limit with
virtually no money for 6 months. I have debts, which
by rights are yours from Brock St. I have been let
down a million times. How you can treat me the way
you do is beyond my comprehension. You should
have repaid me my money after a couple of weeks,
as you said you would. Then at least I could have
had my life back and we might have been able to
get through the rest. This situation is impossible. I
have been kept dangling for over a year, from
waiting to be picked up to go to Ascot/Wimbledon, to
being packed up for 6 weeks waiting to go to Beach,
to having a suitcase packed for weeks waiting to go
to Mallorca, Marbella, Italy etc, and more recently
the Nice fiasco and now this. I can't take any more.
Please return my money to me and then we will see
if we can salvage anything.

Now Mark was the one who didn't respond.

21:37   I don't even have a car to sleep in, let alone get
around in.

I tossed and turned in bed, unable to get a moment's peace as I
felt the heavy weight of fear and despair pressing down on me
again. I desperately fought back the tears.

12th Jun 2013

03:57   I have loved you so much

04:58   Please help me

I lay there for nearly three hours before he responded.

07:49 You told me to cancel the trip

And it took me another half hour before I could focus enough to play the ball back to him.

08:15 Yes. I just need you to repay me what you owe me. Even if you could give me £20k to start to repay these debts, which are accruing interest all the time, it would be a start. If you could repay £50k I could get a car and rent a small place and try to get my foot on the ladder again.

09:03 Darling I am trying to do exactly that

Hence the fact I let you down with travelling

Try to find a rented house for now

I will find the money

I had dared to take off the blinkers, and I saw a landscape littered with broken promises and shattered dreams. It broke my heart when I thought about how I had loved Mark and been so sure of him. I still couldn't work out what was going on, but I knew that I could never share my life with this man. He was the one who had changed – perhaps because of his brain surgery, but now I didn't care. Self-preservation was overriding every other thought. I had always known my heart might get broken, but it had never crossed my mind that every aspect of my life could be destroyed.

09:35   I cannot begin to do anything until you start repaying me. That is all that counts. I don't know what your game is but it is sick. I have been a fool, I admit, but you took advantage of me and abused my love for you. That is horrible and amoral. My sister-in-law was right. I was never interested in your money but I am very interested in having mine returned to me. I don't suppose you will do it but I hope that you can find some grain of humanity in yourself, plant it, let it grow and do the right thing.

He didn't respond, but I couldn't stop thinking about him. I couldn't get my mind on to any other track.

15:15   I have been thinking a lot about you today. I feel very sad about all this. What makes you tick? It used to be money, now it's power and control? Why? That is a sign of insecurity. You said you had never loved or been loved, and you have thrown that opportunity for real happiness away. I feel very sorry for you. I am of course aware that you never loved me.

I was talking to myself really, but I wanted him to know that the silken thread of hope on which my future with him had been hanging for so long was about to give. What if the whole thing had been a sham? But how could anyone conjure up such unusual but convincing scenarios? He was right: his life was like a film. Could it really be that he was writing the script, directing the show and acting the part of leading man? Was everyone else just a puppet in his hands – an extra or a hopeful young starlet, hanging around for hours, days, weeks, months on end, all in the hope of having their wildest dreams realised? Whatever the answer was, you had to give it to him: he was incredibly inventive. All those business deals, the setting up of companies – that had been real; I'd seen it with my own eyes. And MI6 – I'd seen him enter the MI6 building, walking past two armed guards. Yes, credit where it was due, he was quite amazing. I couldn't think of a scriptwriter or novelist who could come up with anything quite as extraordinary. As I let my mind wander through various novels and plays I was familiar with, I resumed texting.

> **15:19   You should go into the theatre. You are highly creative and theatrical.**

Suddenly, he was there.

> Darling stop
>
> That is complete crap
>
> YOU are the one who gives up each time
>
> My attitude now is simple
>
> Get my money back
>
> Pay you
>
> Then see if YOU love me
>
> **I have seen the light. The blinkers are off.**
>
> Thanks
>
> Leave it at that it's stupid to argue

Only time will tell. But it is running out

If we are ever together the harsh words are remembered

That's why I prefer not to argue. It's a waste of time

As are the deeds. Actions speak louder than words

I know.

You will see soon.

I will call later

Arguing is healthy as long as it is honest.

Yes. It is. If you can do it face to face

That is the best way, I agree, but, like Macavity, you're not there. T.S. Eliot

Now Mark was telling me that James would pick me up at three o'clock that afternoon. If it didn't happen, I would call 'time'. I had managed seventeen of his eighteen months, but I couldn't carry on. I didn't have a grain of strength left in me.

At three o'clock that afternoon Mark called to tell me that James wouldn't be picking me up, after all, and the trip was on hold. I didn't even ask for an explanation. That night, once again, I went to bed and lay awake while demons and devils invaded my mind and the weight of darkness pressed down on me. My body now felt so heavy that I was sure I would pass through the mattress, through the floor below and into the bowels of the earth. And I longed for it.

At four o'clock the following morning, I was still awake. The first hint of daylight was filtering through the curtains and I was thinking about James Miller. I didn't know him very well, but Mark had always said that I could call him if I was worried about anything at all. He had told me that James would know everything, and if I needed news or reassurance and couldn't get hold of him, I could always call him.

My fingers fumbled in the dark on the bedside table. I picked up my mobile phone and typed three words:

13th June 2013

04:22   Please help me

Two days later, I found myself sitting with James in Arthur's Bistro on Twickenham Green. It was difficult to know where to begin, but I started by asking him about Mark's work for MI6 as it was that which had kept us apart for so long.

'Yes,' said James quietly. 'He told me he worked for MI6, too, but I don't believe it.'

I told James that at the beginning of the year Mark told me that he had been sent back to Syria where he had been badly wounded, shot in the arm and leg, and that he had ended up in a military hospital in Athens.

'No, that's not true,' James replied, 'He was in Spain trying to do more business deals. I was there some of the time.'

I told James how Mark had introduced me to his young niece, Bianca.

'Bianca's his daughter,' James told me, hesitating slightly. 'He's got two young daughters, and he's married. They were all living in Bathampton, not far from where you were living,' he continued, getting bolder now. 'Then they moved to Bristol. And he didn't own that house you were living in, he was renting it.'

I felt so stupid. I remembered a while ago, when I was telling a girlfriend that I saw so little of Mark, and that we had never actually spent a whole night together, she'd said, 'It's obvious that he's married.' And I just thought, No he's not; you don't know what I know. He's out on a mission or doing this or that, because he has an extraordinary life.

'I knew him initially as Marc Ros Rodriguez,' James continued, 'but then he told me that for security reasons he'd changed his name to Zac Moss. That was the name he was using when he was in Bath and Bristol – to everyone except you, it seems.'

It was all so much to take in, but really there was only one thing that mattered: he was a conman.

'Take a look at this,' James said, handing me his mobile phone. 'Scroll down. I didn't know how much of this I was going to tell you – how much of it you could take – but I think you need to know.'

I took the phone from James and started to read.

Boy Lives It Up in a Spree With Dad's Credit Card

There was a report dated July 1991 of a sixteen-year-old boy, named Mark Acklom, who had rented private jets and flown to Paris, Berne and the Canary Islands, living the high life and treating his friends to champagne and lobster dinners.

I looked up at James.

'I remember this case. I remember hearing about it on the radio. I remember thinking what gall that boy must have to do such a thing at sixteen. And this is him? Mark Acklom?'

'That's him.'

I scrolled down. There was more:

Teenage Conman Given Four Years

The article reported that a teenage boy, described by a judge as utterly selfish and ruthless, had been sentenced to four years' youth custody. At the age of sixteen he had falsely obtained a half a million pound mortgage, having convinced a building society that he was a twenty-five-year old stockbroker earning £250,000 a year. The boy's name was Mark Acklom. He had squandered thousands of pounds on 'self-indulgent pleasures', and even since being bailed had tried to 'obtain' a convertible BMW worth £21,000. He had stolen his father's credit card and had also swindled thousands of pounds from two of his schoolteachers. Acklom, who admitted several counts of theft and deception and asked for 119 other offences to be considered, was described by his defence lawyer, Mr Charles Conway, as 'greatly disturbed' and in need of psychiatric treatment, but, after listening to three hours' mitigation, including professional psychiatric evidence, the judge told Acklom: 'I prefer my own diagnosis, based on many years' experience, that you show all the typical symptoms of a conman telling sophisticated lies to your victims, closely adapted to suit the circumstances of the particular person you are talking to.'

My head was spinning. Charles Conway? Was that where Mark had got the name from? And this article was dated 1991. When did the offence take place? Two years before, in 1989. If he was sixteen in 1989, that meant he was only about thirty-eight when he met me. Thirty-eight! I never would have gone out with him if I'd known that. And there was more.

I couldn't peel my eyes away from James' phone.

Now I was on a Spanish expat blog, reading a report of a British man being jailed in Spain, having been convicted of serious fraud and a £13 million property scam. The Spanish police had discovered that he was wanted in the UK and the name he was using was false. His real name was Mark Richard George Acklom.

It was never-ending. As I scrolled down I read that a man named Marc Ros Rodriquez had scammed his way around Geneva, prior to fleeing Switzerland in 2009. And then another report of Acklom trying to scam unwitting businessmen with gold and oil deals. He had, allegedly, presented himself as being in business with the Russian government, specifically Putin, and claimed to be the illegitimate son of George Soros. Oh my God, I thought, George Soros. I remembered Mark telling me exactly that – and that he knew Putin!

I couldn't take it all in. It just went on and on.

'The guy was nothing but a con artist who told greedy people what they want to hear,' it said. And that hurt. Because I hadn't been greedy. I hadn't wanted his money. But yes, he had told me what I wanted to hear. The veil of mystery through which I had been looking had been whipped away and my worst fears were realised.

Reeling from the shock, I knew I needed to be with my daughters. I called Lara, who was travelling back from Cornwall with Glenn, and they agreed to come and pick me up on their way home. Thankfully, everyone was out when I returned to my friends' house, and I hurriedly packed my bag as I waited for Lara. We drove back to Islington in a deluge of rain and I began to tell them what I had discovered. That evening, Emma joined us at Lara's flat and we tried to grapple with the enormity of the events of the past eighteen months.

Lara searched the internet for more information about the man I now knew was called Mark Acklom. What we discovered was truly astonishing, and Lara compiled a ninety-six-page document on him, listing everything she could find, including a dozen aliases, details of his notorious schoolboy escapades and accounts of his criminal activity in Spain later, where he allegedly committed an €18 million fraud. Alongside this was a rambling, defensive account, apparently written by Acklom, in which he described himself as an 'Author and Script Writer', the victim of a society that won't forgive him his past misdemeanours. In another blog, Acklom cited his 'latest' book, *Needless Destruction*, in which he depicts the business he set up in Spain in 2013 as having been 'needlessly destroyed' by malicious talk about him. It is common for psychopaths to blame everybody but themselves when things go wrong, and it seems to me that this kind of victimhood is just the other side of the egocentric coin. I think about all the people he has conned, robbed and manipulated, whose lives he has calculatedly and needlessly wrecked. It is to them, not him, that the term 'needless destruction' should be applied.

During the final stage of a romantic relationship with a psychopath, the perpetrator feels nothing but contempt for his victim. He will do everything to strip her of her confidence, her dignity and her peace of mind. From the day she falls for his charm, and steps into the world he creates for her, he regards her as unworthy of dignity, respect or any sort of value. His lack of empathy, his callousness, amorality and absence of any conscience enable him to remain completely indifferent to her suffering. She deserves his abuse, and she will eventually be discarded as totally worthless. The psychopath himself will vacillate between feelings of exhilaration and contempt. This sort of 'contemptuous delight' is what feeds his ego and narcissism. The lower he pushes his victim the more contempt he feels for her, and the greater his self-congratulatory regard for himself.

When I look back on everything that happened, I am proud of myself for standing up to Mark Acklom as much as I did. But I can see how he used all the character traits that I thought were my strengths – loyalty, stoicism, discretion – against me, so that, in effect, I was complicit in my own downfall. I am sure the same applies to those bona-fide businessmen and women who also fell under his spell, and the countless women he has 'romanced'.

That night, lying stock-still on Lara's sofa, feeling as if the tiniest movement would cause me to shatter into a thousand fragments, I was unable to sleep. I couldn't stop thinking about Mark and what he had done. From the moment he met me he had scattered the seeds of his deception freely into my mind and my fertile imagination and his expert nurturing had let them germinate, take root and grow. I recalled the things he said, many of which now resonated with a sinister undertone: 'Everything happens for a reason … all your money will run away … I can read people like books … you are perfect for me … I don't really know how to make love … I'm so pleased I met someone with money; it just makes everything so much easier … I love you for being the way you are … my life is like a film … I'm not normal.'

I am in shock. I lie here unable to move a muscle. Every nerve in my body is under attack. I am so tired, but if I close my eyes, I'm assaulted by sickening flashes of psychedelic light. So I lie here, motionless, eyes wide open, hardly daring to breathe.

I want to die. I feel myself being sucked into the vortex of a black hole as white noise crackles in my head and three words spool around my mind, over and over, screaming to get out, louder and louder, until I think I'm going to pass out.

YOU FUCKING BASTARD!

By morning, I still hadn't moved from the sofa. Lara and Glenn were cooking breakfast when my phone rang.

'It's him,' I told them, as I answered the call and put my phone on speaker.

'Baby, I love you so much,' he said. 'James is going to pick you up and fly you out here. We'll be together very soon.'

'Just give me my money,' I replied, in a voice that sounded strange to me – beige and flat.

'You'll have your money. Everything's going to be OK.'

'Just give me my money.'

'It will have been worth all the heartache.'

'Just give me my money.'

The line went dead. I never heard from Mark Acklom again.

9

A SINGULAR WRETCH

Taking no further interest in herself as a splendid woman, she acquired the indifferent feelings of an outsider in contemplating her probable fate as a singular wretch.

Thomas Hardy, *Far from the Madding Crowd*

In the immediate aftermath of the discovery of Mark's true identity I felt as though I was fighting for my life.

I knew it was imperative just to keep going: to get up every day, to wash, to get dressed, to put on my make-up, to eat, to try and step outside and to see a few close friends. Every small goal I set myself took the most tremendous effort to accomplish and – wanting to die, longing for peace that only death could bring, but still feeling terribly responsible for my daughters – I felt condemned to a life I didn't want. In the first few weeks I took each day ten minutes at a time.

On 16 June, the day after my meeting with James, Lara took me to Islington police station to report the crime. I could hardly stand up as we entered the building. I propped myself up against the front desk, feeling dizzy, fearing I might faint at any moment. I tried to focus on what I was saying. 'That's a lot of money,' remarked the duty officer in a rather jocular fashion, as I tried to explain the extent of my loss, but he sent me away telling me that

the police didn't deal with reports of fraud. He handed me a leaf-
let and told me to make an online report to Action Fraud,
marking the beginning of a two-month quagmire of delay. With
no fixed address, I seemed to have become a non-person and had
the distinct impression that no one wanted to take on the case. I
was given conflicting advice, contacted by Action Fraud with the
wrong crime reference number (which, luckily, I spotted) and
tossed around between three police constabularies, until the
matter was eventually assigned to Avon & Somerset police – to
an officer who was on holiday. This set the tone for the first three
years of a so-called 'investigation' that was to drag on for six years.

I knew that to survive I must face my fears as soon as possible,
so after a week I forced myself to return to Tetbury. Thankfully,
when Mark appeared in my life, I passed my old car on to Lara,
and she now gave it back to me, so that I had the means to travel.
A friend – a saviour, who to this day remains anonymous – gave
me £1,000 to get me back on my feet, so for a while I had money
for petrol and food. Uma and Antony said I could stay with them
and, the day after I arrived, Uma persuaded me to see my old
doctor whom she asked to come to the house. I broke down as I
gave him a brief outline of what had happened. He told me that
I was suffering from post-traumatic stress disorder, and that, in
his view, Mark Acklom was a dangerous psychopath. I was (and
remain) dead set against taking antidepressants and he didn't
think they would help either. Nor did he think counselling would
be beneficial at that time, although he felt it could be useful
further down the line. He did, however, recommend that I establish some sort of normal sleeping pattern and prescribed me a
month's course of sleeping pills. I didn't know him well, but
before he left, he hugged me and told me that he hoped he would
never again have to listen to such a story as mine. I mention the
hug because even at the time it surprised me that any man would
have the courage to make physical contact with a distressed and

highly emotional, vulnerable woman (and I can't imagine it would happen post-'Me Too'). But he did, and I will remain eternally grateful to him for that. It was a spontaneous, human response – a comforting, empathetic gesture – and, having been deprived of affection or any sort of comfort for so long, it meant more to me than I can adequately express.

Although I had been very friendly with Uma and Antony, it now felt strange to be in their house as, apart from the bed itself, the room in which I was staying was furnished entirely with my furniture and belongings – my old wardrobe, chest of drawers, mirror, bedside tables, chair, duvet and bed linen – and it made me feel unbearably homesick.

James Miller offered me an appointment with his solicitor (whom he had already spoken to about his own losses in relation to Acklom) for advice about what I could do. Having taken a sleeping pill in the early hours of the morning on the day of the proposed meeting, I felt like a zombie when I woke up – so much so that I didn't think I could drive safely. I asked Uma and Antony if they could help by driving me to Cirencester, if necessary, and they agreed, but when the time came to leave, I felt much better and decided to go alone. I felt it was important to try to do as much as I could by myself.

As I was preparing to leave, going through my suitcase, on the bedroom floor, Uma stood over me. She had been insisting that Antony accompany me to the solicitor but I was determined to go by myself. She couldn't accept this and told me in no uncertain terms that if I was going to stay with them I had to 'abide by our rules'. Hearing raised voices, Antony came into the room and asked what was going on. I told him that I wanted to go to Cirencester by myself and repeated what Uma had just said.

'Damn right you will!' he asserted, standing over me.

Perhaps they thought they were helping me (and I desperately needed help), but it seemed as though I was being controlled all over again, and I told them that in that case I would have to leave. I started to pack my suitcase and told them I would return after my appointment to finish packing and collect my belongings. I felt totally devastated.

Half an hour later, I was sitting in the solicitor's office, fighting back the tears as I told him about Mark Acklom and outlined everything that had happened. But I got none of the reassurance and help I was hoping for.

'My advice to you', he told me, 'is to try to forget all about it. You've reported it to the police, and that's all you can do. But the police are useless; don't expect any sort of a result. You will never get your money back, believe me.'

I was completely stunned. What about the law? What about justice? At the time, I thought the solicitor must have been involved in some sort of conspiracy with Acklom and was trying to stop me from pursuing him. When I look back at that meeting now though, I realise that his was possibly the best advice I was given. But of course, I was completely unable to heed it.

I felt exhausted by the meeting and the falling out with Uma and Antony. I hoped that the row had blown up in the heat of the moment and that we could make up and come to some sort of understanding. On the way back I bought some flowers and a bottle of wine as a peace offering, but when I returned to the house nobody was home. There was, however, a note pinned to the back door.

It expressed sorrow at what had happened, and I was told that to avoid any awkwardness they had placed my packed belongings in the outside laundry room. They were sorry I was unable to accept their help and wished me luck for the future. They said they were not bullying me or trying to pry into my affairs, and that they only wanted to help. I have sometimes wondered how things would have turned out if they had been at home and we could have talked things over, but, as it was, far from feeling that any awkwardness had been avoided, their decision not to see me and to remove my belongings from the house made me feel totally rejected, as though the door had been slammed shut on our friendship.

It was early evening. The rain had been falling relentlessly for the previous few hours and I didn't know where to go. I thought about returning to Amersham or Chesham, but I was so exhausted that I didn't think I could safely make the journey. In the end, I contacted my brother, who I knew would be home alone that evening as Annalisa was away in Cornwall, and asked if we could meet. He told me he was going to be rather late home, but I made my way to his house anyway, and sat outside in the car with the rain lashing down, drinking the best part of the bottle of wine I had bought for Uma and Antony.

When he arrived, I went into complete meltdown. He was welcoming, and seemed genuinely pleased to see me, but during our conversation, when I commented that if my house had burned down and all my possessions been destroyed, at least I would be covered by insurance, he replied, 'Not if you set fire to your own house.' This told me exactly what he thought about my predicament, and where he thought the blame lay.

Knowing that he would be leaving the house to join Annalisa for the weekend, I asked if I could stay on for a couple of days. I told him I would be gone by the time they returned home and, after making a phone call to Annalisa, he told me that I could, adding that I should wash the sheets before I leave. This felt like another massive rejection, and it demonstrated how far apart our worlds were. Mine had collapsed and I was left with nothing: their biggest concern was not to have to deal with my dirty linen. To me, at the time, it felt as though the connotation was that I, myself, was dirt.

In fact, a couple of days after discovering the truth about Acklom, I had phoned Annalisa to acknowledge that she had been right all along. It was a very difficult call for me to make, as I had had no contact with her since the previous October. I suppose I was looking for compassion, but there was none to be found there. She reprimanded me severely for having put her family in danger and demanded to know everything I had told Acklom about them, saying I 'owed it' to her. Feeling belittled and fighting back the tears, I hung up on her.

In the few days that I was in Tetbury I forced myself to see a few people, and an old neighbour offered me somewhere to live for the summer. In a strange twist of fate, I found myself living in an attic that overlooked the beautiful cottage I had rented when I first moved to the town, and where, for the first year, I had been blissfully happy. Kerry offered me a Sunday job back at the shop, so I had a small income of £50 a week to keep me going. I was so grateful for the work, but although I still made an effort to dress the part, I knew that I was a shadow of my former self when it came to engaging with customers. Completely lacking in confidence, I dreaded seeing anyone I knew and generally hoped that nobody would go shopping on a Sunday.

Unbeknown to me, Lara contacted an online forum, Antifraud International, where she met 'Charlie's Angel', someone who seemed to know a great deal about Mark Acklom and was determined to bring him to justice. Lara was worried about how I would react to this as she knew how much I distrusted internet encounters, but eventually she told me and, with nothing left to lose, I too decided to engage with the online world and was soon in daily contact with Charlie's Angel. I told her everything about my relationship with Acklom, and she gave me a lot of information on him in return, including copies of two passports in different names, and his Spanish residency permit. She also put me in touch with 'Mike', allegedly another victim of Acklom's in Poole, who told me he had gone 'from two Porsches to one', when I subsequently met him at a service station on the M4. Charlie's Angel and Mike thought we might be able to help each other, but I felt very exposed as I didn't really know who they were.

Over the course of the next six months, I met James Miller about once a week for coffee. Initially, I was wary, but I soon came to look forward to these meetings and I found James' presence calming. He was the only person who really understood what I had been through, and how such a thing could happen, because he had experienced something similar himself, and knew exactly how Acklom operated.

Soon after I arrived back in Tetbury, James showed me an account he had prepared for the police about his association with Mark Acklom. It was an eye-popping read.

I learned that James, a mining engineer by training, had met Acklom a few years previously. At that time, Acklom was posing as a gold dealer and James had visited him in some of the most expensive and exclusive properties imaginable in London and, later, in Poole, Dorset, but nothing had come of any gold deal because Acklom wanted the gold delivered before any sort of payment was made. Their paths crossed again early in 2012 when James 'went into business' with him, the hook being, for him – a vintage aircraft enthusiast – the promise of finance to facilitate the acquisition of Kemble airfield, then Colerne airfield and finally an airfield in Spain.

During the first six months of 2013, when I'd believed him to be in a military hospital, and then on the run in Italy, Acklom was, in fact, in Spain (where he had moved his company, now called EnOrg), making grand plans for an extravagant celebration of the 200th anniversary of the battle of Vitoria, at which Wellington beat Napoleon's brother, King Joseph Bonaparte of France, while simultaneously trying to get Ferrari to move all their vehicle testing from Italy to Spain. James told me of a lunch he had attended with Acklom and the Ferrari team, as well as a meeting with local Spanish government ministers. James said he had been run into the ground by Acklom, who wanted him to organise marching bands and all sorts of other extravagances for the anniversary celebrations, as well as drawing up business plans for the venture with Ferrari. Acklom had rented luxury offices in Alicante, persuading his secretary (whom he claimed to have fallen in love with, saying that he would leave his wife for her) to use her life's savings for the deposit. He had hired her, as well as accountants and lawyers, on vastly inflated salaries, which, of course, he never paid. He ordered €30,000 worth of office furniture and, as usual, secured himself a luxury apartment, owned by an innocent Spanish business acquaintance, but never paid the rent.

James discovered Acklom's true identity when he received a call from Mark's secretary, Fernanda, to say that the police had arrived at the office and Mark had been arrested, but that the name they had used was Acklom. An internet search led to Mark's true identity and James was left to wind up the company and mop up the mess, trying – in vain – to save his own reputation. James told me that Acklom claimed to have been released from the police station. He had then gone to to Italy, where James still believed him to be. James had tried to keep tabs on Acklom as he was trying desperately to recover his losses; he even had an address for him, which he passed on to the UK police when he reported Acklom to them.

Meanwhile, I carried out my own investigations and discovered that the house in Brock Street had been rented in my name, with my signature badly forged on the tenancy agreement (a copy of which I acquired); and I also found out that a year's rent had been paid up front out of my money, and that Acklom had posed as my agent, telling the lettings agency that I was a member of the wealthy Spanish family who owned Heathrow Airport. The owner of 1 Brock Street was given the same story. I suspect that I was supposed to be María del Pino y Calvo-Sotelo, the fifth-wealthiest woman in Spain at the time, who is the same age as me and was pictured on the internet with the same dark bob that I had when I moved into the house.

During 2012, when I was living at Brock Street, unbeknown to me, Acklom was living nearby with his wife and two young children, as James said, in another rented property that he purported to own. This was the Old Rectory at Bathampton, where he spent £25,000 on renovations, thereby impressing all his new business acquaintances with his taste, style and wealth. James Miller had visited both properties in 2012; he told me that the Old Rectory was swarming with building contractors. He was initially told by Acklom that Brock Street was his new office, and subsequently informed that he was letting a wealthy American investor live there. I now realise that Acklom used the property to entertain or impress other people, when I was not there, which is why he was so adamant that he should know my movements at all times.

James' account also revealed that Acklom had offered a young model from Bristol a £60,000 contract with InOrg. She never received a penny, but – as I later worked out – she was involved in a photoshoot that took place at Brock Street during one of my absences. When she arrived for the shoot, she discovered that she was to model lingerie, and that Acklom himself was to be the photographer. I also believe that, as well as taking advantage of my planned absences, Acklom engineered events so that he could use Brock Street if necessary, phoning me and arranging to meet me away from the house, and then failing to show up. In retrospect, I suspect this is what he did when he said he would take me flying on a second occasion, telling me to meet him at Kemble airfield. He never showed up, but I was away for probably three hours, giving him plenty of time to use the house for a business meeting or other assignation. There were other occasions when Paul would turn up to take me here or there (the waterfront in Bristol and the Celtic Manor Resort near Newport in Wales) to meet Mark, who would then fail to appear.

James' account gave me the 'backstory' of what Mark Acklom had really been doing between January 2012 and June 2013. He was for a while working with the Prince's Trust, and I later discovered that he had offered them a donation of £8 million, but he was eventually rumbled by his contact there, Rick Libbey, who was ex-military and realised there was something very wrong with Dr Zac Moss's claims about being involved with MI6.

Acklom had, indeed, been heavily involved with fund-raising for Clifton College, and had also ensnared a judge, promising funding for the restoration of his collection of boats and the setting up of InMaritime.

Everything Mark Acklom turned his hand to he did on the most lavish, extravagant scale, and he is a master at insinuating his way into the highest social circles.

Eight weeks after I first tried to report Acklom to the police I had a meeting with the investigating officer. I took a mountain of paperwork with me and any other relevant information, including a memory stick with CCTV footage of Acklom and me in the shop (I later learned that Kerry had kept this, after a conversation with Annalisa that took place not long after I met Acklom, during which they both expressed concern for my wellbeing).

I was shown into a room with two male police officers. I handed them a copy of an outline of the fraud, which ran to nine pages, but they seemed totally uninterested, jotting down no more than a line or two during my interview. I asked if my phone and laptop could be examined, as I feared that Acklom still had access to them and might be monitoring my every move, but the police were only interested in the phone I had before I met Mark.

That was examined and returned to me a few days later when I also emailed them copies of Acklom's passports, received from Charlie's Angel, one in the name of Marc Ros Rodriguez, the other in the name of Mark Acklom, together with his Spanish residency permit in the name of Marc Ros.

The so-called investigation hardly seemed to progress at all until 22 January 2014 when I received a telephone call asking me to come to Bath police station to sign a statement which the police needed before they could interview Acklom's accomplice, whom they had at last found. This was the man I had known as Paul Deol, but who was known to everyone else as Paul Kaur, and whose birth name was Paul Wiggins. He was due to be interviewed on the afternoon of 27 January and I agreed to attend the same morning.

I arrived at the police station at the appointed time, but when I was shown the statement that had been prepared for me to sign I was appalled. Not only was it full of grammatical errors and barely coherent, but it was also factually incorrect. I was shocked that I was not allowed to write my own statement. The investigating officer was aggressive towards me, treating me more like a criminal than the victim of a horrendous crime, and initially refused to change the statement, telling me that it was based on what I had said in my original written report. I challenged him to show me that initial report, which he did, and I proved him wrong, whereupon he reluctantly agreed to change one paragraph of what he had written. At one point, when the officer went out of the interview room, leaving the statement open on the computer, I hurriedly changed as much as I could to make the document readable and factually correct, but I was not at all happy with it.

I had been in the police station for a couple of hours and was very upset and tired. The police officer repeatedly told me, in a very accusatory tone of voice, that £850,000 was an awful lot of money for anyone to have in the bank, and I, in turn, repeatedly said that most of it was the proceeds of the sale of my house. Eventually, with the officer insisting that he needed the statement that very afternoon, I agreed to sign it. It was still nothing like I wanted it to be, but at least now it was factually correct. When a printed copy was put in front of me, however, I noticed that it was dated 20 September 2013. I drew this to the officer's attention and said it needed to be changed, but he told me that the date should remain as it was. I said in that case I would put today's date next to my signature, at which he became visibly angry and swept up the pieces of paper from the desk, saying that he would have to amend the date and reprint the statement. He returned with a revised copy, which I signed, but found that there was now a blank page at the end, which he was also demanding that I sign. I didn't want to do so because it could easily then have been used to make it seem as though I had put my signature to something I had never even seen. The police officer became extremely aggressive, to the extent that I signed the piece of paper, against my better judgment, just so that I could get out of there.

When I left the police station I felt totally dejected and vowed that I would never allow myself to be in such an intimidating situation again. As soon as I arrived back at my attic 'home', I emailed the police officer to complain about the way the meeting had been handled, and to document the fact that I had been forced to sign a blank page.

In September 2013, I had conducted my own research in Bath, visiting the lettings agency, about whom I subsequently complained to the Property Ombudsman. The manager asked me all sorts of questions, maintaining that she hadn't been taken in by Dr Moss for one minute. Why then, I wondered, had she done so much business with him, enabling him to rent at least three properties through her agency? She later changed her tune, however, claiming that she was another of Acklom's victims, and that she had been present at 1 Brock Street and had met me when he first showed me around the property. This was not true. What she told *me* that day in September 2013 was that Paul Kaur had been very aggressive towards her and had insisted that she did not come into 1 Brock Street. She told me that she had waited in the offices of Cobb Farr, directly opposite the front door of 1 Brock Street. She may have seen me, but she certainly didn't meet me, and I had never set eyes on her until I visited her in her office eighteen months later.

Thinking back to the day when Acklom showed me around the house in Brock Street, I now believe he told me to wear my expensive clothes because he wanted to parade me in front of the lettings agent, who he knew would be watching from the Cobb Farr offices when we arrived at the house, and later when we went for a stroll, to demonstrate to her that I existed and that I was a woman of considerable wealth. She said that she had been told I was a member of the Spanish family that owned Heathrow Airport, that I was a very private person and that Dr Zac Moss was my agent. Now she suggested that if I wished to know more about him, I should visit two exclusive designer clothes shops in Bath – Christopher Barry and Kimberley – where Acklom had done a lot of shopping. She also told me that a doctor friend of hers, whose name I recognised, might be interested in talking to me. I visited the clothes shops, establishing that Acklom had spent thousands of pounds there on designer clothes for himself and his wife, and also learned that he had bought a £60,000 Porsche Cayenne (paid for with my money, as I later found out from the police) from a dealership called Cameron Cars, run by the son of the husband-and-wife team who owned the clothes shops.

Everybody I spoke to remembered Dr Zac Moss. I was told he always paid cash and that his purchases were delivered to the Old

Rectory in Bathampton. On one occasion he apparently became 'quite shirty' when he was asked to settle his account.

I also visited Gem Solutions, a specialist lighting company in Bath, and had a conversation with a man called Andy who told me that Zac Moss had spent a small fortune on lighting for the Old Rectory and had promised Gem Solutions £5 million of work installing lights on the runway at Kemble airfield. He'd tried to get them interested in some sort of business partnership, but, luckily for them, they declined.

'What a great guy,' reflected Andy, as we sat in his office chatting. 'He took us out to Hudson's [a steak restaurant in Bath] and entertained us all evening. He had so many amazing stories to tell.'

Regarding 1 Brock Street, he told me that he had heard two stories about the property: first, that someone very important from Heathrow had rented it; but then, that it was an 'upmarket knocking shop'. He also told me that the manager of the lettings agency, and another woman, Suzanne, had been taken to London in Acklom's helicopter.

Every day I hoped to hear of some progress in the police investigation, but nothing seemed to happen, and I was told that until there was sufficient evidence to charge Acklom, nothing could be done to try to find him. In the meantime, I continued to be made to feel more like the criminal than the victim in the case.

I stayed on in Tetbury for nine months, but after the initial relief at having a roof over my head, I found myself as isolated as ever. There had been conditions attached to the offer of a place to live, namely that nobody except my brother and my daughters were to visit me, or even know I was there. I'd been trying to hide my real feelings from my daughters, to protect them, and my relationship with my brother was almost non-existent. So, when in November 2013, Charlie's Angel cut me off with no explanation, I experienced a terrible sense of abandonment and betrayal.

I had given her everything I had on Acklom, including some very personal material, and I felt horribly exposed.

Now, spending six days a week on my own, I began to feel like 'the mad woman in the attic' – literally the rooms where I was living. I was terribly alone, slipping back down into deep depression and so, at the beginning of 2014 – just as I had recognised it a year before, when I left Bath – I knew it was time to make a change.

10

REFUGE FROM MYSELF

Bathsheba became at this moment so terrified at her own state of mind that she looked around for some sort of refuge from herself.
Thomas Hardy, *Far from the Madding Crowd*

In January 2014, I returned to Buckinghamshire, staying with my friends Bridget and John. Immediately after my discovery that I had been defrauded and was on the brink of total ruin, Bridget had helped me out more than anyone else, insisting on lending me the money to pay off my credit-card bill. I had moved in with her and John for a few days then, and they'd said at the time that their spare room would be mine any time I needed it.

I had asked the police if they were going to investigate the lettings agency's involvement with Mark Acklom, as I felt that by accepting a vast sum of my money and a forged signature on the tenancy agreement for Brock Street, without carrying out any identity checks, they had been complicit in the fraud. But the police told me that on the contrary – the lettings agency had been most helpful and would not be the subject of any investigation.

They had been anything but helpful to me, however, and I had no doubt that they had behaved in a most unprofessional manner, so I decided to report them to the Property Ombudsman. Despite my strained relationship with my brother, we were still in touch, and it was he who first suggested I make a formal complaint, as in his view this was the only way I might be able to claw back some of my losses. He helped me enormously by drafting a letter to the ombudsman in a clear, concise way, something that I found very difficult to do myself at the time.

One day in February, I picked up two voicemails – one from the investigating officer in Bath asking me to call him, and one from my brother. I called my brother first; he told me that someone purporting to be a detective constable had telephoned him ordering him not to take any civil action against the lettings agency in Bath, and not to help me in any such action. The caller refused to identify himself by any verifiable means, nor would he commit to writing what he was saying over the phone. My brother described him as being aggressive, with a particularly protective attitude towards the lettings agency (and, as my brother pointed out, for all he knew it could have been someone from the agency claiming to be a police officer). I then returned the officer's call. He was aggressive towards me too, warning me to take no action against the lettings agency. I asked him what authority he had to make these demands and told him that in my opinion, this was a civil matter and nothing to do with him. He repeated that I must not take any action, then hung up on me. I had my phone on speaker during this conversation and Bridget, who had heard everything, was dumbfounded. She couldn't believe the hostile manner he had displayed towards me. And I was learning to ensure I had witnesses to all my encounters with the police, and to keep a detailed record of everything.

I had kept in touch with James and, now that I was in Buckinghamshire, was missing our weekly get-togethers over coffee, which had developed into something more romantic at the end of 2013. I think that under normal circumstances this would never have happened, but everything was far from normal and we were trying to make the most of the very difficult circumstances we both found ourselves in by discovering some enjoyment in life. James was in dire straits himself and was surrendering his house voluntarily to the mortgage company and trying to find somewhere to rent. He asked me if I would consider coming with him and I told him I might. You would never have put us together on paper, but Fate had brought us together, we enjoyed each other's company and, with nothing left to lose, we both thought it was worth taking a chance on one another.

There were very few affordable rentals that held any appeal for us, but we viewed three and James asked me which I would choose. There was one that I liked. It was a property that I knew from one of my many walks when I'd first moved to Tetbury – a tiny, detached, dark, damp lodge, in need of renovation, but with romantic appeal, situated in an idyllic location on the outskirts of a pretty Cotswold village, with a river running by and only one close neighbour. James told me he would do his utmost to secure it and I said that if he did, I would join him there. I felt sure that the peace of the place, the beautiful surroundings and James' calming presence would enable me to begin to recover.

On 14 April 2014, we moved, from different directions, into Yewtree Lodge and felt incredibly lucky and happy. It is an extraordinary feeling to enter a relationship with another human being when you each have nothing to offer, except yourself (and I felt a large proportion of me was missing). I revelled in being able to do the most ordinary things. I could do the laundry in a washing machine and hang it out to dry, I had a house to clean and make homely and a very neglected, overgrown garden to clear. That evening, we lit candles, we cooked steak, we pulled crackers, we wore paper hats and we felt like the luckiest people in the world.

The following few months were a time of great happiness for me, compared to what had gone before, and I derived great pleasure from both being in a beautiful rural location and also from feeling that I had something that felt like home. I almost felt like a child 'playing house' as I went about normal, everyday domestic activities that would previously have held little appeal for me. And James and I tried to make the most of a house and garden that were definitely in need of some TLC. The spring and summer of 2014 were warm and sunny, and I spent as much time as possible out of doors, exploring my new surroundings and taking hundreds of photographs. Looking back over the years, I can see that during my happiest times I get out and about with my camera and take photos; when I am low, I take virtually none. 2014 was a very good year for photos!

For two people who barely knew each other, James and I got on remarkably well and the house and garden at Yewtree Lodge frequently resounded with gales of laughter and much silliness as we made the most of everything that was good in life: we were genuinely happy and it felt like a miracle to me. James had managed to salvage his aircraft-restoration business and we fell into a very comfortable and old-fashioned way of life, with him going off to work each day, while I cooked, cleaned, gardened, baked innumerable cakes and became a veritable domestic goddess. We also took to the skies as often as we could, and I felt elated every time we flew over the glorious Cotswold landscape. But all the time I had to keep the pressure up on the police who didn't seem to have any sense of urgency, nor any real interest in building a case against Mark Acklom or finding him. In fact, they seemed determined to bark up the wrong tree.

On 12 June, I travelled to Bath for a meeting with the investigating officer and a financial investigator, who told me that he had traced the movement of my money. He shocked me when he said that he thought it was Paul Kaur who was the mastermind behind the scam, together with a bank insider. Acklom, he said, was just the 'pretty boy' used to lure me in. I disagreed vehemently – after all, I had been there! It was obvious to me from my own experience and what I had since discovered about Acklom that he was a master criminal who'd been honing his skills for over twenty years and was now at the top of his game. But they just would not listen to me.

The financial investigator told me he had been investigating fraud for thirty years, and he knew better than I did. He also implied that the whole thing was a property scam, and that I was complicit in it, asking me if I knew the word 'trapesco'. I said I'd never heard it before, but he insisted that I had, claiming (falsely) that the word appeared numerous times as a reference on my bank statements, against transfers of money I'd made to Paul Kaur. I asked him to show me the statements, which he failed to do, but he continued to maintain that he was right and I was wrong. Years later, I came across the Spanish word '*trapaso*', meaning transfer, on the Antifraudintl website where it appeared on some anonymised bank statements (not mine) relating to transfers made to Mark Acklom (under the name Marc Ros) and others.

During the meeting, there was also some discussion about how demands for money were made, and I explained (again) that requests were usually made by Acklom via text message. Once again, I asked that my mobile phone be examined for evidence of these, but I was told that text messages would not be admissible as evidence as I could not prove that they actually came from Acklom, even if they came from a number that I claimed he used. The brick wall against which I was hitting my head just got harder and harder.

The meeting lasted over two and a half hours and when I left the police station, once again, I was totally exhausted and thoroughly dejected. I felt as though I was being stitched up and my faith in the criminal-justice system slipped a few rungs further down the ladder. Not only did the police not listen to me, it appeared they didn't read what they were given either: it had become clear that the investigating officer knew nothing about Acklom's arrest in Spain or his jumping bail, despite the facts having been detailed at length in the report James had given to him ten months previously.

The day after the meeting, I received an email from the acting detective inspector, telling me that the police were going to concentrate their efforts on Paul Kaur. I contended again that Mark Acklom was the mastermind behind everything that had happened during the eighteen months I was in a relationship with him, but the police insisted otherwise, directing me to alter a Victim Personal Impact Statement I had drafted, so that Paul Kaur assumed as much culpability as Acklom. I was also told that the Crown Prosecution Service needed more evidence before they would authorise any charges against either man. In the meantime, I sent the police my report about my investigations in Bath, told them I had a copy of a £60,000 contract between a model from Bristol and InOrg and also that a judge, who I named, was also conned into a business relationship with Acklom, with the promise of a large cash injection to save his collection of boats.

During the summer of 2014, I eventually completed the paperwork to send to the Property Ombudsman, and made a complaint against the letting agency on five counts, three of which were ultimately upheld.

Although I didn't really want to think about Mark Acklom, I had to, and over the course of the year, as I recalled more and more, and all sorts of things filtered slowly down through my mind, I realised that not only had I been the victim of a financial fraud, I had also been the victim of the most horrible domestic abuse. As Women's Aid points out:

Domestic abuse isn't always physical. Coercive control is an act or a pattern of acts of assault, threats, humiliation and intimidation or other abuse that is used to harm, punish or frighten their victim. This controlling behaviour is designed to make a person dependent by isolating them from support, exploiting them, depriving them of independence and regulating their everyday behaviour.

A law was introduced in December 2015 to make this type of behaviour a criminal act, and perpetrators can be sentenced to up to five years in prison, but unfortunately for me, the law was not in existence when I was in a relationship with Mark Acklom, and I was told that he could not be charged with this offence, despite my repeated attempts to persuade the police otherwise. I also asked if he could be charged with sexual abuse. I don't think the police ever took this seriously but, as I pointed out, I gave consent to sexual relations with a man called Mark Conway who was forty-six years old and single: I never consented to sexual relations with Mark Acklom, aged thirty-eight, a married man and convicted criminal. He fraudulently and knowingly misled and deceived me (and many other women) into having a sexual relationship with him. Although I could not persuade the police to pursue this either, I think it warrants serious consideration, now more than ever (especially in the light of the 'Me Too' movement), and I would dearly love all the women Acklom has lied to in order to get his hands into their knickers, as well as their wallets, to take a group action and pursue this through the courts.

In September 2014, by chance, I came across Jon Ronson's book *The Psychopath Test*, which led me to Robert Hare's *Without Conscience*. Reading Ronson was a revelation in itself – a proper light-bulb moment. The light shone even brighter as I read *Without Conscience*, which confirmed to me that Mark Acklom displayed so many symptoms of psychopathy that he must, by definition, be a psychopath. Hare is a world expert on psychopathy and is responsible for devising the Psychopathy Checklist, now the Psychopathy Checklist-Revised (PCL-R), which 'lets us discuss psychopaths with little risk that we are describing simple social deviance or criminality, or that we are mislabelling people who have nothing more in common than that they have broken the law. But it also provides a detailed picture of the disordered personalities of the psychopaths among us.'

The PCL-R lists twenty character traits:

- Glibness/superficial charm
- Grandiose sense of self-worth
- Need for stimulation/proneness to boredom
- Pathological lying
- Cunning/manipulative
- Lack of remorse or guilt
- Shallow affect
- Callous/lack of empathy
- Parasitic lifestyle
- Poor behaviour controls
- Promiscuous sexual behaviour
- Early behaviour problems
- Lack of realistic long-term goals
- Impulsivity
- Irresponsibility
- Failure to accept responsibility for own actions
- Many short-term marital relationships
- Juvenile delinquency
- Revocation of conditional release
- Criminal versatility

Although Hare warns against non-professionals making diagnoses, it was impossible for me not to do so, and I have no doubt that Mark Acklom would score highly on all counts, if only someone would test him. Hare's book also helped to explain how and why I, as his victim, fell so quickly and easily under his spell. Reading these books marked the beginning of me regaining confidence in myself. I felt absolved of all charges of having been stupid or done something wrong, and I reached a turning point in my struggle to regain my identity.

Looking back over my relationship with Mark Acklom, I can see how once I had fallen in love with him, not content with defrauding me of all my money and possessions, he carried out a cruel and deliberate psychological and emotional assault on me, gradually chipping away at my confidence and sense of self, until not only did I not *feel* like myself, I didn't even recognise myself when I looked in the mirror.

It started with little things, like dismissing a beautiful evening dress I had as being totally unsuitable to wear to accompany him to a Prince's Trust dinner (which, of course, I never attended anyway). Very soon, he'd completely taken over the way I dressed, telling me to get rid of all my clothes because if I was going to be with him I would have to 'look the part'. Making appointments for me to have my hair done at Nicky Clarke seemed wonderful at the time, but now I can see that not only was he painting a picture of himself as a wealthy, generous future husband, he was actually just taking more and more control away from me, ridiculing me when I said that I had always received compliments on my hair when it was cut by my regular hairdresser and telling me I had to leave my old life behind.

When he had finished with the physical transformation (thankfully, failing to persuade me to have Botox or cosmetic surgery), he used psychological tactics to undermine me, saying I was selfish, demanding or hysterical whenever I challenged him.

The games he played, making me believe he was in Syria, that he had been wounded and that he had a brain tumour – all backed up with 'evidence' – were designed to break me down. The high level of planning and theatrical scene-setting show that Acklom is no common fraudster. He is a highly dangerous narcissist and fantasist who demonstrates all the characteristics of the psychopath listed in Robert Hare's checklist. He is capable of wreaking havoc in other people's lives, engineering things so that the tsunami that follows is almost guaranteed to render his victims completely helpless, continuing to unleash total mayhem long after the initial storm has passed. I believe he does all this for two reasons: first and foremost, for monetary gain and the sense of control he has over his victim; and second (a close second), just for the hell of it, for the feeling of power it gives him, for the kick he gets from it – for fun.

To my mind, the way Mark Acklom operates is deeply sinister, and it worries me greatly that despite the fact that he is a serial fraudster, known to be totally amoral, with a pattern of reoffending, to date he has only been faced with short prison sentences. When he is released, he invariably just starts up again, living the high life at other people's expense.

Acklom has seldom shown remorse for any of his crimes (I believe any he has shown was just an act designed to get a reduced prison sentence), and he always presents himself as the victim. He has been at it for over thirty years now. Surely with his history, more effort should be made to stop him? He has spent a few years in prison, but does anyone think of the countless years his victims have lost? As I write this, at the beginning of 2020, apart from having lost everything I had (the accumulation of over thirty years' work and mortgage repayments) I have also lost eight years of my life – first as a result of his appalling abuse, and then in what I can only describe as an ongoing battle: trying to report the crime in the first instance, then getting the police to take it seriously, and latterly some sort of justice and closure. And I have had to do all of this while attempting to deal with my own loss of identity and all the associated problems that are a direct result of my involvement with that despicable man.

It is very easy to glamourise people like Mark Acklom. They are charismatic and engaging and they live the high life. They are very clever and convincing, and people are fascinated by them. Everything appears to sparkle around them. But let's never forget that they are also parasitic and entirely self-serving. They laugh in the face of all things decent and they get a kick out of seeing their victims' despair. In short, they are utterly diabolical, and society needs to be protected from them.

In November 2014, the police decided that they did, after all, need to examine the mobile phone that Acklom had given me, but although I had asked them to check it at the beginning of the investigation, and again at the meeting with the financial investigator, I now found, with my growing mistrust of the police, that I was reluctant to hand it over.

At the end of January 2015, I received an email from a Detective Inspector Adam Bunting telling me that he was now supervising the investigation, and a meeting was arranged for him to introduce himself to me in person. I forwarded him an email that I had recently sent to his predecessor, outlining a number of concerns I had about the investigating officer, and he responded saying that the detective constable was committed to the case. I had already asked the DC what data would be extracted from my phone, telling him that I was reluctant to hand over all my personal information (which included my photos, about which I was particularly sensitive, and all my contacts, which included the names and addresses of a number of people who had helped me, but had expressly told me they wanted nothing to do with the police). The police wanted evidence of the numerous text messages that Acklom had sent me with instructions to transfer money, all of which – apart from the very first which had been sent to my original phone – had been deleted, either by Acklom himself or by me on his instruction. The DC had assured me that they would only extract deleted data from my phone. Now, as I didn't trust him, I decided to ask DI Bunting the same question. He gave me a different reply, saying that it was not possible to extract only deleted data from the phone, and that all the data from the phone would have to be retrieved.

With my confidence in the police by now non-existent, I started to think about other ways of finding Mark Acklom. I contacted Stuart Higgins, who had been Editor of the *Sun* newspaper in the mid-1990s, and whom I had met some years before, thinking that the media might raise awareness of Acklom and increase the chances of him being found. And so it was, that in February 2015, Stuart introduced me to Martin Brunt, Crime Correspondent for Sky News.

11

WATCHING THE DETECTIVES

And with the voicing of his question, Garp heard the cold hop of the Under Toad thudding across the cold floors of the silent house.
John Irving, *The World According to Garp*

On a cold, grey February afternoon, I met up with Martin Brunt and Stuart Higgins in London and told Martin my story. He was fascinated and thought that it would lend itself well to an hour-long documentary, particularly as he soon found out that Sky had archive footage of Acklom during his trial in London back in 1991.

Two days later, I attended a long meeting with the police in Bristol (the police station in Bath having now closed down). I took my friend Chris with me, so that there would be a witness to everything that happened. I had been asked to bring my phone for examination and was told that the police wanted me to sign another witness statement. But the main purpose of the meeting was to meet DI Adam Bunting, and to establish a level of trust between me and the police.

DI Bunting introduced himself and Detective Sergeant Helen Holt. The detective constable was also in the room, sitting away from the main table at a computer, typing up a statement for me to sign. I was surprised that this had not been prepared beforehand, particularly as it transpired that it related to information I had given him six months previously. DI Bunting only attended the first half of the meeting, and I disappointed him when I told him that I had just brought my BlackBerry phone in for examination (one that Acklom had given me to use when he was in Syria). He emphasised the importance of trust in the relationship between the police and me, was at great pains to reassure me that they were working hard on the case and stressed that I could have absolute faith in them. He told me, again, that it was imperative that the other phone was examined.

The meeting dragged on for four hours and was exhausting. I was asked to look through my previous statement and confirm that it was accurate. Reading over it, I remarked that I would need to check the number of Barclays Bank transfers that had been made from me to Acklom via his accomplice, Paul, as I couldn't remember offhand, at which point the DC turned around and looked straight at me, exclaiming in an exasperated tone of voice, 'Trust me, there are fifty-four. I counted them, *and so did my daughter.*' I was aghast. The DS had just stood up and was leaving the room to get some water. I scribbled a note to Chris on my notepad. 'Daughter went through my bank statements!' Chris nodded and mouthed 'Wait.' I waited until DS Holt returned to the room and then repeated what the DC had said and asked her for an explanation. At this point the DC interjected and said that his daughter had only been counting the highlighted transactions on the bank statements. He then shielded the left-hand side of the statement that was uppermost in the file and said that she had only seen the right-hand column. I asked him if his daughter was a police officer and he said no. I asked for some time out and DS Holt escorted Chris and me to the canteen where I explained to Chris that I wanted to leave. I was very upset, and astounded that an unauthorised person had been given access to confidential evidence in a police investigation.

It begged all sorts of questions: where had this happened? Had the DC taken the files home? If not, what was his daughter doing in the police station? What else had she seen? The questions flew around in my head, a blizzard of stinging hailstones.

Chris and I returned to the meeting room to say that we wanted to leave. Both the DC and DS Holt were there. I hung back in the doorway as Chris went in to get his coat. Brandishing a sheaf of papers, the DC spoke to him.

'Let me explain,' he said. Showing Chris a letter from Barclays Bank, he went on to say that all his daughter had been doing was counting the pieces of paper that he now held out in front of him.

I challenged him saying, 'You've changed your tune: that's not what you said before!' but he went on, still addressing Chris, ignoring me, telling him that there was no identifying information on those pages.

Once again, I asked to leave, and DS Holt escorted us to the front door of the police station. I felt sick – sick to the core with anger. As we were leaving, I turned to DS Holt and looked her squarely in the eye.

'And you wonder why I don't trust the police?' I said, trying hard to keep my voice from faltering. 'Do *you* find this acceptable?'

DS Holt said she would have to speak to the DC's 'supervisor at the time'.

Chris and I made our way back to the car. I still couldn't get my head around what had happened. The primary purpose of the meeting was to establish trust between the police and me, but I felt thoroughly betrayed, my level of trust now non-existent. There was no way they were ever going to get their hands on my phone after this.

The following day, I received an email from Adam Bunting who had spoken with the DC and DS Holt and seemed to unquestioningly accept the DC's version of events. 'I have explained that his action was unwise,' he said, 'but I see no malice in it.' He also said that it was clear to him that my working relationship with the DC had broken down and that he had made the decision to move the investigation to a new investigating officer, adding that 'due to the vast amount of work already carried out, and his in-depth knowledge of the investigation, [the officer] will need to have some further involvement'. He went on to ask me, again, to hand over my phone for examination, saying, 'I understand your concerns re privacy but repeat my promise that we will only look for relevant information and will delete all other personal information.'

It still seems incredible to me that Adam Bunting thought I would believe anything he had to say about promises, or that I would think for one minute that any information I gave him would be handled in confidence. I replied at some length, asking him to clarify various points that I did not understand in relation to the investigation. And regarding the DC's behaviour, I commented, 'I find it totally unacceptable that anyone other than a police officer, or someone working for the police, should be given access to confidential police evidence. You say you think [the officer] was "unwise" to give his daughter such access; I think it is more serious than that.'

In the meantime, a new investigating officer, DC Clare Ball, was assigned to the case. On 12 March, I had an introductory meeting with her and DS Helen Holt, during which we completed the statement that was being prepared at that fateful previous meeting. I was pressed again to hand over my phone, but couldn't bring myself to do so, finding the thought of the police having access to years of photographs, emails and text messages unbearable. It felt like another violation and I still didn't trust them at all. They had a meeting planned with the Crown Prosecution Service on 7 April and I was disappointed to hear that the original investigating officer would be attending, together with DS Helen Holt. A further meeting was arranged for 27 April for Clare and Helen to tell me the outcome.

At that meeting Clare told me that no charges had been authorised and explained that the CPS had stated that they would only consider doing so if all three suspects (Acklom, Kaur and a female bank insider) could be charged together. Consequently, Kaur and the bank insider's bail had been cancelled. I was shocked and dismayed, as for many months I had been under the impression that the evidence against them was compelling, and I could not understand how justice would be served if they were allowed to walk away scot free just because Mark Acklom had not been found. To add insult to injury, I was told that the CPS would not authorise a European arrest warrant (EAW) for Acklom to be raised in this country. As the news sank in, I felt profoundly depressed. Clare explained that I could appeal the CPS decision and I asked if I could have sight of the CPS report, so that I could fully understand what I would be appealing against. I was told that unfortunately this would not be possible, as it was confidential. However, she said I could apply to the CPS for details of it.

I had been asked to bring in various documents with me, including the ombudsman's report relating to the lettings agency. Clare reminded me that the previous DC had asked for a copy of the report and I had failed to provide it. She said my behaviour looked suspicious. I explained to her that the reason I had not handed the document over at that time was because I'd had serious doubts about his behaviour (I had since made a formal complaint about him).

Towards the end of the meeting, I was shocked to discover that neither Clare nor Helen was aware of the CCTV footage of my first encounter with Mark Acklom in the shop. Neither were they aware that my signature had been forged on the tenancy agreement for 1 Brock Street – in fact, they knew nothing about the agreement. I gave them a copy of the document and they scrutinised the relevant page and agreed that the signature was nothing like mine. I was appalled that neither officer had any knowledge of these crucial pieces of evidence. They did not even appear to have read my original 'outline report', a document I had given to the police when I was first interviewed in 2013 and which, in my view, was fundamental to any understanding of what had happened. The CCTV footage and the tenancy agreement had been given to the police at the same time, along with a mountain of other information about Mark Acklom, and it soon became clear that they had no knowledge of any of it. I realised that they lacked the most basic knowledge of the facts of the case.

The discussion moved on to the examination of my mobile phone and I was told that I had to be seen to be 'whiter than white'. I stressed that it was only because the police had proved to be untrustworthy that I was now so reluctant to hand it over, repeating that they had previously had every opportunity to examine it, but had refused to do so. I suggested that I could arrange for the phone to be examined by an independent body, but was told that if I did that and produced any 'evidence', it would be assumed that it had been doctored. I told Clare and Helen that in my view the business with my mobile phone had been blown up out of all proportion and I felt I had become a scapegoat. I did not go on to elaborate, but what I meant was that the emphasis on my phone, and casting doubt on my character, were being used to take the spotlight off the totally incompetent handling of the investigation, which had resulted in two suspects – against whom I had been told the police had compelling evidence – walking free.

I also informed Clare and Helen that there *was* something they could do to help their understanding of what had happened between me and Mark Acklom, which was to read Robert Hare's book *Without Conscience*, a copy of which I had with me. I explained that I was convinced that Acklom was a psychopath and that reading this book, or even just some short extracts from it and a couple of other texts I had with me, would shed light on the crime. Hare is particularly keen to educate the police about the dangers of the psychopath, but neither officer seemed interested.

I have never kept a daily diary, but during the course of the police investigation I sometimes put pen to paper, usually when I was feeling very low, so that in the event that I took my own life there would be some record of how I was feeling. Not exactly a suicide note (although that is how I used to refer to these entries), more a howl of pain and anguish. The one I penned in the early hours of the following morning was one of the loudest.

Meanwhile, Martin Brunt at Sky News was still hoping to make a documentary. At the end of April 2015, resources at Sky were stretched, with a massive amount of attention being given to the election, the Hatton Garden heist and an earthquake in Nepal. But on 12 May, I received an encouraging email from Martin:

Everything held up by election coverage but some progress and going to Spain tomorrow. Acklom is in jail there, on remand for crimes he fled from two years ago. Will know more when I arrive and whether I can see him. Details of previous jail terms and in pursuit of victims.

I was delighted to hear of Martin's progress, but I was also worried that if he were to meet Acklom, he would be duped by him, even with the knowledge he had. So, I responded with some advice:

I hope all goes well in Spain and that you get some good leads. Do not be taken in by Acklom if you get to meet him (which I hope you do). He is a master manipulator and utterly convincing.

Martin returned having interviewed Mark's secretary, Fernanda, and an accountant, and he was chasing various other leads, but he still didn't know for certain where Acklom was being held, although he suspected Murcia. James thought this was likely as he knew that Acklom's wife's family lived there.

On 5 June, there was a breakthrough when Martin called me to say that he had had it confirmed that Acklom was in the main prison in Murcia. I immediately called Adam Bunting to pass on the news and asked if he could verify it. DI Bunting said he had no idea where Acklom was and asked me what led me to believe that he was in Spain. I told him that a journalist friend had given me the information, but he seemed unimpressed as I had no proof. Once again, he asked me why I was still reluctant to have my phone examined, when a year ago I had been asking the police to do just that. I told him that perhaps I valued my life a little more now.

On 22 July, Lara (who was proving herself to be a natural sleuth) discovered video footage on the internet of Mark Acklom in court in Spain. Here was the evidence I needed, and I sent it to DI Bunting, wondering why we had been able to find it when the police had not. He emailed me the following day, saying, 'It is good news that we know where he is now,' and went on to tell me that the examination of my phone was now critical.

In August, I was told that the Sky documentary wouldn't happen, due to lack of funding. This was a blow for Martin and me, although he told me that he would continue to do what he could to follow up his investigations. And as Lara continued with hers, she unearthed a five-page spread about Acklom, written for *GQ* magazine by Nick Cohen, back in 1992. It was a fascinating, though chilling read and reinforced my belief that Acklom is a psychopath. Entitled 'I was a teenage fraudster', the article's byline read: 'While his peers were busy picking their spots, 16-year-old Mark Acklom got grown men to part with thousands and took a building society for £446,000. Nick Cohen meets a bright young sting.' The article began:

> The pallid face of Britain's youngest yuppie criminal broke into a grin of pure adolescent delight. I can still do it, the smile said. Despite my father and girlfriends leaving me in the shit, despite the poxy press building me up into some kind of teenage Robert Maxwell, despite the judge throwing the book at me, despite being jailed, beaten and humiliated, I can still make people trust me. *Believe in me.*
>
> 'You'll never guess what I'm going to do,' he said, his eyes shining behind his thick accountant's glasses.
>
> 'Go on.'
>
> 'Be a priest. Can you imagine it? Me a priest?' …
>
> Now this financial *wunderkind*, this emblematic product of the late Eighties, is sitting there saying that he has got religion and will become a wet member of the caring Nineties.
>
> It's so clichéd, I'm almost disappointed. But a second later he adds, 'It's a brilliant idea. They can't refuse parole to a priest, can they?' Ah, so that's his game. That explains the triumphant laugh. He's still conning them. He's enrolling in theological college because the Roman Catholic authorities can dig him a tunnel straight out of prison.

Cohen was obviously disarmed by Acklom, not really knowing what to make of him, but ultimately coming to the conclusion that he was a spoiled little rich kid who had had too much too soon. I thoroughly recommend reading the whole article as it is utterly gripping, illustrating many of Acklom's psychopathic traits. I passed the article on to the police, again wondering why they had not found it themselves.

* * *

In October, Martin visited Acklom in prison in Spain and I was still genuinely fearful that despite my warnings, he would be taken in. Reporting back to me, Martin said that Acklom talked at high speed, virtually non-stop, presented himself as the victim in his own life story, showed off his 'IRA torture wounds' (which he had also shown me, and which, as I later found out, he had shown Rick Libbey of the Prince's Trust – a move that had made Rick very suspicious of him) and described my allegations against him as 'rubbish'. After the meeting, Acklom wrote Martin a number of letters in which he promised to lead a good life and spoke about the love he felt for his wife and children – all the old tricks, as far as I was concerned. After all, what type of man would use his own two-year-old daughter as a prop in his charade? Martin subsequently admitted that he had felt some sympathy for him.

The police investigation didn't seem to be progressing further and I found it galling to think of Acklom – a sitting duck in a Spanish jail – every day getting one step nearer to his release date, whenever that might be. In July, he had been sentenced to three years, but had spent months on remand and I feared that he would be released before the police here had compiled their case against him. Unusually, although the CPS had not authorised any charges at that fateful meeting back in April, the police had not closed the file. My relationship with them, however, remained strained. On 12 November, I attended yet another meeting with them, this time in Amersham police station, at which I met Detective Chief Inspector Gary Haskins who told me that he was there because he wanted me to know just how seriously the police were taking the investigation. Adam Bunting and Clare Ball were there too, and this time my friend West came with me for moral support and to be my witness.

DCI Haskins did everything he could to convince me that the police were determined to bring Mark Acklom to justice, and there was some good news: I learned that the CPS had finally assigned a solicitor to the case. The deadlock between the police and me was broken at last, and I agreed to my phone being examined and to a further meeting with Clare Ball. I found it frustrating that I was never given an agenda for these meetings with the police, which often went on for three or four hours, and I suggested to Clare that at our next meeting we begin by going through my original report of the crime, which I was convinced she still hadn't read. That, I told her, would lead to all sorts of other conversations and should help her to understand exactly what had happened between Mark Acklom and me.

On 24 November 2015, we sat down in a large, non-descript meeting room at the High Tech Crime Unit in Bristol, and I relinquished my phone, which was taken away for examination. I had brought a vast amount of paperwork with me – everything I had previously given the police and more, and I got out the report that I'd originally supplied at my first meeting over two years earlier. Seeing Clare empty-handed, I asked if she had her copy. She appeared confused. 'I've not seen that document,' she told me. 'It's not in the file.' I was stunned, and as we started to discuss the case and I produced more and more documents, including James' detailed report, the response was always the same: 'It's not in the file.'

I gave Clare a number of documents to copy, and later emailed her others, including links to the Clifton College fund-raising promotional video and Lara's ninety-six-page document giving detailed information about Acklom. I thought back to the meeting eight months before, at which the police had admitted to having no knowledge of the CCTV footage of my first encounter with Mark Acklom in the shop, or the fraudulent tenancy agreement for Brock Street. At the time, I'd thought they just hadn't bothered to read up on the case, but now it was clear to me that most, if not all, of the documentation I had given the police was missing. On 26 November, Clare emailed me to thank me for all the information I had sent her, saying, 'I will review all the new material and let you know if I need anything else from your files (which at present appear far more comprehensive than mine!).'

A few days later I got a copy of another extraordinary document – the fund-raising briefing papers for Clifton College for the year 2012. It was clear from this that Acklom, using the name Dr Zac Moss, infiltrated the college and was, for a while, involved in the fund-raising activities there, as he told me he was at the time. With regard to the Classic Car Wheeze he was credited with providing a demo plane, Nicolas Cage's Rolls-Royce, the Spitfire flypast that he had told me about (which was, in fact, organised by James, who never received a penny back from Acklom), prizes and celebrity attendance. It was noted that a local celebrity 'made a promotional video and attended the Car Wheeze with her family as a guest of Dr Moss.' Another high-profile TV celebrity 'also appeared after a conversation with Dr Moss – CC [Clifton College] had asked her several times'.

Regarding a proposed *son et lumière*: 'Dr Moss offered his help and guidance on promoting the event … The "names" that could be brought to the event were discussed and Dr Moss used his contacts to approach a number of people: Coldplay, Julio Iglesias, Gary Barlow, etc. … In the meantime Dr Moss approached a number of TV companies to broadcast the event – the income from this alone would have offset any artistes cost and generated a significant profit … Dr Moss also approached several other big potential sponsors such as Chubb and Coca-Cola who were interested in the event if televised.'

It is my belief that Acklom viewed the college as a pot of gold, using it as a gateway into Bristol's high society. As James described in his account, Acklom certainly became very friendly with a female member of staff, whom I believe he was mining for information, and whom I am told he visited at home. The judge with the collection of boats was on the school's fund-raising committee, and John Bresnahan, the property developer and director of InOrg, was a parent at the school. For years, Clifton College declined to be interviewed by the police about any of the above (although I believe they did eventually give a brief written statement), and I was told that the high-profile celebrity claimed to have no recollection of ever having met Dr Zac Moss.

In a final push at the end of another year I emailed DCI Haskins expressing my concerns about the vast amount of evidence that seemed to have gone missing from the files. I told him that I felt there was a conflict of interest that was making it difficult for Clare to be completely open and honest with me as she would not want to highlight any failings in police procedure. It took nine days for him to respond and he didn't address any of my queries, only saying that he agreed with me about being open and honest, and reassuring me that the police were 'striving to secure all available evidence to support bringing Acklom to justice'.

On 10 December, Martin phoned me to say that he had received a scribbled note from Acklom saying that he was due to be released later that month. I told Martin that it was quite likely that Acklom would be playing games with him, but you never knew, so I emailed Clare to tell her. I then asked her if the police had any information about Acklom's sentence, his release date or anything else, but they knew nothing at all about anything.

12

SPEAKING THE TRUTH

If you can bear to hear the truth you've spoken
Twisted by knaves to make a trap for fools
Or watch the things you gave your life to, broken
And stoop and build 'em up again with worn-out tools

Rudyard Kiping, 'If'

Every new year I think to myself, This is the year that everything will turn around. But 2016 was the year in which nothing seemed to happen, and everyone, including me, seemed to be 'off sick'.

The year kicked off for me with a four-hour meeting with Clare during which she took down yet another statement. I was done in and my head was fizzing by the time we had finished, but on 8 January, Clare phoned me with good news: she had had a meeting with the CPS lawyer and he had agreed to apply for a European Arrest Warrant (EAW) in Acklom's name. At last! But my spirits, which had been briefly lifted with this news, soon sank again, when on 21 January, Clare emailed me saying that she had chased the CPS lawyer to see if he'd completed the official charging advice, only to find that he was off sick, and not expected back until the beginning of February. On 4 February, she emailed once more, saying that she had tried to contact him again, but he was now signed off until the end of the month. She told me she had 'requested that a different lawyer progress matters in his absence and highlighted the urgency'. She said she would let me know as soon as she had any news. I felt sick as I thought of the note Acklom had written to Martin telling him he was going to be released towards the end of December. Nobody seemed to know if this was true though, or have an actual release date, and all the police were able to tell me was that he was still in prison on 28 December.

Back at Yewtree Lodge, James and I were in dire straits. His business had folded and with no money at all, we were forced to claim Job Seekers' Allowance, which turned out to be another lesson in frustration, incompetence and never-ending bureaucracy. It saved our skin and we received housing benefit for a few months, but my health was suffering and I felt as low as I had at any time since the whole nightmare had begun. On 9 February, I emailed the DCI asking what, if anything, was being done to further the investigation, but I received no response for two weeks, when he told me he too had been off sick.

I was now feeling so bad that the panic attacks returned. A further email to the DCI went unanswered. Two diary entries written at this time reveal that I was deeply depressed.

8th February 2016

I feel unwell and have felt the 'black dog' of depression overtake everything. There is no money, James and I have signed on, the police are useless – everything is a massive battle and I don't want to live. This has come as a shock because I thought I had climbed high enough out of the pit of despair not to slip back in, but here I am. I am on the verge of tears the whole time. I can't cope and I think of death. I just want to go to sleep and never wake up

11th February 2016
I slept in the living room – or rather I lay awake and slept
intermittently. The panic attacks have returned. I felt I was going to
disappear through the floor, and a heavy weight bore down on my
chest and I had difficulty breathing. I dreamed of Daymer Bay and
wondered if I could go there and just walk into the sea. I just want
to be left alone. I can't take any more. All morning tears have been
streaming down my face. I can't even put on a brave face any more.
I give up.

On 12 February, Clare emailed me to say that the CPS had advised that they had no more staff to review their sick employee's workload and that we were just going to have to wait until the end of the month for him to return to work when, hopefully, things would move on. On 16 February, I asked Clare if she could let me know if Acklom was still in prison and, if so, could she tell me when his release date was? She replied: 'The National Crime Agency have not advised us otherwise and we have still had no direct contact from Spain as requested.'

Some time before this I had made an appointment to see the doctor. I hadn't spoken to a doctor since I was staying with Uma and Antony, and I did it now because I was sure that if I didn't get help, I would take my own life. I don't know exactly when I tried to make the appointment, but I seem to remember that when I called, the earliest appointment they had was not for another three weeks. I didn't think for one minute to say it was an emergency, but I did think clearly enough to book a double time slot, as there was going to be a lot to explain in a very short time. I arrived at the surgery punctually, but they were running late. When I eventually saw the doctor, I broke down in his consulting room, but I caught him glancing at his watch as I tried to explain what I had been through and how I was feeling, and he told me he was running late for a meeting. I think he thought I needed help, but I don't think he believed a word I said.

I don't know how I kept going. I seemed to be back in the surreal world of Mark Acklom, where nothing made any sense, and where I had learned that however bad things seemed, they could always get worse – and so they did.

On 19 February, Clare emailed me to say that, through the NCA, the police had made a further request to the Spanish authorities to establish when Acklom was due for release and advised them of their intention to acquire an EAW. I was also told that Adam had been in touch with the CPS who had agreed to assign 'a replacement lawyer from the serious complex case unit' to the case if the lawyer currently assigned to it had not returned to work by the following week. But at 6 p.m. on 29 February, four years to the day since I had proposed to Mark Acklom, Clare phoned to tell me that he had been released from prison the previous Wednesday, 24 February. It was the call I had been dreading. I felt a screaming pain in my head – as though someone had punched my lights out.

On 2 March, once again I wrote to DCI Haskins requesting a comprehensive update on the case, asking why no direct contact seemed to have been made with the Spanish authorities, expressing my dismay that Acklom had been released and telling him that with the benefit of hindsight, it now seemed to me that the original investigating officer had lost the files on my case after I made my complaint about him – and many other points besides. I asked for a written response in order to avoid misunderstanding, as I had found that with no record of telephone conversations it was easy to misinterpret what was being said. I chased him twice for an answer before he eventually called me on 15 March, but he seemed evasive and skirted around the points I had raised in my lengthy email. And he would commit nothing to writing.

The CPS lawyer returned to work on 15 March, hoping 'to sort Acklom's advice in the near future', and over the next few weeks Clare made contact with Rick Libbey of the Prince's Trust who, she said, was very helpful.

On 15 June, the European Arrest Warrant was finally obtained. I felt no reason to celebrate this landmark; quite the opposite. It had taken three years to produce a bit of paper, which as far as I was concerned, was now useless, because Acklom had had four months in which to travel wherever he chose and reinvent himself.

I had given up with doctors, who only wanted to prescribe antidepressants, and thankfully, the days of claiming benefit were over. I was beginning to feel stronger and had even managed to enjoy a few sunny days, going out on my bike, feeling the wind in my hair and enjoying the beautiful Cotswold landscape. But my emotions were still on a very uneven keel and I sometimes had nightmarish dreams. One I can still recall, it was so bizarre. Acklom was there, dressed as a Gestapo officer and looking menacing. His parents were both there, his father looking ashen, lying in a bath of vomit. I was there too. I remember a lot of white laundry – towels and sheets hanging out to dry – and a grotesque woman was begging me not to resist, although I can't now remember what I was resisting. I awoke with a start, cold and clammy and feeling distinctly disorientated.

Over the next few months, after the granting of the EAW, everything seemed to grind to a standstill once more, until one Sunday afternoon in October I decided to do a bit of my own internet research. This time I concentrated on Acklom's wife, Maria Yolanda Ros Rodriguez. In just a couple of hours, I discovered that within days of Acklom's release from prison, a luxury estate agency was registered in Murcia, with Maria Yolanda named as sole director. I had no doubt that this was the work of Mark

Acklom. The properties, advertised on Prime Location, were all yet to be built, with computer-generated images depicting the latest state-of-the-art designs. There was no telephone number or website for Ross Luxury Estate Agents, just a contact form for interested potential purchasers. It had ACKLOM stamped all over it and I was sure it was a lure to attract people to put down a deposit on land that Acklom didn't own, for a development project that was either completely fictitious or owned by someone else.

I was so furious that the police had not discovered this that I called Martin to tell him what I had found. It turned out that Martin was about to call me himself, to say that he was going to Spain for a press conference to mark the tenth anniversary of the crime-fighting charity, Crimestoppers, and that the National Crime Agency would be naming Mark Acklom as one of the UK's Ten Most Wanted fugitives. The police had mentioned 'Operation Captura' back in September, first saying that Acklom was going to be featured, but then that the NCA had contacted them again saying they should 'hold fire'. I was informed in a subsequent telephone conversation that he would be featured but had heard nothing since.

Martin told me that he would investigate Ross Luxury Estate Agents when he was in Spain and asked if I would agree to give an interview, to be included in a news item about Acklom, due to be broadcast on 19 October. I have always valued my privacy and hated the idea of being exposed in this way, knowing that I would then have an internet presence – something I had always tried to avoid – but I agreed to the interview. It seemed to me that it was the only way to uncover Acklom, and that the publicity it would generate might just lead to his arrest.

When I had finished speaking to Martin, I sent Clare a detailed email about the estate agency I had discovered, giving her links to the company registration information and to the properties on Prime Location. I rounded off saying:

Everything points to this being the work of Mark Acklom. I don't suppose he is actually going to work and sitting at a desk in this office every day, but this is a good lead, and I have to ask why nobody responsible for this investigation in your office, or at the NCA, or in the Spanish police force has picked this up when I managed to do so in a few hours on Sunday?

I have never wanted any sort of fame, preferring to go through life with total anonymity, and I was totally unprepared for the media storm that erupted on 19 October 2016. Even when Martin arrived with a cameraman to interview me, a few days before, I felt very nervous. My hopes for an hour-long documentary in which Acklom's history could be explored in some detail had been reduced to a short news item, but I felt that I had to take the chance to expose him. I also very much wanted to draw attention to what I saw as the failings of the police investigation – but one step at a time.

Even in the familiar surroundings of my 'home' my mouth felt dry and my hands felt cold and clammy as the camera operator set up his equipment, including a horribly bright light. Knowing that I was not at all keen to be photographed, Martin told me that I could be filmed in silhouette, or be pixelated, but I decided that for maximum impact, and so as not to appear afraid (particularly to Acklom, should he see the interview), I would show my face and speak directly to the camera.

I didn't like the intrusion into my 'safe space'. As I stared into the mirror, I thought I looked terrible, and I knew that my appearance would be the first thing that would register in viewers' minds. With my confidence only marginally restored since my eighteen months of surreal hell with Acklom, and still suffering an identity crisis, I pulled my features into something resembling a smile, subsequently worrying that I looked too upbeat and that I had completely failed to convey the catastrophic nature of what had happened to me. I knew that most of the news item would be devoted to Acklom himself, that I would probably be given no more than a minute of edited footage and that I would have no control over the editing.

The exposure I felt that day, as I sat talking to Martin under the glare of a floodlight, with the camera rolling was, however, nothing like when the story broke. I don't know how these things work, but news of the upcoming story had obviously filtered through the media. I was told there would be a news blackout until the morning of Martin's broadcast, but the afternoon before it went out, I received a call from *This Morning* asking if I would appear on the show the following day. I knew that the whole story might be dead within a day or two and that I had to make as much of the opportunity to expose Mark Acklom as possible, even if it meant exposing myself, so I hurriedly packed a bag and made my way to the station.

And so it was that from a hotel room in London, at six the following morning, I tuned into Sky News as I was getting ready to depart for the *This Morning* television studio. My heart was in my mouth as the item kicked off and I heard Martin's voice:

'*Since he was three years old, conman Mark Acklom has been pretending to be someone he's not.*' On the television screen was a black and white photograph of a little boy, marching in profile, dressed as a Queen's Guard, with a real guardsman standing to attention behind him. The news item only ran for a few minutes, but everything seemed to go into slow motion as I sat, glued to the screen, now seeing archive footage of Acklom as a teenager: '*At sixteen, he posed as a stockbroker, stole his father's credit card and hired private jets for jaunts around Europe. He bought this small mansion by duping a building society to give him a half a million-pound mortgage. The public-school, classroom conman was briefly infamous. He went to prison, then he disappeared.*'

Martin went on to talk about Acklom's criminal career, explaining that the British police were now looking for him, before telling the viewers about my involvement with him. The footage cut to me. My mouth felt dry and my hands felt clammy as I watched myself and heard my own voice.

'The bell pinged on the door, I looked up, and there he was. I think the thing to say about him, when you first meet him, is he is someone with great presence and charisma.'

Now Martin was talking again and the CCTV footage of my first encounter with Acklom was showing on the screen. I sat motionless on the hotel bed, riveted.

I felt very strange when the report came to an end. Rather disconnected from it. The whole business with Mark Acklom was surreal enough, but now, having heard the gist of the story told in just a few minutes and having seen myself on television, it felt even stranger. But I had to go and get breakfast before making my way to the television studio and going through it all again, with presenters who I was not sure would be as understanding as Martin was.

I was overjoyed when I got to the hotel lobby to find that Lara and Glenn had come to join me for breakfast and give me some moral support. Glenn said that he could come with me to the TV studio too, which I thought would help enormously. There was a lot of hanging around, and I spent nearly an hour in make-up, emerging feeling even more estranged from my 'self'. Eventually it was time to go into the studio.

I was interviewed by Phillip Schofield and Christine Lampard. Both presenters were sympathetic towards me, and while it is all a bit of a blur to me now, I can confirm that it is incredibly daunting when you have no experience of this sort of thing to find yourself in a television studio with bright lights and cameras rolling, knowing that the broadcast is going out live. At the end of the brief interview I felt exhausted. Glenn and I went to get a coffee and I was then taken to Paddington Station to get the next train home. I kept my head bowed as I caught the train and sat for the duration of the journey with my eyes lowered or staring out of the window. I felt so exposed, I could have been sitting there naked. It was not a pleasant experience at all.

We were only about ten minutes out of Paddington when Stuart Higgins called me to say that the *Mail on Sunday* wanted to interview me, and could I get myself to their offices immediately. I explained that I was already on the train, but agreed to an exclusive with them if they could come to me. It seemed wise to take every opportunity to create as much publicity around the case as possible. When I got home I changed into jeans and a jumper. I had the most terrible headache and really needed to rest, but there was little time for that because a journalist and photographer from the *Mail on Sunday* were hot on my heels.

I liked Claudia Joseph, the interviewer, although she talked non-stop and my head was really splitting. She immediately managed to establish a rapport by telling me she knew the village in which I was living and had a photograph of herself at the village school in the 1960s, which she showed me. We talked for hours as she took notes, and she looked through some photographs on my laptop, telling me she would like a selection to accompany her article. (My advice to anyone who finds themselves with a newspaper reporter: give them nothing – you will regret it otherwise; and ideally, don't speak to anyone if you are tired and have nobody to act as a sounding board.)

As the sun started to go down that afternoon, the photographer said he needed to take some pictures as the light was going, and I was asked if I could change into 'something more colourful'. I was reluctant, as I normally wore jeans and a jumper at home. Perhaps I could put on my leather jacket – good, sensible clothing for life in the country? But no, they wanted something to draw the readers' attention. Claudia had seen a photograph of me at a wedding wearing a red and white dress and asked if I could wear that. It seemed a very odd choice to me, for an October evening, as it had a Bardot, sweetheart neckline and was obviously a summer dress. Nevertheless, despite my own misgivings, I capitulated and went off to change. My legs hadn't seen the sun for over two years and I had no tights, so I said that I did not want my legs to show in any photograph that was used. That was agreed, verbally, and we went outside for what I hoped would be a quick, discreet photoshoot. No such luck. The photographer had lights and a light reflector with him, and I could hardly have drawn more attention to myself if I had tried. I hoped that no walkers would appear on the footpath that cut through the property, but of course they did, including my landlord. I acknowledged him with a wave but felt acutely embarrassed. Eager to get the whole thing over as quickly as possible, I just did what I was told. In retrospect, I don't know why I just didn't refuse to do anything other than what I would have liked – a natural-looking picture of me smiling, wearing jeans, boots and a jacket. I was told not to smile though, and the following Sunday, when I saw the article, I was horrified. The photograph made me look ridiculous: wearing the red and white dress, sitting on a Cotswold stone wall, looking haggard and miserable. Worst of all, my legs were displayed for all to see in their pallid, unshaven glory! When I spoke to Claudia about it and told her I thought the photo made me look terrible she responded saying, 'I think that was the idea.'

Prior to publication, Claudia sent me the first draft of her article, which I thought was rather good. There was a problem though. She'd been asked for 2,000 words, but she had delivered 4,000, and by the time it had been edited, it was far less than half as good, the editing giving it a bias towards the salacious and sleazy. I learned a lot from the experience and would handle the situation much better now: I was on a very steep learning curve.

The story ran for ten days and was picked up by just about every newspaper, grabbing bold headlines everywhere it appeared: 'The Real Catch Me If You Can con artist', shouted the *Sun*; 'He even fleeced his own mum'. 'Conman's trail of planes, cars and broken hearts', cried the *Sunday Times*. 'Ex-public schoolboy fraudster "fleeced lonely divorcée out of £850k life savings",' yelled the *Daily Mail*. 'If a middle-class woman like me can be duped into sex – and out of £850,000 – by a fake MI6 spy … so can you,' shrieked the *Mail on Sunday*. I received many requests for interviews, which came via Martin, the police and Lara, but I couldn't really cope with the pace of it all. So, having done interviews for Martin, *This Morning* and the *Mail on Sunday*, I only agreed to one more.

The coverage in the media was generally sympathetic, although the focus of interest, of course, was Mark Acklom and his life of deception. What I most objected to was the way in which, across all media, I was described first and foremost as a 'divorcée', which carries with it a whole host of negative connotations (she's old, she's sad, she's lonely, she's desperate, she's fleeced some poor man, she's a gold-digger) – a term which, in the masculine form, is virtually never used to describe a formerly married man who hits the headlines. I also felt that the reports in the press were inherently misleading, saying I had lost my savings – as if I'd had a spare £850,000 sitting in the bank. Seldom did they make it clear that the bulk of the money was realised from the sale of my house, and that I had been left destitute.

I tried to avoid viewing any comments about my story on news websites, feeling sure they would all be negative, but occasionally I couldn't, and – even expecting the worst – I was quite shocked at how nasty and misogynistic some of them were. They were nearly all of the 'stupid woman' kind, and one read, 'She is divorced, so was it even her money?' – a remark that to me was so totally ridiculous I had to laugh. But really it is no laughing matter, just another very sad example of a deep vein of misogyny running through society, and not a comment that would ever be made about a man.

For a few days after the Sky broadcast and the ensuing media flurry, once again I found myself indoors with the blinds down, and rather hoped that nobody living locally would realise that the person staring out of their newspaper was me. But once all the fuss had died down, I actually felt a lot better, not only for having exposed Acklom, but also for having 'come out' myself. I was surprised at the number of friends who saw me on Sky News, *This Morning* or in their newspaper, and it really boosted my confidence to receive their messages of support and encouragement. There were many people with whom I had lost contact since meeting Mark Acklom, as although I wrote to my closest friends in the immediate aftermath, I didn't have the energy or the will to contact everyone, and I think that a lot of them didn't really know how to respond when they heard the news. Also, although I tried to appear 'normal' when I met people, for a long time – even now, sometimes – I shied away from socialising at all, because it was just too exhausting and difficult. I felt that many people didn't realise that however I appeared on the surface, I wasn't able to function normally. Things are much better now, but it is still very much a work in progress. In any case, at the end of October 2016, I just hoped that all the publicity would help to make people aware of Mark Acklom and maybe lead to his arrest.

Soon after the Sky broadcast, I received a phone call from Clare Ball. The police, who knew nothing about my interview with Martin, had seen the news coverage and were fielding calls as a result.

'Why did you do it, Carolyn?' she asked me.

'Because I was so frustrated at the apathy of the police,' I replied. 'It was I who told you he was in prison in Spain. You should have been telling me. He was a sitting duck for eight months, but even then, you didn't get him. And it was I who told you about the estate agency in Murcia. That should have been the other way around too. The story needs to be out there.'

Clare said she could understand how I felt but warned me that I might be jeopardising any court case, as Acklom would claim that with all the publicity, he would not receive a fair trial.

And what court case is that? I thought to myself. We're nowhere near a court case. But I said nothing.

After the flurry of activity sparked by the media interest, many leads came in to the police, but they all seemed to be dead ends. Then, after a few weeks, everything died down and the year limped to an end.

In mid-November, I discovered from the Spanish expat website, Olive Press, that Acklom was now using the name Mark Long. I emailed Clare and she responded saying that she did a weekly search, but could I send in any new information as 'it's still easy to miss stuff'. In mid-December, Clare and Adam were at last supposed to be meeting with the doctor who had been in a relationship with Acklom, who I knew had given him money, and who I suspected of having bandaged his arm and head when he was feigning gunshot wounds and brain surgery. But when I contacted them to ask how the meeting had gone, they said she had cried off at the last minute and there was nothing they could do to make her talk. It seemed that everything had ground to a halt once more.

Just before Christmas, I emailed Clare to say that the police hadn't relayed any information to me from the Spanish authorities since I'd told them I believed Acklom to be in prison in Spain back in June 2015. I asked for an update, saying: 'It seems to me that nothing whatsoever is being done to try to find Acklom, either here or in Spain and elsewhere.' She responded:

Despite multiple emails to the NCA I have had no update re what proactive action is being taken to try and locate Acklom. I think I will have to escalate with Adam in the new year as it is somewhat ridiculous that we are getting nothing back from Spain at all.

This did nothing whatsoever to reassure me, and I ended 2016 feeling proud of what I had done to shine a spotlight on the case, but once again that the police didn't really have any interest in it.

13

PROOF OF STRENGTH

It might be desirable to die; but this privilege was evidently to be denied her. Deep in her soul – deeper than any appetite for renunciation – was the sense that life would be her business for a long time to come. And at moments there was something inspiring, almost exhilarating, in the conviction. It was a proof of strength – it was proof that she should some day be happy again.

Henry James, *The Portrait of a Lady*

Another new year dawned. In my mind's eye, I had given myself a maximum of five years to come to terms with the events of 2012/13, and thought that by my sixtieth birthday, surely, I would be feeling like myself again. Perhaps I might even have a job and feel like having a birthday party and seeing some old friends. As the time drew nearer, however, I had no job, and although I told myself it might do me good, the thought of organising a party filled me with dread.

Approaching my sixtieth made me realise just how much Acklom continued to dominate and control my life. Not only had he stolen all my money and possessions, he had robbed me of five years. But the more I thought about it, the less I blamed him, and the more I felt let down by the criminal-justice system. I remembered the meeting I had had with James' solicitor in the immediate aftermath of the discovery of Acklom's true identity, and how he had advised me to put all my energy into trying to get my life back on track. I have often thought back to that day, and in my darkest hours have thought that his was the most sensible counsel anyone has given me.

Having been through what I have been through with the police, my advice to anyone thinking about embarking upon a quest for justice might well be 'Don't do it!' The recent bestseller about the workings of the criminal-justice system, *The Secret Barrister*, draws attention to the plight of witnesses:

> Nearly half of all witnesses surveyed said that they would not be willing to take part in criminal proceedings on a future occasion. If they witnessed your daughter being mugged, they would not assist in bringing her assailant to justice. If you were falsely accused of assault, they would not come forward to say that they saw you acting in self-defence. If they were themselves a victim, they would not entrust the justice of that crime to the state, preferring, one infers, that the miscreant go unpunished, or be subject to a more immediate, possibly divine, form of retribution.

I think that it would have been impossible for me at the time not to involve the police and not to keep on at them in the hope that they would get a result, and that justice would eventually be served, but there have been times when I wish I hadn't. I wanted Acklom stopped in his tracks. I didn't want anyone else to go through what I'd been through, and yes, I hoped for the return of my money. What I felt at the beginning of 2017, three and a half years after my initial attempt to report the crime, was that the police had robbed me of that time, that they weren't fully on my side and that Martin and I had been doing the job they should have been doing.

On 11 January, I once again wrote to Clare asking for an update. I didn't mince my words:

Hi Clare

I have heard nothing from you since 23rd December and would appreciate it if you could let me know what is being done by you, the NCA and the Spanish police to locate Mark Acklom? Please could you also let me know what was done after I informed you, on 11th October 2016, that I believed Acklom had set up a company, Ross Luxury Estate Agents, in Murcia, and was operating there? Was this ever followed up and investigated? Is anybody still working on this case as I get the impression that the investigation has been more or less shelved.

Again, I heard nothing, until Clare called me on 2 February. She still didn't have any information from Spain but there were some new leads in Bath. I was told that around the time I met him, Acklom had been renting a property in Widcombe, owned by David Hadfield, a local architect, and Clare wanted to know if Acklom had taken me there. Very early on in our relationship he had taken me to a property on the outskirts of Bath that he said he was renting with a view to buying, but we had gone there after dark and I wasn't sure where it was, although I could clearly remember driving along a very narrow road, the approach to the property from the road and the property itself. Clare sent me some photographs of the house Acklom had rented and it definitely wasn't where I had been taken, but I was intrigued. I opened up my laptop to look the address up on Street View. It was impossible to find the rented house (which I later realised is not visible from the road), but as I made my way along the road on Street View it felt familiar, and suddenly, I was sure I was at the end of the drive of the property Acklom had taken me to. I remembered that we had turned right into a drive, going downhill past a large Bath stone house on our left, bearing right until we came to a long, low outbuilding, which I recalled him saying was a converted dairy. The back of the building was parallel to the road, set down below it, and I thought it must have been up against the boundary, because as far as I could remember, there had been no windows in the back wall, and only a gravel drive-way at the front. When we arrived, the front of the house was illuminated by a mass of fairy lights. Mark had explained that he was in the process of moving out. He seemed agitated and we stayed there no more than ten minutes.

Now, on Street View, I could see a building below me to the right, and it looked just like the place Acklom had taken me to, but it wasn't the house the police were talking about. As I moved along the road, I couldn't find any house name at the end of the drive – only the name of the large Bath stone house that I felt sure was the large house we had driven past as we had headed down the drive to Acklom's bachelor pad.

I emailed Clare and told her that I'd looked at the photos she'd sent me of the house Acklom had rented and it wasn't the place he had taken me to; but I also told her about the other property that felt familiar. She replied saying that the rented house had a two-bedroom annexe, and she wondered if that was where Acklom had taken me. Without any photos of the annexe I couldn't say, but I told her about the long, low building that I had seen on Street View and sent her some screen shots. It was later confirmed that this was indeed the annexe of the house that Acklom had rented from David Hadfield.

During my conversation with Clare that day my jaw dropped as she revealed a treasure trove of new information. The police had discovered that Acklom had been reported to them back in April 2012, around the time I moved into Brock Street. A private investigator had been employed by Hadfield to find out about Dr Zac Moss and Clare now gave me some of the details. Acklom had rented a house from Hadfield on a short-term let in December

2011, initially introducing himself as Mark Moss, an international banker who piloted his own plane and was having a house built in the New Forest. No sooner had he moved into the house than he expressed an interest in buying it and commissioned Hadfield to draw up plans for a £3 million extension. By all accounts, Acklom was very keen to integrate into Bath society and was soon getting to meet some of his well-off neighbours, now introducing himself as Dr Zac Moss, a paediatric neurosurgeon. Among many other claims he made, he said that a well-known female television personality was buying a 'second penthouse' from him. Acklom's wife, Maria Yolanda Ros Rodriguez, was introduced as Mary Moss, a prominent Spanish property developer. It transpired that Hadfield's partner, a property developer in Bath, became suspicious of Mark Moss/Dr Zac Moss and persuaded him to hire a private investigator to dig into Moss's past. In February 2012, at just about the time I met Acklom, the private investigator submitted his report to his client, explaining that what he had discovered was so alarming that it was imperative it was reported to the police. This duly happened in April 2012, when the PI's report was passed on to two police constabularies – Gloucestershire and Avon & Somerset.

'Of course, we didn't know who we were dealing with,' Clare told me, 'because we didn't have his name.'

But they *did* have a name, Dr Zac Moss, and he could easily have been found under that name had anyone bothered to investigate him at that time. Then I could have been spared all the misery I have been through, and possibly not have lost anything – other people too. The worst-case scenario, in my view, should have been that Dr Moss was identified as already having been reported to the police when I reported him and gave the police a number of aliases, including Dr Zac Moss, in June 2013. Why did it take almost four years for them to realise that they already had a detailed private investigator's report on him, warning that he was building up to a big scam? And why did they do absolutely nothing about it at the time?

At the end of February, Clare met the private investigator, the CPS appointed yet another solicitor, as the previous one had been promoted and wasn't going to take his current workload with him, and I decided to make an official complaint about the vast amount of documentation that was missing from the police files.

A week later, I received a phone call from the detective inspector who was dealing with my complaint. I told him that I could send him copies of numerous emails to show that I had raised the issue with the police on many occasions and had received no satisfactory response, but he said that would not be necessary. He explained that it was important to keep focused on the investigation and implied that conducting a full inquiry into my complaint now would hinder the ongoing work being done by the team. He asked if I would be happy to receive a letter, and I said that I would if it demonstrated that my concerns had been investigated and dealt with appropriately. I had not named anyone in particular on my complaint form, but the police named the original investigating officer in their response (which suggested to me that they already knew he had done something wrong), and I confirmed that I suspected that he was responsible. I explained that I just wanted to know what had happened to all the documents that I knew had gone missing from the files. The DI said I had been very reasonable and told me he would be in touch again soon.

On 11 April 2017, I attended a meeting with Clare, the purpose of which was to show me that the police had all the documentation I had given them. I had previously said that I thought this meeting would be rather pointless because I had already supplied the police, for a second time, with any documents that I knew were missing, but it went ahead anyway.

About half a dozen lever-arch files were brought into the meeting room, and conversations were had around some of the documents. Most discussion, however, centred on the fascinating document that I knew about but had never seen before: the private investigator's report on Acklom – or Dr Zac Moss as he was calling himself to everyone, except me, at the beginning of 2012. I was sure that this was designed to distract me from the primary purpose of the meeting, and if that was so, it had the desired effect.

I was not given the report to read myself, but Clare went through it, reiterating what she had originally told me. As well as getting David Hadfield to draw up plans for an expensive extension to the house, Acklom also told him that he would need an architect to redesign Kemble airfield, along the lines of Farnborough. I was told that Hadfield was taken to the restaurant at Kemble, where Dr Zac Moss was greeted like an old friend. It seems that Acklom was using Hadfield as an unwitting conduit into Bath society. Clare said that there was also a report of a woman in Cheltenham who 'lost' £1 million, in similar circumstances to mine.

Clare also referred back to the police visit to the Little Coach House and the phone call I had received from the female police officer when I had been sitting in the car with Acklom and Paul Kaur just prior to the visit to MI6 in April 2012. Neither the police nor I had been able to work out what had been going on. Before the case was assigned to Avon & Somerset police, I had gone for an interview at Cirencester police station and I had told the detective sergeant that there should be a record of me on file because two officers from that police station had visited my cottage the previous year. I also said that I had been contacted by an Officer Harding. The DS told me that there was nobody of that name at the police station, and when I gave her some details of the telephone conversation, she said that the bank would never have contacted the police in that way. I subsequently went to Barclays Bank and spoke to an assistant manager there, who confirmed what the DS had said. For years, as I'd tried to work the whole thing out, I believed that the visit by the police and the subsequent telephone call were staged by Acklom. Now, however, Clare said it had come to light that Cheltenham police had contacted me in April 2012 because of the PI's report. If it was they who contacted me, it seems incredible that police making enquires at that time were satisfied by a phone call during which the police didn't identify themselves to me, or me to them, by any verifiable means, also bearing in mind that when I took the call I was sitting with 'Dr Moss' himself, who was directing my side of the conversation. In theory, I should have been alerted to what was happening and given some details about the alleged perpetrator – the police should have met me in person. Acklom could have been apprehended and I could have been spared the subsequent years of hell that I had to endure. At the very worst, when I reported Acklom to the police in June 2013, the name Dr Zac Moss should have flagged up, but it took another four years for the police to even realise that Acklom had already been reported to them, with a serious warning about what he was up to, and that they had made contact with me at the time.

In mid-May, I received a letter from the DI who was dealing with my complaint about the loss of documents I had given to the police. He summed up by admitting that some items of evidence had gone missing and mistakes were made, but said, 'I am satisfied there are no misconduct issues to consider for any serving member of this organisation.' I immediately saw through what seemed to me to be a smokescreen, for as far as I was aware, the original investigating officer was no longer a 'serving member' of the police force. I pressed the point but was told: 'If [name] was responsible for any of this he cannot be dealt with in this process as he is no longer a member of the organisation.' Surely,

I thought, if anyone was suspected of losing evidence, they should be investigated and not be immune just because they had left the police force? I was told I had a right to appeal the decision, but again, I didn't have the energy to jump through more and more hoops in a complaints procedure that, it seemed to me, was designed to run the complainant into the ground.

At the end of May, Martin called to say he had been contacted by someone who claimed to be a past victim of Acklom, who had spotted him with another man outside a café in Geneva and had a photograph to prove it. Martin wondered if I might recognise Acklom's mystery companion. I told him that I was aware of a sighting a couple of weeks before, and that I had understood from the police that Acklom was under surveillance, but I'd heard nothing more. Martin sent me the half of the photograph he had received; it showed the profile of a man with his hand over his mouth, but I didn't recognise him, and we wondered if he might be Acklom's next victim. By the next day, Martin had seen the complete photo and confirmed that it also depicted Acklom, and the day after that, 2 June, he was at the café in Geneva, on Acklom's trail, and a news item was broadcast on Sky that day. Once again, media interest was sparked, but Mark Acklom was nowhere to be found. Once again, the trail went cold.

Martin, meanwhile, thought he knew who Acklom's companion in Geneva was. On 8 September, he contacted me to say that the Spanish police had confirmed he was José Manuel Costas Estévez, one of Spain's most wanted fugitives, suspected of an €11 million fraud. We wondered what scam he and Acklom were cooking up between them.

2018. Yet another new year, and I wondered if this would be the one in which I could finally shut the door on Mark Acklom. You get to a stage where you have invested so much time and energy in something that you feel you can't give up, but there comes a tipping point, too, where you feel there are more important things in life to focus on, and I was nearing that point.

In January, the police told me there was 'live information' coming into the office, which was being acted on by officers in the relevant country. I didn't know which country this was, but in February I was told that 'the male who we believe is in contact with Acklom is still in the location, and more is being gleaned about him daily'. I thought the male in question was a property developer whom the police had mentioned before, and I knew Martin was investigating.

I contacted Martin who said he was now in touch with 'Charlie's Angel' and they were being helped by the estranged wife of a man they believed to be working with Acklom. They thought Acklom was in Switzerland or Liechtenstein, and Martin said they'd discovered some flashy websites which they believed to be his. I asked Martin to send me links to the websites, one of which, Swiss Disks, immediately caught my attention. There were strong similarities to the InOrg website, with images of fast cars, planes, expensive watches and references to James Dyson, Bernie Ecclestone and other well-known public figures, and I was in no doubt that it was the work of Mark Acklom.* I also recognised some photographs that I had previously seen posted online by Acklom's wife. The website was full of waffle and badly written – all gloss and no substance – but I liked the Swiss Disks motto, 'Being Defeated is Optional', which I decided to alter to 'Defeat is Optional' and claim for myself in my continuing quest to bring Mark Acklom to justice. The police told me that the new CPS lawyer, Alyson Harris (an absolute stickler for detail, they said), was reworking the European Arrest Warrant to include more charges – a highly unusual development, according to Martin.

---

* There is no suggestion that James Dyson or Bernie Ecclestone were acquainted with Mark Acklom.

At the end of March, Martin said that Charlie's Angel had been trying to engage the National Crime Agency to act on what she and Martin discovered about Acklom's companies in Switzerland, but they were making little headway. At the end of April, I heard from Clare, saying she was going to court to finalise the first stage of obtaining the new EAW. Containing twenty charges, all relating to me, it was a much better reflection of the case against Acklom, and by the end of the first week in May, she'd confirmed that they had the new EAW. She said there was lots going on and that they were 'working with authorities on the ground in more than one country to collectively try and catch Acklom'.

Martin wanted to run another story and thought the investigation may have moved to Portugal. He wasn't 100 per cent sure though, and asked if I could confirm it, but I couldn't. In the meantime, I was finalising another statement for the police, and drew their attention to Acklom's post in an internet chatroom only a week after I met him, which proved his intent and demonstrated just how callous he was. He talked about 'desperate women who do not think', adding, 'nobody is going to get engaged and marry you in a couple of months unless you have something to offer like money or connections'.

By June, I was feeling better than I had for the previous six years. We were experiencing the most glorious summer and I was spending as much time as possible out of doors, feeling my spirits rise day by day as I delighted in the sights, sounds and scents of summer.

It was 1 July and Lara was staying with me for the weekend. For the past six months, James had increasingly been working away from home, and I now only saw him one week in three, so I was especially pleased to have her company. On Sunday morning, we were in my bedroom and I was telling her that I would be concentrating far less on Mark Acklom and everything to do with him, when my phone rang. I looked at the screen – number unavailable. I usually didn't answer these calls unless I was expecting to hear from the police, but Lara couldn't understand my reticence. 'Just pick up, Mum,' she chided.

Detective Inspector Adam Bunting was on the line. He had some news, he said, and I could not believe my ears, as he calmly uttered the words I'd been waiting five long years to hear.

'Mark Acklom has been arrested.'

14

THINKING WELL OF HERSELF

After this she held her head higher than ever again: for it was of no use, she had an unquenchable desire to think well of herself.

Henry James, *The Portrait of a Lady*

Acklom was arrested in Switzerland late on 30 June 2018, but the press release was delayed by the Swiss authorities until 3 July, when Martin broadcast the story, after which it was quickly picked up across all media. The *Daily Mail* online said his arrest was described by a neighbour as 'like something out of a Netflix drama', with Acklom jumping over a balcony in an attempt to escape. It was also reported that his mother realised there was something wrong with him when, aged two, he kicked the puppy she had brought home. She also revealed she had put a sign on his bedroom door that read 'Why Be Normal'.

With the news of Acklom's arrest I became focused on him again, only now I could see light at the end of the tunnel. But the roller-coaster ride was not over yet and at the end of the month, Martin told me that Acklom was now being investigated in Switzerland in connection with his company Swiss Disks and also historical fraud. Nevertheless, we decided a celebration was in order, and in the late-afternoon sun of 1 August, we met at Gordon's Wine Bar in London for a celebratory bottle of champagne, congratulating ourselves and each other for our dogged determination to see Acklom brought to justice.

A week later, Martin told me that Acklom was being investigated in two Swiss cantons and that the investigations centred around reports of fraud involving six or seven people who had invested in Swiss Disks. Acklom, now going under the name of Manuel Escolar, had reportedly claimed to be 'the brains behind Elon Musk', and his wife had allegedly told neighbours that Musk had invested 5 billion Swiss francs in Acklom's company. Extradition was now on hold and, once again, I found myself in limbo, with no idea as to when he would be brought to trial in the UK.

On 10 August, Martin broadcast an interview with one of Acklom's investors, Harald Herbon, a Swiss banker, who was appointed CEO of Swiss Disks and invested and lost 500,000 Swiss francs – all this having never met Acklom in person. Martin also broadcast from inside the luxury apartment where Acklom and his family were living at the time of his arrest. He had rented it through Harald Herbon, paying only a deposit, the payment for the rent being promised when the millions upon millions of Swiss francs' profit started to flood into the new company. It all sounded so familiar to me – all the same old tricks – but I was very pleased that Herbon had had the courage to be interviewed, as I knew that Acklom's victims usually felt too embarrassed and ashamed to admit publicly to having been duped. Herbon summed Acklom up, saying, 'He is brilliant in operating with persons. He tells you a story and after a few minutes you believe in it.' Interestingly, now that a successful businessman was talking about how convincing Acklom was, a number of people, including my brother, told me that they were beginning to understand what had happened. A female, it seemed was just a 'stupid woman', whereas a businessman was worth listening to!

With an investigation in Switzerland under way, Martin reported that extradition was on hold indefinitely, and my heart sank. The light at the end of the tunnel had been extinguished.

Nothing much happened over the following three months, although a lengthy and interesting article was published in *Der Bund* in Switzerland on 22 September, giving a very detailed account of Acklom's activities and claiming that a former federal councillor had been 'dragged into his machinations'. It was impossible to get any information from the police and I was told that they now had no direct contact with the Swiss authorities and that everything had to go through the CPS. I asked for contact details of whoever was dealing with the matter at the CPS and the NCA, to no avail. I was trying to keep positive and focus on getting my life back on track, but it was hard. It was, however, gratifying to think of Acklom locked up at last, and I felt a sense of achievement in that. At least behind bars he couldn't find more victims, and I gave myself a pat on the back for having been the driving force behind his arrest.

On the evening of 21 November, I was with my friend Anne at her home in West Sussex. We were preparing supper when my phone rang. It was Clare Ball, and what she had to tell me was astonishing: she said that the Swiss were not continuing with their investigations into Acklom's activities there, and that extradition had been granted. It was somewhat confusing because she said she had received two emails: one saying that Acklom had run out of time to appeal this decision, the other that his lawyer would be in court the following day to lodge an appeal. However, he had run out of time, so as far as we were concerned that was that.

The next day, she called again to confirm that extradition had been granted and told me that Acklom would be picked up on 30 November. She said she would call me when he was safely banged up in Bristol. He would appear in court on 1 December.

Five days later, however, Adam Bunting called to say that somehow or other, despite having run out of time, Acklom had been granted the right to appeal, after all. Martin had also been told independently by the Swiss authorities that extradition had been granted, so I felt totally bemused. This was a massive disappointment for me. Having had my hopes raised and the end in sight (again) just a week before, I now found myself not knowing when/if Acklom would be extradited. This sent me into a black mood that I carried with me into the new year. It didn't ruin Christmas, but it tainted it, and despite all my best endeavours, I was on edge and tetchy and no fun to be around. Lara and Emma were spending Christmas in Australia and I missed them. James was back home, but on top of everything else, I was finding it increasingly difficult to manage the way we were living. With him being away two weeks out of three, I was getting used to my own company and had settled into a routine of my own. So, when he came home, I found his presence quite disruptive and it took a few days to readjust. Then, by the time I'd settled into having him around, it was time for him to depart once more.

Everything seemed to be in flux. I was generally feeling much stronger – much more myself – but I was restless. James and I talked about relocating to where he was working. It was hundreds of miles away and I was disinclined, but we could not carry on as we were, and I felt the winds of change upon me once more.

The first couple of weeks of 2019 were the quiet before the storm. On 16 January, I heard from Clare that Acklom had lost his first appeal in the Swiss courts, but was now appealing to the Supreme Court. She said that this was likely to take another couple of weeks or so, but she was confident that we would get our man. On 15 February, she called again. The Supreme Court had rejected Acklom's appeal (he'd appealed on the grounds that in a post-Brexit Britain his human rights could not be guaranteed!), and extradition had been granted. The police now had ten days in which to pick him up, and four days later Clare called again to tell me that extradition would take place on the 22nd. She explained that he would be brought back to Bristol Airport on an easyJet flight and I thought I could work out which one it would be. She also said that the NCA wanted to publicise Acklom's extradition, the message to criminals being that there was no place to hide – they would eventually get caught. She said that they would contact Martin and give him the scoop. This time, I was quietly confident that Acklom would indeed be brought back, but after the last fiasco, I remained more quiet than confident and decided to tell very few people of this latest development.

One of the people I did contact – immediately – was Martin. I told him that I'd heard it was all booked for Friday and that it looked like the 16.55 departure from Geneva. It seemed to me that the police wanted the publicity but couldn't give out too many details themselves. Martin said he wanted to be on that flight, with a photographer, and asked me to let him know if there were any changes. A couple of days later, he told me that the Avon & Somerset police press office phoned him and virtually told him which flight Acklom would be on. It was the one we thought, and Martin was booked on it.

At 10 a.m. on 22 February, Martin texted to tell me he was at Geneva Airport. I was like a cat on hot bricks, and I wondered how Clare was feeling. Over the years, I had come to like and trust her as she, more than anyone else, gave it to me straight and was prepared to admit when things went wrong. It was she who would be arresting Acklom, and I knew she was nervous about finally coming face to face with the man I'd described as a charismatic, mind-altering magician. I too was nervous, hoping that he wouldn't be able to charm her – after all, according to author Robert Hare, even professional psychologists working in prisons, with full knowledge of their patients' psychopathic natures, have been taken in.

Soon after his text, Martin was on the phone, telling me that his camera operator had just bumped into a Bristol cop – their sons played rugby together. The cop wondered if they were there for the same reason, and Martin suspected that they were, fearing the element of surprise they were hoping for was lost. That evening, Martin called again, this time from Bristol, telling me that there had been a bit of a commotion on the plane, but he had seen Acklom, who looked good – a smart haircut, a neatly trimmed beard and not too thin (as he had been when he was being tried in Spain, back in 2015). He broadcast the news of the extradition, with footage of Acklom at Bristol Airport, being escorted down the aircraft steps to a waiting police van. I watched the clip a few times and wondered where Clare was, as there was no sign of her in the footage. I was at home, by myself, but didn't celebrate. I was waiting for confirmation from Clare that Acklom was safely banged up, but this didn't come until 1.30 a.m., in the form of a text message, when I was asleep.

The following morning, Acklom appeared at Bristol Magistrates' Court to confirm his name, and to have the twenty charges read out to him. Clare called me and I got her side of the story of the pick-up and flight home. She told me what an anti-climax it had been when the cell door was opened. She was expecting some superhuman, hypnotic superstar, but all she got was 'some ordinary bloke wearing green Crocs and terrible jeans with embroidery on one of the pockets. I mean, GREEN CROCS!' She couldn't get over it. She was also affronted because after she charged Acklom he thanked her, invading her personal space and putting his hand on her arm. She really didn't like that. She described him as 'schmoozing' and 'smarmy' and disliked him intensely. She told me she could overhear him talking to the cop next to him on the flight back, trying to get information about the prison he was going to. He also said that the issue of not repaying the loan was a civil matter, not a criminal one. Clare told me that there was a reporter on the plane and that there had been a 'bloody kerfuffle', resulting in the pilot switching the seat-belt sign on, so that everyone had to go back to their seats. I told her I had seen footage of Acklom walking down the aircraft steps but hadn't been able to see her anywhere; she explained that she had managed to 'totter down the steps' in her heels and had taken refuge behind the police van.

She explained that the trial would have to take place within six months and that Acklom would appear at Bristol Crown Court on 25 March for a pre-trial hearing. Now I could see not just a flickering candle at the end of the tunnel, but a bright, guiding light. I didn't know how Acklom would plead, I didn't know what verdict a jury would come to if he pleaded not guilty, but what I did know was that one way or the other, within six months, I could close the door on this prolonged and painful chapter of my life.

On 25 March 2019, Mark Acklom pleaded not guilty to all twenty charges against him. This came as no surprise to me, as I was sure that his arrogance would override any other considera-tion, and that even though the police had told me that the CPS barrister had said Acklom had 'very little wiggle room', he would fight me every inch of the way. I really did view it as a personal battle: me against him.

There was a flurry of activity leading up to the trial, the tension mounting steadily as the weeks passed by. In May, I was staying in London and made a trip down to Bristol for a court visit, and to meet Charles Thomas, the prosecuting barrister. This was very beneficial as I was shown into a courtroom and could see how it was configured – the high bench from which the judge would preside, the benches below where the legal teams and the police would sit, the public gallery, the bench where the clerk of the court and some of the journalists would sit, the witness stand from where I would give evidence and the glass screen behind which Mark Acklom would sit.

I had been asked if I would like to give evidence via video link or from behind a screen. I knew I wouldn't want a video link, and initially I had been certain that I wouldn't want a screen, but latterly, I had wondered if the presence of Acklom, within view, would put me off. Perhaps I would be better able to concentrate if I couldn't see him, and he couldn't see me. I wanted to stand up to him, literally, but now I wondered if he would be able to undermine me, just by looking at me. I remembered the intensity of his gaze when he first walked into the shop, how his eyes had held mine, and I didn't want to feel them upon me again. Now, when I saw the screen in place, however, I knew that I didn't want one. It turned out to be a curtain on one side of the witness box, which, as I stood in it, already felt claustrophobic.

Accompanied by Helen Holt and Clare Ball, I had a very brief meeting with Charles Thomas, and I was pleased that he already seemed to grasp a couple of key aspects of the case. I knew that he would be unable to tell me very much at all, as it had been stressed all along that I must be kept 'sterile', but he made it clear that he knew from the case files that in my relationship with Acklom, I had always stressed my wish to retain my financial and domestic independence. I warned him that Acklom was extremely clever, but he told me that he would find it hard to convince a jury that when he met me, he had forgotten his own name, and that he was a married man with two children.

There were two points in particular that I wanted to convey to Charles Thomas, and I wasted no time in speaking out.

'I know people tend to think "stupid woman",' I said, 'but I'm not stupid.' And I also told him that I believed Acklom to be a psychopath.

'In the true sense of the word?' he asked.

'Yes,' I replied, and I was confident that he understood exactly what I was saying.

I was pleased I'd made the effort to travel to Bristol. Court visits and initial meetings with lawyers are often left until the day the trial starts and it had been suggested that I could leave it all until 5 August, but I'd thought that would be stressful on top of everything else. As I climbed aboard the train back to London, I felt encouraged, and a little better prepared for what lay ahead.

The next three or four weeks were relatively tranquil, but this period soon came to an abrupt end. On 19 June, just six weeks before the trial was due to start, I was in a buoyant mood, riding home on a bus, when I received a message from the police asking if they could call me. I emailed back saying that I should be able to talk to them in about an hour.

'Just to let you know we are recording this conversation,' Clare told me when the call came through. I tensed, red lights flashing in my head, spelling danger – my telephone conversations with the police had never been recorded before. I had thought this was going to be a courtesy update, but it was obviously something much more significant. I was immediately put on my guard.

The conversation started and I was asked if I had made any money out of my association with Mark Acklom. I must say I nearly choked at the absurdity of the question. 'I lost everything,' a voice screamed out in my head, 'absolutely everything!' But somehow, I kept calm and asked them to explain what they meant. They asked if I had been paid for any newspaper articles, and if I'd ever written a book or a film script. If so, who had read it? Did I have any contracts with publishers?

I began to get the drift of where this was going. Acklom and his lawyers were obviously going to argue that I had benefitted from my relationship with him. How ridiculous, I thought. But I had to take the question seriously and answer it. It was difficult to remember exactly what I had been paid back in 2016, but I thought it was something in the region of £6,000. Regarding, a book I told them that I had written a draft of a manuscript in 2014, as a way of reminding myself of all that had happened, but that I hadn't written a film script. Off the top of my head, I could only think of one person who had read my manuscript in full – my daughter Lara. I told them that I had made about twenty submissions to literary agents at that time, but that nobody had been interested. I felt really annoyed at the question and told them that if Mark Acklom would like to give me my money back, I would have no desire to publish anything. What was I supposed to do? I thought. All I'd been left with was a story, and it seemed totally reasonable that I would try to do something with it.

I was then told that the police would need evidence of all the payments I had received for anything in relation to Mark Acklom, and I felt sick to the core – more hoops for me to jump through! Of course, as soon as I hung up, I remembered that another three people had read my manuscript, and so I spoke to the police again, immediately, to 'confess'. When I searched my bank records, I saw that I had been paid not £6,000, but a total of £9,000 from various media, so yet another 'confession' was necessary. I felt as though I was the one on trial. It was a horrible experience, but it was a good lesson. I realised just how tough things were going to be when I took the witness stand. Although I anticipated that the cross-examination in particular would be gruelling, I reminded myself that I would just be telling the truth, so it would be relatively straightforward. But what if I couldn't remember? After all, I was going to be questioned about events that had taken place up to seven and a half years earlier? What if I 'failed to mention when questioned' something that I later relied on?

The following day, I noted in my diary that I was 'feeling really crap and depressed after yesterday's call from the police, and thoughts of Acklom', and from then on, I spiralled down into a deep depression, drinking too much, eating rubbish and willing the days to pass until the trial, so that I could just get it over with and put it all behind me. I had intended to get fitter mentally and physically, but I found it impossible to motivate myself. I did, however, try to prepare for what might happen during Acklom's trial by reading *The Secret Barrister*, an alarming, eye-opening account of the parlous state of the criminal-justice system. It should be read by everyone: I found it invaluable preparation for what was to come, and my expectations were substantially lowered.

Over the next couple of weeks, there were more calls from the police, another one of which was recorded. I was told that Acklom's defence team were not convinced that the photographs they had been sent of my wedding dress actually depicted a wedding dress.

'But you have the receipt for the dress,' I said.

'Yes, but it just gives the style of the dress. It doesn't actually say "wedding dress", and the lawyers think it just looks like a dress in the photographs: they want to see the real thing.'

How ridiculous, I thought to myself. Thank goodness I had kept the dress – they were probably banking on the fact that I wouldn't be able to produce it. But I didn't have it with me. It was hanging in a wardrobe at Bridget's house in Buckinghamshire, so arrangements had to be made for it to be collected and taken to Bristol. Added to that, I was now being asked if I could send my 2014 manuscript to the police, so that the prosecution could take a look and see if it should be disclosed. I had offered it to the police years before (they had declined, telling me that they didn't want to be influenced by 'a work of fiction'), but now I felt a terrible invasion of my privacy once more. As with the examination of my phone back then, I didn't want to hand over my innermost thoughts and feelings to the prosecution, let alone the defence. I felt stripped naked; worse than that, I felt stripped to the bone.

This is the reality of 'disclosure'. You have to be prepared for your whole life to be opened up, dissected, scrutinised and passed around, so that the defence stand the best possible chance of discrediting you, or just upsetting and humiliating you. It seems to me that they end up holding all the cards. I had already been told that it was lucky that I had never joined any internet dating sites as my whole dating history could have been trawled through. And I was subsequently told that given Acklom's final defence statement, had there been a history of any sort of mental illness in my medical records, this may have needed careful examination by the CPS – and if it was considered helpful to the defence, it would have had to be disclosed. Why, I wondered, was there this burden of disclosure on key witnesses but not on the accused?

I find the whole system completely baffling. However, in these matters a witness has no choice, so I dutifully, but very reluctantly, sent my 2014 manuscript off to the police, and twelve chapters of it were disclosed to Acklom's lawyers. Then I was told that I would need to bring all my records of the police investigation, and anything else I had on Mark Acklom with me when I came to court. This seemed crazy to me as this included printouts of all the correspondence I had had with the police (I had been so worried about my email account being hacked and my electronic records being destroyed that I had made hard copies of everything) – all stuff that they would have in their files. But again, I had no choice in the matter; failure to comply would look suspicious – as if I had something to hide – and I had to 'be seen to be whiter than white'. And so it was that I had to drive hundreds of miles with a box of lever-arch files, three mobile phones, various other books and documents and my wedding shoes. I also had to pack enough clothing to last three weeks.

15

THE SERPENT IN A BANK
OF FLOWERS

*Under all his culture, his cleverness, his amenity, under his
good-nature, his facility, his knowledge of life, his egotism lay
hidden like a serpent in a bank of flowers.*

Henry James, *The Portrait of a Lady*

On 5 August, I had to be in Bristol to meet the police around lunchtime. Lara and Emma met me at my hotel and DC Clare Ball and DS Helen Holt came to collect the files and other items that I had brought with me. We also completed one final statement relating to the recorded telephone conversations, and they handed me copies of all my earlier statements, dating back to 2014, so that I could refresh my memory before I was called to the witness stand. The wedding dress had been collected and was already in court. A jury had been selected (but not sworn in) and dismissed, and we were told that it had emerged that morning that the judge was going to be away Monday to Wednesday the following week, so that court would not sit until the Thursday of week two. I was dismayed because the way things were looking there would now be a five-day break between me and the next witness giving evidence, and possibly three weeks between my evidence being given and the summing-up. Would the jury remember a word I'd said? It was also now likely that the trial would run into a fourth week.

I was told that Acklom was running his barrister ragged and legal arguments were ongoing and likely to carry on for the rest of the day, so as long as we were contactable and within half an hour of the court, we could have the afternoon to ourselves. We were also informed that Acklom's barrister was staying in the same hotel as me and were warned to be very careful about discussing the case, especially in the hotel or the vicinity of the court.

It was a beautiful afternoon and, after Lara and Emma had been to the court to familiarise themselves, we wandered around Bristol old town, eventually making our way to an upstairs terrace on the waterfront where we enjoyed a drink in the evening sun. I thought that if it hadn't been for the circumstances of our being together, I could have believed we were on holiday. But that feeling of wellbeing was to change dramatically the following day, and the next forty-eight hours would be a roller-coaster ride of highs and lows, hope and despair, clarity and confusion.

The next morning, Helen and Clare came to meet me at the hotel and we made our way to the court. As we emerged on to Small Street, the police officers spotted a paparazzi lying in wait for us. I heard the shutter of the camera clicking away like a football rattle, getting progressively louder as it loomed towards me, until that camera was literally in my face. It was a horrible experience and I was unprepared for it. Next time I'll be prepared, I thought. Another steep learning curve.

The trial was to take place in Court Number 1, the largest of all the courtrooms, and configured slightly differently from the others. It had two public galleries, one behind glass, above the jury, looking directly down on the witness stand, and although just as bland and soulless as the court I had viewed before, it was more intimidating, purely by virtue of its size, so I was glad I had had sight of it before going in 'officially'.

I had a brief meeting with Charles Thomas and met Alyson Harris, the prosecuting solicitor. We were joined by former DI

Adam Bunting, now semi-retired, who had remained closely involved with the case. I was told that Acklom was not denying that he knew me, but he *was* denying the extent of the relationship, saying that I knew all along that he had no money. Legal arguments were ongoing and I was informed that it was unlikely I would be called to give evidence that day.

I returned to my hotel, but before long the police were on the phone telling me that I was needed in court. They came to escort me back to the witness suite. Lara and Emma came with me (I had asked them to be my eyes and ears), and we wondered what was going to happen next.

There were eight of us around the table: Clare, Helen and Adam, Charles Thomas, Alyson Harris, Lara, Emma and me. Charles began to speak.

'Well, there've been some developments and it's possible that Mark Acklom might plead,' he started. He went on to explain that Acklom might plead guilty to five of the counts against him. I said nothing, but inside my head I was screaming, 'No! He's guilty of them all!'

Charles proceeded to outline the plea bargaining that was going on, and to explain why the prosecution were in favour of accepting the pleas. The key points seemed to be that by pleading guilty to these five counts, Mark Acklom would be labelled a 'lifestyle criminal', and that the sentence he would receive would, in all probability, not be a great deal less than if the case went to trial (in which case he would plead not guilty to all twenty counts). If he pleaded guilty to these five counts, it was anticipated that he could be sentenced to six years, minus 10 per cent for pleading, but if the case went to trial, even if he was found guilty on all twenty charges, the maximum sentence that could be handed down was ten years, and the lawyers felt that something in the region of eight was more likely. It was also emphasised that having Acklom admit his guilt, even if it was only to a quarter of the charges against him, was of great benefit in itself, and it was stressed that I would be spared the potentially upsetting and humiliating ordeal of taking the witness stand.

I asked what would happen regarding the remaining fifteen charges. Would Acklom be presumed innocent (I could not bear the thought)? Would they be wiped out? It was explained that the charges would simply remain on file. I then asked whether, if these fifteen charges were left on the file, I would be able to tell my story and publish a book. Charles Thomas told me that he used to specialise in defamation, and that I would be free to tell my story. There was no way Acklom could come after me, he said. I asked the police if they too were in favour of accepting this plea, and they said that they were. We were then asked if we'd like some time alone to discuss the matter and we said we would. It was so much to try to take in: I had so many emotions bubbling away inside, all the while trying to preserve a façade of poise and control – why do we always feel we have to be on our best behaviour, even when we want to rant and rave, scream and shout?

Lara, Emma and I sat mulling over everything that had been said. They had taken notes and I was so pleased that they were there with clear heads, because mine was in turmoil. We felt under considerable pressure to come to a decision quickly. Charles had made it clear that ultimately the decision was theirs, not ours, and I sometimes wonder what would have happened if we'd come to a different conclusion, but after about half an hour of deliberation, we were all in agreement that, all things considered, this was a reasonable outcome. The lawyers and the police came back into the room and I asked them, once again, if they were sure we should accept Acklom's five guilty pleas. They assured me they were, and I told them that we agreed. As we left, we were told that legal arguments were likely to rumble on after lunch, but that we should, again, remain contactable and within striking distance of the court.

The mood was flat that afternoon. As the day wore on, I found myself feeling more and more dispirited. By the time evening came, I was feeling quite depressed and struggling to remain civil with my family and my friend Anne and her son, Nick, who had come to support me. We were trying to decide where to eat, but I had no appetite, and anything that anyone suggested I rejected. Eventually, we wound up at the same place that we had been to the evening before. I had hoped that the vibe would be the same and that my mood would lift, but it didn't. We were all decidedly downbeat, and when I got back to the hotel, I was feeling like hell.

That night, I didn't sleep. I had terrible cramps in my legs and spent much of the night in pain, pacing around my room. When I lay down, I tossed and turned. I felt so short-changed by the events of the day. My six-year struggle reduced to plea-bargaining, and, it now seemed to me, the CPS just wanting to save the expense of a trial. I also knew that the only reason Acklom would agree to what was being proposed was that he knew he was likely to be found guilty on more counts and sentenced to more time in prison if we went to trial. For there is only one thing that motivates psychopaths: self-interest. Acklom knew that this way he'd get the best possible deal for himself.

I was due to meet the police at nine o'clock on the Wednesday morning, and as I got ready, I struggled to fight back the tears that were welling up, pricking the backs of my eyes. I was exhausted and frightened that I was going to panic and be unable to cope with the events of the day. I knew that anything was still possible and that until Acklom actually stood up in court and answered the five charges with the word 'guilty', he could change his mind and I could still find myself having to give evidence. As usual, he was pulling the strings, creating drama where there need be none, and I imagined how he would be enjoying having everyone running around, keeping us all on tenterhooks.

I was in the hotel lobby at nine o'clock, but there was no sign of the police. I sat there, tense and tearful, concentrating on my breathing. Time almost drew to a standstill. I kept looking at my watch, only to find that it was just a minute or so since I had last checked it. At 9.29 a.m., a text message pinged in. It was from the police, saying that they had been held up, but should be with me shortly.

Lara and Emma arrived, but still no police, and we all felt that this delay did not bode well. When Helen and Clare did eventually appear, an interminable ten minutes or so later, I felt the hot tears pricking at my eyes again. We were told that it was still unclear how events would unfold. They were hopeful that Acklom would enter his guilty pleas, but they couldn't be certain. There was still a lot going on behind the scenes. They explained that the judge would not tolerate much more in the way of delays, but also that if nothing happened imminently, and if Acklom decided not to plead, it was likely that the trial would be postponed for two months, as the witness sequencing was now so out of kilter that, with the judge being away the first three days of the following week, it would be impossible to get all the witnesses in court again during August.

Although I had prepared myself for most eventualities, I hadn't entertained the thought that I could be leaving Bristol with no result. The prospect of having everything on hold for another two months, of having my hopes dashed once again, was more than I could bear – but it helped sharpen my mind and I realised that I would much rather get the whole thing over and done with and accept the guilty pleas than go through yet another delay. I also thought that Acklom was just trying to spin the whole process out for as long as possible, because he would prefer to be in prison on remand than as a convicted criminal. The longer he could spin things out, the better it would be for him. Each day he spent in jail now would be deducted from his eventual sentence, and he knew that once he was convicted, his conditions would become considerably worse.

As we were sitting there, the police received notification that court was being reconvened and so they left with Lara and Emma to see what was about to unfold. I was still a potential witness and not allowed into court, so I stayed behind. Lara and Emma were to be my eyes and ears again, and they subsequently told me what had happened.

The proceedings started at 10.45 with Gudrun Young, Acklom's barrister, raising the issue of a leaked blog on Monday night, which she said was in contempt of court, and Judge Picton warned the court about the seriousness of leaking information outside the courtroom. An application was then made to the judge for a 'Goodyear indication': an indication of the maximum sentence Acklom would receive if he were to plead guilty to five counts of fraud. The judge said he was prepared to give a 'Goodyear indication', and that the maximum sentence would be six years. However, he also said that this was not binding unless the defendant acted upon it promptly.

The court was then adjourned for twenty minutes and Lara and Emma had a private discussion with Charles Thomas. He explained that part of the delay was caused by a blog on Antifraud International by Charlie's Angel. Charles speculated that Charlie's Angel could have been in court on Monday and could be a man. Indeed, on Monday we'd received two independent reports of a suspicious-looking man in the public gallery and had been warned by the police to be very wary of him. I had often privately wondered whether a man could be behind this internet alias, and now it seemed even more likely.

At 11.30, Emma phoned me to say that it looked as though Acklom was, at last, going to plead, and she came with the police to escort me to court. We entered the building through the side entrance from where we could see the main entrance, where there was a strong press presence. Thankfully, nobody ambushed us this time. We entered Court Number 1, where three seats had been reserved for Lara, Emma and me in the public gallery in the courtroom itself. As I entered, I saw two or three rows of familiar faces, mainly friends, who had travelled from London, Buckinghamshire, Sussex and Wales, and also a couple of friendly journalists. Martin Brunt was there from Sky News and Martin Jones, from BBC Points West. I tried to acknowledge everyone with a fleeting smile. Seeing my friends there, rooting for me, instantly lifted my spirits. These were good, decent people who all knew me well, who knew my story and believed it and wanted to see justice done.

The atmosphere was strained, with an undercurrent of hushed murmuring and tense anticipation. The jury was ushered in, and I tried to make them out, but only got as far as registering that there were only four women present. (I had always hoped for at least half the jury to be women, as I thought they were likely to identify with me, so already I felt the jury weighted against me.) We all rose for the judge and, as we sat down, I dared to turn my head over my shoulder to take a look at Mark Acklom. It was important to me that I looked at him to verify that he was really there. I was taken aback by what I saw. The man behind the glass screen was the most ordinary-looking bloke you could imagine. He was thinner than when I knew him, sporting facial hair, but not the closely trimmed 'designer stubble' of 2012. He was dressed in a grey hoodie and looked totally unkempt. Would he have turned my head now if he had walked into my shop? Not at all!

The tension was palpable as the clerk began to read out the charges, starting with count 5.

'Mark Richard George Acklom between eighteenth day of January 2012 and the twenty-second day of March 2012 committed fraud in that dishonestly and intending thereby to make a gain for himself or another, or to cause loss to another, or to expose another to risk of loss, he made a false representation to Carolyn Woods which was and which he knew was or might be untrue or misleading and which included that he was in a committed relationship with Carolyn Woods and that he was free to marry her and that he needed £29,564.36 as a loan to renovate property that he owned and that he was developing, in breach of section 2 of the Fraud Act 2006. How do you plead?'

Acklom's thin, watery response was barely audible, but in the tense atmosphere of Court Number 1 we heard him mutter, 'Guilty'.

The clerk continued, reading out the remaining four charges, and each time we had to strain our ears to hear Acklom respond. His voice was so quiet and his enunciation so poor that on the fourth count I thought he had changed his mind. The clerk started to question him again and was interrupted by another muffled 'guilty' response. And then I got it. Of course! Acklom's scruffy appearance and downcast demeanour were all part of another charade. In his chameleon-like way he was adopting the persona of an ordinary guy, wearing street clothes to make him look as young as possible, mumbling as though he was down-trodden and lacking in confidence. All a cold, calculated performance designed to convince the court that there was no way that he could ever be taken for a suave, handsome, exciting, dashing, multi-millionaire, thereby persuading people that I, not he, was the liar and the fantasist.

Court was adjourned for lunch and when we reconvened at 2 p.m. for the summing-up and sentencing the proceedings began with my Victim Personal Statement. I had vacillated between wanting to have this heard in court and thinking it was just a waste of time, because I had been given conflicting information.

Originally, back in 2014, I had been told that if I wrote a VPS, it could be read aloud in court by the CPS barrister, or I could deliver it myself. I had assumed that my statement could influence the sentence that was handed down and I had decided that for maximum impact I would deliver it myself. Latterly though, I had become confused, as I was told that the purpose of the VPS was to let the defendant know what effect his actions had had on me, and that it would most likely have no bearing on the sentencing because the judge would have already listened to all the evidence and drawn his conclusions. When I was told this, I decided that there was no point in my delivering a VPS, as the last thing I wanted was to give Mark Acklom the satisfaction of hearing directly from me how he had devastated my life and wreaked havoc with my emotions and mental wellbeing. But I still wanted to have my say, so I had asked Charles Thomas if my VPS could be delivered in writing, in private, to the judge, and he told me that it could be. Up until the day before, this was what I thought I would do, but that was when I had thought that we would be at the end of a three-week trial, during the course of which the judge would have heard my account of my relationship with Mark Acklom. Now I found myself in court with Acklom about to be sentenced 'on a basis of plea which significantly reduced Mr Acklom's level of criminality' (as his barrister's chambers' website subsequently so neatly put it). Under these unexpected circumstances, I suddenly felt it much more important that my statement *should* be heard by the court, especially as I had now been told in the witness suite by one of the volunteers that the VPS definitely would be taken into account, and that it could play a key part in sentencing.

The VPS that the police had on file had been written some time before and I had thought that I would probably like to write a new one, but I hadn't yet done so, thinking that the trial was going to last three weeks and that I would have plenty of time to redraft it, but here I was on day three having to decide whether it was worth delivering it at all. I had discussed my concerns briefly with the police and the lawyers, and Alyson Harris had said that she thought I would feel better if my statement was read out to the court, and that at least I would feel I'd had some say in the proceedings. She also confirmed that it could have a bearing on sentencing, and that was the clincher for me: I decided that my statement should be delivered in court. But I then unexpectedly found that I didn't want to take the witness stand to deliver it myself, so I asked Alyson if she would do that for me, and she graciously agreed.

Through Alyson, I told the court how I believed Acklom had acted deliberately and in a calculated, premeditated way to defraud me of all my money and nearly all my personal possessions, and to deprive me of my home and my job, thereby rendering me totally helpless and at his mercy. I told how he also deliberately isolated me from my family and friends and played psychological games to deceive me and engender a sense of fear in me, and how I believed it was an act of the utmost cruelty, designed to destroy my life for his personal gain.

I described the violation I felt, sexually and emotionally as well as financially, of the loss of identity and the ill health I had suffered and of my struggle to keep going, explaining, 'Emotional and psychological wounds are not obvious in the way that physical wounds are, and it is in my nature to put on a brave face. However, if the assault I have suffered had been physical I would look as though I had been beaten to a pulp. Psychologically and emotionally, that is what has happened to me.'

I concluded by trying to explain how in my relationship with Mark Acklom what I normally thought of as my strengths had been used against me. I told the court that I had felt a terrible sense of injustice and how I hoped that in the end justice would prevail and Mark Acklom would be stopped from destroying more lives in the way in which he had destroyed mine.

Charles Thomas then listed Acklom's previous convictions

before delivering his case summary. I listened to what he said and found myself wanting to shout out 'No! That's not correct!' as the court was told that when I met Mark Acklom I had about £800,000 sitting in the bank, 'largely from a bequest from her parents and her divorce'. I have a real bugbear about the depiction of women like me, particularly in the media, who are invariably described as 'divorced', and whose material wealth is nearly always attributed to a divorce settlement. This just doesn't happen with divorced men. The 'divorced' adjective is rarely used to describe a man, and any assets they have are seen as their own, never as 'part of a divorce settlement'. It makes me mad! I had been divorced for nearly nine years when I met Acklom and my divorce settlement was half of a 50/50 split of combined assets after twenty-two years of marriage and hard work on both sides. My husband received exactly the same. A more accurate explanation would have been to say that the money in the bank was mainly from the sale of my house (which had increased significantly in value between 2003 and 2010), and a bequest from my parents, but frankly is it even relevant to know why I had this money in the bank? In his description of Acklom's past misdemeanours, Charles Thomas said that as a teenager, he had duped a building society into giving him a mortgage of around £350,000. 'No!' shrieked a voice inside my head. 'It was nearer five hundred thousand pounds. Get your facts right!' But, of course, I remained mute.

When it came to the defence's mitigation, I had to exercise even more self-control as I listened to what I thought was a pathetic string of excuses, peppered with a number of vague assertions that were just left hanging in mid-air. It was as though Gudrun Young had produced a bubble wand, through which she blew Acklom's assertions and lies, some big, some small, and left them floating in the courtroom, until they popped and vanished into thin air.

It all began with a plea to include the time spent in prison in Switzerland awaiting extradition (237 days) and the 167 days in the UK as part of the whole sentence. Then she talked about the unwarranted level of publicity the case had attracted, saying that Acklom had been portrayed in the media as one of the ten most wanted fugitives in Europe when clearly, the level and type of crime he had committed was not commensurate with being on a list with dangerous criminals. She herself referred to him as a 'catch-me-if-you-can' character. She told the court that Mark Acklom did not accept that everything he had said to me was a lie (I had never made that assertion), and it was pointed out that he *had* worked for a financial institution in Switzerland, he *did* know Nicky Clarke, he *did* speak seven languages, he *did* have a photographic memory, and there was a reference to HM Government, implying that he may even have been in MI6. Gudrun Young gently blew this last bubble into the air, where it hovered tantalisingly, and then said she would say no more about it – we were left to draw our own conclusions.

Attempts were made to pull at our heart strings, as we learned that although Acklom had been born into a privileged background, his childhood was 'insecure and unstable'. His father had worked at Lloyds and had made and lost large sums of money. There was little love or affection at home, we were told, and Acklom had been sent to boarding school at the age of eleven (so had I). All this had resulted in him feeling unloved and insecure. He admitted to having defrauded his family but said that his father had been aware of him using his credit cards. He said that his past was not as it had been depicted and that he had forged documents to raise money for one of his children from his first marriage who had cerebral palsy (no mention was made of the fact that he deserted his first family when the children were very young). We were told that he was a devoted father to his children (so devoted that he used them as props in his charades, I thought) and that they and his wife were now suffering as a result of all the press attention. His wife had even sent a letter to the judge.

The court was informed that Acklom admitted to taking advantage of me but claimed that the initial attraction had been genuine and that I had become infatuated with him. He admitted also that he had lied about his familial responsibilities but said that I knew he had no money and that I was aware that he was not able to enter into a full-time relationship because of his personal circumstances. Gudrun Young then announced to the court that 'they never had sex' (if only that were true, I thought to myself). Evidence for this, she said, was written in my own hand in a letter to Acklom where I had complained that he had 'never seen my naked body' and that we had 'never spent a night together'. Was anyone in that courtroom so naïve as to think sex was not possible without the removal of every item of clothing, or that it necessitated spending the night together? Let's not forget that Mark Acklom was always a man in a hurry.

The court was also asked to bear in mind that Acklom hadn't spent all the money on himself; much of it had been used to make me happy – for example, by housing me in a luxury mansion in Bath! This was a low-level, opportunistic fraud, we were told. Acklom took advantage of a woman who was besotted with him. He wasn't fraudulent from the outset and was now very sorry. We were told that he had been using his time in prison well, helping other prisoners to read and write, and that he had produced some pamphlets to help them in business. The pamphlets were offered to the judge who, I have to say, did not appear to be very impressed. Throughout the proceedings, Mark Acklom sat with his head bowed, expressionless and inscrutable, scribbling on a piece of paper behind the glass screen.

Once more, the court was adjourned while Judge Picton considered what sentence he would hand down.

Twenty minutes later we were back to hear the judge's summing-up and sentencing. He accepted that Acklom had not targeted me from the outset – I suspect otherwise, but I guess we'll never know – but he said that he was happy to spin me a number of lies and that he had no intention of paying the money back at the time and had made no effort to do so since. 'Money slipped through your fingers like water,' he told Acklom. Mark Acklom was only here today because of the efforts of others. He had prior convictions, numerous identities and had done his utmost to avoid capture.

Judge Picton saw through most of Acklom's lies. In terms of sentencing, he said that he must take into account the enormous harm Acklom had caused me, and the fact that he had avoided being brought to justice and chosen to hide and evade the authorities. There was precious little by way of mitigating factors, he said. By pleading now, Acklom had saved a little public money and avoided me being put through a trial. He was unpersuaded that Acklom should get more than the statutory 10 per cent off his sentence for a guilty plea. The circumstances that his wife and family now found themselves in, he told him, were entirely of his own making: 'She and your children are just collateral damage.'

'After a trial, I would have awarded six years and four months. However, by pleading now I sentence you to five years and eight months. Your time in custody will be taken into account and the fifteen outstanding counts will be kept on file.'

Court was dismissed and as we filed out, it dawned on me that my Victim Personal Statement *had* made a difference to the sentencing – by four months. I was glad that it had been read to the court. It hadn't made much difference, but Acklom would have to spend a few more days behind bars because of it. More importantly, I felt pleased that I had let people know the effect that my relationship with Mark Acklom had had on me. Behind my brave face was a fragile woman. I was brought up not to show vulnerability – but vulnerability makes you human, and people can help you more easily if you show it.

There was a bit of hanging around inside the court building before I emerged, flanked by Clare and Helen, together with Adam Bunting and Alyson Harris, to face the press. Friends had gathered outside and were chatting and smiling broadly. I felt rather stunned that the whole thing was now over. I felt no sense of victory or elation, no sense of real justice, but I did feel as though a great weight had been lifted from my shoulders. Adam was going to say a few words, and I stood rather dispassionately expecting to hear the usual 'We have been working for some time with the CPS and our counterparts in other countries …' But what he said was something quite different – much stronger and to the point.

'Mark Acklom is a career criminal fraudster. He is a pathological liar and fantasist who, over many years, has left a trail of destruction in his wake. He is a very manipulative and selfish man. He has funded his own and his family's hugely extravagant lifestyle by destroying the lives of others.

'Mark Acklom has fought this prosecution every step of the way. He has only pleaded guilty today, at the start of his trial, when faced with overwhelming evidence. I would like to publicly thank Carolyn Woods, the victim in this case, for her bravery, her resilience and her determination to bring Acklom to justice. I hope that the sentence passed today gives her some form of closure and she is able to start rebuilding her life.'

Ten minutes later, back at the hotel, I walked in to find my friends, who we'd all thought would be buoying me up at the end of my first day of giving evidence, smiling and laughing and ordering champagne. As we sat together celebrating, I felt truly happy. I knew that Mark Acklom, for all his years of living a millionaire's lifestyle, had nothing compared with me. What he had told me as we lay in bed only forty-eight hours after meeting, resounded in my head: 'I have never loved or been truly loved before.' I had thought him wrong at the time, but now I knew he was incapable of love, and who could ever truly love a man like him? I, on the other hand, had done both, with my family, friends and lovers, and I knew that whatever my financial circumstances, my life was infinitely richer than his.

The following day, Lara, Emma and I had arranged to meet Adam, Helen and Clare, informally, for lunch, and Adam had said they would try to answer any questions we had about the investigation, and what had transpired in court.

It was another warm summer's day in Bristol, and we settled ourselves at a table in a waterfront restaurant. The waitress came to take our order, and when she asked what I would like to drink, I hesitated momentarily, feeling slightly self-conscious in the company of people with whom I had always been on my best behaviour and had never let my guard down.

'I'd like a glass of white wine,' I said.

'Regular or large?' the waitress asked, pen poised.

I hesitated again.

'Go large!' said Adam, and that broke the ice. Large it would be.

We then slipped into a relaxed but captivating conversation about what had been going on behind the scenes – the things they hadn't been able to reveal to me before. I found out some information about Paul Kaur, who I had been expecting to be a key witness. It seemed he had corroborated my story but the police decided he was likely to simply be a pawn in Acklom's game and they made a decision to release him. He didn't appear to have profited from the crime. In the end, they felt that Acklom was the bigger fish and that they would use Paul Kaur as a witness. However, the prosecution decided ultimately that using Kaur as a witness was too risky and might confuse the jury, making them question who the real criminal in the room was, particularly as Acklom was more intelligent, more articulate and perfectly capable of play-acting and appearing to 'break down' in tears in the courtroom to garner pity from the jury – something he had done in a previous trial. So, Paul Kaur was pulled out only about four weeks before the beginning of the trial.

Having failed to discredit the extradition on a technicality and finding themselves unable to cast doubt on Paul Kaur's credibility as a witness for the prosecution, Acklom's lawyers started to build a new defence. In their defence statement they raised concerns as to whether I was attempting to control the investigation, withholding information from the police and/or drip-feeding them. This was when they asked for disclosure of all material relating to meetings and conversations I'd had with the police. They were going to argue that I was a fantasist who had misunderstood the nature of my relationship with Acklom. Having seen chapters of my original manuscript, the defence would have known my version of events exactly, and using it, I can see how the jury might have been persuaded to think that my account of my relationship with Mark Acklom was a fantasy, especially with him presenting himself in court as a rather unkempt ordinary bloke who nobody would look at twice. It is a chilling thought. I agree that on the face of it my account might sound somewhat fanciful, but how they thought they would get away with that, given the evidence that the prosecution had to back up my claims, I just don't know. And it seems that in the end they didn't either.

My determination to see justice done was never primarily about getting my money back; it was about not letting this despicable man get away scot free with what he did to me. I wish others besides me had had the courage and felt morally bound to speak up, and I hope that my example will help people to stand up against all kinds of wrongdoing in the future. We live in times in which looking out for number one, whatever the cost to others, seems OK. It is not. We all need to be brave and expose wrongdoing when we see it. We need to reset our moral compass and not pass by or look the other way when we see people abusing others for their own personal gain. It is said that we live in a world where there is a generally weaker sense of conscience, responsibility and empathy among us. This is particularly prevalent online, but it affects the real world too, and we are all diminished by it.

The police described the case as 'very challenging' and it was the longest investigation any of the officers involved had ever dealt with, undoubtedly complicated by the fact that the police in the UK had to deal with other European jurisdictions. The Swiss, we were told, were relatively co-operative, but the Spanish authorities were a nightmare, as they failed, time after time, to communicate what they were doing, if anything.

Meeting the team informally after four and a half years of formal contact was extremely useful as, probably for the first time, I saw the three officers for what they were: three decent people trying, against the odds, and with limited resources, to make the world a better place. I think there are serious failings in the whole of the criminal-justice system, and they need to be addressed, but I can't blame these three individuals for that. As *The Secret Barrister*, points out (with regard to the Crown Prosecution Service):

> There can be no organization in any field that, from a starting position of being underfunded, then loses a third of its workforce and has its budget reduced by a quarter and still performs as it should. When that organization depends on the investigative prowess of a national police force which, over the same period, has lost nearly 20,000 officers – a fall of 13 per cent – and has sustained budget cuts of 20 per cent, the window for error is opened wider.

Adam personally apologised for the blunders made at the beginning of the investigation, admitting that the case wasn't allocated quickly enough or taken seriously, because it was just considered to be an everyday fraud (nobody likes dealing with a fraud case). He thanked me for my strength in seeing the case through and told me I was the driving force behind the investigation. In his opinion, Acklom backed down at the eleventh hour because he knew he didn't have a case. He thought I would be the one to break at the last minute and find myself unable to take the witness stand and face him, and when he realised that I really was going to stand up to him, he decided on damage limitation and chose to plead. According to *The Secret Barrister*:

> One of the reasons that many defendants plead guilty only on the day of trial is that they will bide their time, hopeful that a prosecution error or a key witness losing their resolve – a crushingly prevalent problem in allegations of domestic violence – will free them at the last.

For many years, as I've said, I thought that the character traits I had always regarded as my strengths (my stiff upper lip, my resilience and stoicism, standing up for what I think is right) were used against me by Mark Acklom and contributed to my downfall. However, it seems that in the end, I was stronger than he ever imagined, and eventually, it was all those qualities in me that beat him.

16

A PLACE OF BRIGHTNESS

She had a fixed determination to regard the world as a place of brightness.

Henry James, *The Portrait of a Lady*

In my account of my relationship with Mark Acklom, I have tried to explain how I think he operates, and how he sowed the seeds of his deception. I found him fascinating and that is the main reason I was hooked. To fascinate: to attract the strong attention of someone. Synonyms: engross, captivate, absorb, enchant, beguile, bewitch, enthrall, enrapture, entrance, hold spellbound, transfix, mesmerise. Mark Acklom did all these things to me.

But not only did he fascinate me, he puzzled me. I like solving puzzles, and for eighteen months I had been trying to put the puzzle together, to come to some sort of understanding of what was going on, trying to build the 'big picture', not knowing that there were crucial pieces missing. Even at his most outlandish, Mark was convincing – perhaps all the more so because his stories were so astonishing that you thought that nobody could make them up and convey them so compellingly. In retrospect, I can see that he even planted that thought in my mind as we sat in the Hare and Hounds on our first date. When I remarked that his life was extraordinary, he responded saying, 'You're right. It is totally extraordinary. My life is like a film; you couldn't make it up.' He always had an answer for everything, without a glimmer of hesitation. I could never have imagined that anyone could lie so easily or go to such lengths to deceive. Looking back at the fascination Acklom held for me, knowing what I know now and realising that he is utterly diabolical, I think the archaic use of the word 'fascinate' best describes the power he held over me – for it was used especially to describe a snake that deprives its prey of the ability to resist or escape by the power of its gaze.

As Robert Hare says in his book *Without Conscience*:

One question runs like a refrain through the stories told by the victims of psychopaths: 'How could I have been so stupid? How could I have fallen for that incredible line of baloney?' And when victims aren't asking themselves, somebody else is sure to pose the question. 'How on earth could you have been taken in to that extent?' The characteristic answer: 'You had to be there. It seemed reasonable, plausible at the time.' The clear – and largely valid – implication is that had we been there we too might have been sucked in ... The sad fact is that we are all vulnerable. Few people are such sophisticated and perceptive judges of human nature that they cannot be taken in by the machinations of a skilled and determined psychopath.

Even before I realised who Mark really was, I felt as if my brain had been scrambled (a feeling that intensified the more I discovered about him) – and I think it had been. It took a very long time for thousands of thoughts to filter through that scrambled brain, and for new neural pathways to develop and healing to begin. I didn't fall in love with Mark Acklom. I fell in love with Mark Conway, a character Acklom created just for me; that was a very difficult thought to get my head and heart around with a scrambled brain and mashed-up emotions. Mark Conway was brave, he was honourable, he was funny, he was hard-working, he had integrity and he always put others before himself. Mark Acklom is the polar opposite: a parasite, feeding off his unsuspecting victims, motivated by power and control, intent only on gratifying his own perverted needs. There is absolutely nothing admirable or heroic in that. It was the fictitious Mark Conway who walked into the shop in January 2012, but before long Mark Acklom had stepped in and taken over. Acklom is one man with multiple personas, and if he introduces one of them to you, you are likely to find yourself taken in, turned inside out, smashed to pieces and wondering if you will ever find yourself again. The journey back to anything like normal is long and hard.

Before I met Acklom, I was a happy, sociable, positive person; by the time he was through with me, I could barely function and had become deeply suspicious of most people. I suffered panic attacks, claustrophobia, agoraphobia, terrible mood swings, deep depression, and I found it virtually impossible to concentrate on anything, unable even to read a book. For about a year after discovering what had happened, I couldn't listen to Radio 4 because I couldn't bear all the financial reporting, which only served to remind me of how much I'd lost financially. I couldn't bear to see 'For Sale' signs outside the kinds of houses that, by rights, I should have been able to buy. I have come a long way since then. But I still have a long way to go.

I look back on the six years of the police investigation and sometimes think, what a waste of time and effort. Had I known what a struggle it would be, and the toll it would take on my health – both physical and mental – would I have done it? It is impossible to know. There were many times during the investigation when I felt like giving up – when I thought that I was just wasting my time and that justice would never be served. With the granting of the EAW, Acklom's arrest in Switzerland, his eventual extradition and finally, his conviction, I felt a sense of pride and achievement for having persevered, but no sense of elation. The personal cost to me in terms of time and my own health has been immense. Acklom was sentenced to five years and eight months, only half of which will be served in prison, but it is gratifying for me to have stood up to him and to have brought him down, even if only for a couple of years. Unfortunately, I am sure that as soon as he is released he will be back to his old tricks again, but I just want to forget all about him. He is very clever, he is very convincing, but scratch beneath the surface and he is just a common criminal. He truly is beneath contempt.

My dream now is the same as ever. I want a place of my own, somewhere I feel safe and secure. I always thought that if I ever found myself in dire straits, I would do any job to keep going, but since finding myself in this situation, I recognise that I would rather do nothing than something that holds no value for me. It took thirty years of mortgage payments to own my own home before, and I don't have that time left now, so my dream may never be realised – but one step at a time.

In the recounting of my story, the emphasis has been on the struggle and the pain, but even in the darkest of times there have been many moments of wonder and joy, and even occasions when I have had to laugh at the audacity of Mark Acklom.

Luckily for me, I derive great pleasure from the natural world. Out walking, it will make my day if I see a hare, a water vole, a stoat, ducklings, cygnets or any other wildlife. I enjoy seeing the sheep and cattle in the fields. I appreciate the scent of fields of flowering broad beans, or an avenue of lime trees in bloom in July. I love walking through fields of buttercups in the spring. I gaze at the moon and the stars in the dark, inky skies that I tumble into as I listen to the owls calling from the woods across the field. Living in a rural setting has been more therapeutic to me than anything else, and not a day goes by when I don't look out across the landscape and thank my lucky stars that I have been able to live in the midst of such beauty.

My address book has been severely culled over the past few years. Initially, I was deeply upset by the way some so-called friends reacted to me. All this has been very hurtful, but having had time to think about it, I am now glad that the maggots in the rosy apples of superficial fair-weather friendship have been exposed, and those apples are no longer in the basket.

On the other hand, many people rushed forward with offers of help, whether that was accommodation for a while, food, clothes, all manner of things. I will never forget the kindness shown to me by these people – from my oldest school friends to previously unknown strangers who have now become friends. Even the messages of encouragement that I have received from people when the story has been in the media have helped me enormously.

And what has happened to the various characters that I have mentioned in this story? Some relationships have fallen by the wayside, some have faltered, but are now gathering strength, and others have remained firm through thick and thin.

I haven't seen Uma and Antony since the day we rowed and they put my belongings outside for me to collect. We had a brief exchange of two text messages in 2014, when I texted Uma to ask if she could spare any of the things I had given her in 2012. About a month later, I received a reply from her saying that she would like to know more about my situation and suggesting that we meet for lunch. I didn't respond.

Anne and I remain the best of friends; we still holiday together with our very grown-up children and continue to enjoy all the delights of the British outdoors.

For some years I had a very uneasy relationship with my brother, Nick, and his wife, Annalisa. I believe that when I first met Acklom, they really did want to help me. Somehow or other, even though they never met him, they immediately saw him for what he was, and I can imagine how exasperating it must have been for them that I wouldn't listen and appeared to turn my back on them. In 2012, Nick had drawn my attention to two lies that Acklom had told me, one to do with a Churchill quote that was painted on the hall wall in Brock Street, the other relating to the ownership of the house (Nick had checked the title at the Land Registry). I challenged Mark about both these discrepancies but, as usual, without a trace of hesitation, he gave me answers that seemed reasonable at the time, and I chose to believe him and resent my brother for his interference. At one stage, Nick and I went for two and a half years with virtually no contact, and until the Christmas of 2018 I had only seen Annalisa twice since she visited Brock Street in October 2012 – once at the funeral of my ex-husband in 2016, and again in September 2018, at the wedding of one of their daughters. I can't say how or why, but things recently have become less strained. We all spent some time together over Christmas in 2018 and everyone seemed happier for it. Surprisingly, there was no awkwardness and I certainly enjoyed myself very much indeed. We still have a way to go, and nothing will ever be exactly as it was before, but I am confident that we will continue to see each other and enjoy family occasions, because deep down, that is what we all want. In the autumn of 2019, Nick and I spent a couple of days on our own, walking, talking and mulling over the past and our hopes for the future.

Martin and I have become friends and remain in touch. He eventually got to make his documentary, *Conman: The Life and Crimes of Mark Acklom*, which was aired on a new Sky Crime channel in September 2019 and is available to view on YouTube. I can thoroughly recommend it. He even got to meet and interview Charlie's Angel who, he confirmed, is 'definitely not a man'!

I expect that he and I (and she) will keep our eyes and ears open for news of Mark Acklom for some time to come, and my advice to anyone who finds themselves in the sort of predicament I was in is to get hold of a really good investigative journalist to help them.

On 1 November 2019, it was announced on the Avon & Somerset police website that DI Adam Bunting, DS Helen Holt and DC Clare Ball were given awards for their work in locating and apprehending Mark Acklom.

At the time of writing (January 2020), Mark Acklom is in prison. Investigations are being carried out under the Proceeds of Crime Act to try to ascertain whether he has any assets. Unsurprisingly, he says he has none and it seems unlikely that I will ever see a penny of the money he owes me. Since Judge Picton sentenced Acklom in August 2019, the 120 days deducted from his sentence for time served on remand have been added back on, as it transpired that when he was investigated in Switzerland after his arrest in 2018, he was convicted of cheque and credit-card fraud (committed in Switzerland in 2014) and given a short prison sentence which he tried to offset against the one he is serving for crimes committed against me! It has also transpired that he is 'wanted' back in Spain, as he never completed his sentence there in 2016. Incredible though it seems, he was allowed out while he appealed his sentence – and, of course, he did a runner. I am told he is now trying to appeal his sentence here on the grounds that he wasn't given the correct information about the evidence the prosecution had against him, particularly 'unused material', and that had this information been made available to him, he would have pleaded guilty much earlier in the proceedings and thereby received a shorter sentence. My own view is that he should be locked away for ever, as he is a known repeat lifestyle offender – a total menace to society – but in all probability, he will soon be out of jail, once again living the multi-millionaire lifestyle at someone else's expense. Whose assets will he have his sights on next, I wonder?

When I look back over the past eight years, I know that there is one thing that has kept me going, above all else – the fact that I am a mother. There have been times when I have felt condemned to a life I didn't want, but even in my darkest hours, I knew that I just couldn't leave my daughters. They have been on this terrible journey with me and they, too, had the security they had known all their lives taken away. They have seen me in a way that no child wants to see their mother, and no mother wants to be seen. As Lara wrote in an article for the *Telegraph*:

> In the days and weeks that followed, Mum stayed with me and slept on my sofa. It broke my heart to see her lying there in tears as I left for work every morning. In the most awful role-reversal it felt as if I had become the parent and she had become the child.

She summed up saying:

> Mum has lost everything: her money, her job, her home, her security, her self-confidence and her belief in the kindness of others. But the one thing he couldn't take away from her was the love of her daughters. Everything that's happened over the past few years has strengthened our relationship, not broken it, and deep down we know that this matters more than anything else.

It is that two-way love that has kept me going. As I said to Mark Acklom, my daughters are beautiful, in all senses of the word. I am very lucky to have them, and I want us to enjoy many more years of normal family life together.

Despite being sorely tested, my characteristic optimism is still there and grows stronger every day. I still daren't look too far ahead because life is so precarious, but I no longer live life in ten-minute bites; I can think ahead to next week, or next month, and sometimes I can even think ahead to next year and wonder if this book will become a best-seller? Perhaps, one day, I might even be able to buy myself a home to call my own – a place in which to settle and begin to live my life to the full once again. You just never know.

And what about James? Reader, I didn't marry him, but we are still together. You may remember that I felt the winds of change upon me again at the end of 2018 and talked about the first couple of weeks in 2019 being the calm before the storm. Well, in addition to the sudden flurry of activity with regard to Mark Acklom's extradition, my personal life also changed dramatically. At the end of January, James and I went to view a truly lovely house for rent in a beautiful part of Scotland. We moved in on 1 March and we love it. The house came with a resident cat who gives me more pleasure than I can describe (it is so lovely to have a pet again), and I have a whole new landscape to explore and a beautiful (if temporary) home from which to do it. I have already walked miles and taken hundreds of photographs. The health barometer is set fair. Over the six years that James and I have been together, life has been a struggle, but we support each other as best we can. We have enjoyed many happy times together and we're looking forward to many more. Ours was a match made in hell, but we have managed to find our own little corner of paradise, and we count our blessings every day.

AUTHOR BIOGRAPHY

Carolyn studied Comparative Literature and French at the University of East Anglia. She believes in thinking for herself, in taking responsibility for her actions, and in trying to see the world from different points of view. She has been told that three of her best characteristics are that she is fun, generous and resilient, and that three of her worst are that she is volatile, stubborn, and will cut off her nose to spite her face. A natural optimist, she tries to retain a positive outlook, even in the most challenging of times. She lives in the country with a beautiful ginger cat and finds that life in the slow lane has plenty to recommend it.

ACKNOWLEDGEMENTS

I would like to thank everyone who helped me in the aftermath of my association with Mark Acklom, by offering me a place to stay, work, food, money, clothes, moral support, or by treating me to a haircut or some other luxury to make life more bearable. Without your help I would not be here to tell my story.

With regards to getting the book published, I would like to thank Stuart Higgins for his interest in my story; his help over the years has been invaluable. Stuart introduced me to Martin Brunt, whose hard work and determination kept the story alive in the media and contributed to Acklom's arrest. Both Stuart and Martin encouraged me to keep going throughout the police investigation and during the writing of the book.

Martin introduced me to Andrew Gordon at David Higham Associates and I cannot thank Andrew enough for giving me the chance to write this book and get it published. He has challenged, encouraged and advised me in equal measure. When I have faltered, he has given me confidence and has been a pleasure to work with.

I would also like to thank my editor, Kelly Ellis, at HarperCollins for her wonderful enthusiasm when she acquired the story. I would like to thank her and all the team for getting the book to print under what have been extremely difficult circumstances during the Covid-19 pandemic.

There is only one person among my family and friends who read my manuscript prior to publication – my daughter Lara. She has been an infinite source of help, encouragement and enthusiasm, and I cannot thank her enough. I also want to thank Emma for her encouragement and for her forbearance when I talked, too much at times, about a man we all abhor.

Finally, I would like to thank James for keeping calm when I was not, and for his kindness.

CREDITS

While every effort has been made to trace the owners of copyright material reproduced herein and secure permissions, the publishers would like to apologise for any omissions and will be pleased to incorporate missing acknowledgements in any future edition of this book.

Text Credits

Page 29, extract from *The Cider House Rules* by John Irving. Reproduced by permission of Transworld, a division of Penguin Books. Copyright © John Irving, 1985

Page 126, extract from *South of the Border, West of the Sun* by Haruki Murakami © Vintage, a division of Penguin Books, 2000

Page 229, extract from womensaid.org.uk, reproduced with permission.

Page 236, extract from *The World According to Garp*, by John Irving. Reproduced by permission of Transworld, a division of Penguin Books. Copyright © John Irving, 1978

Pages 265 and 306, extracts from *The Secret Barrister*. Reproduced by permission of Profile Books. Copyright © 2019

Pages vi, 231 and 309, extracts from *Without Conscience*, by Robert Hare. Reproduced by permission of Guildford Publications. Copyright © Robert Hare, 1993

Page 244, extract from *GQ* magazine, 'I was a teenage fraudster' by Nick Cohen (1992), reproduced with permission

Page 315, extracts from the *Telegraph*, 'My mother was victim to one of Europe's most wanted men' by Lara Woods, (2016)

Picture Credits
Page 1: Sarah Gawler
Page 2: (Top) The Sun/News Licensing; (Bottom left and right) SWNS
Page 3: (Top) Sky News; (Bottom) Tim Stewart News
Page 4: (Top) SWNS; (Bottom) Sky News
Page 5: (Top) The Sun/News Licensing; (Bottom) Sky News
Page 6: (Top and bottom) SWNS
Page 7: Ken McKay/ITV/Shutterstock
Page 8: Author's own